Amazing

Magazine Illustrations

WONDERFUL COPYRIGHT-FREE

ILLUSTRATIONS FOR

ARTISTS AND DESIGNERS

Volumen I

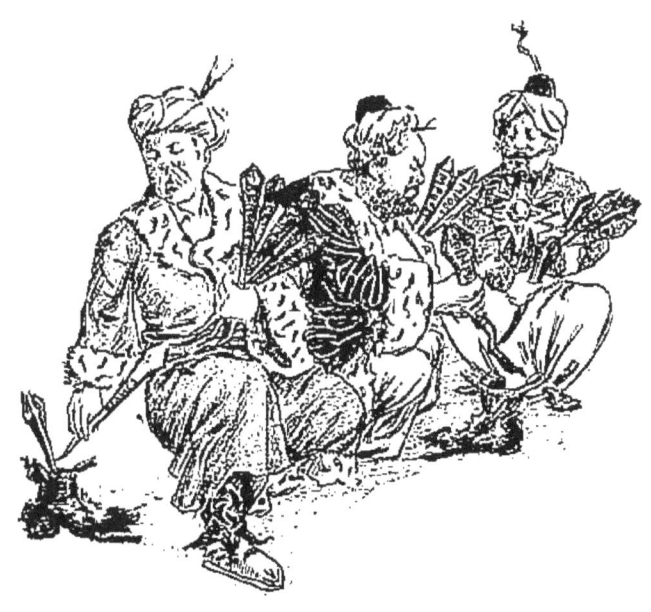

Old Century Books Publications.

Montevideo, Uruguay.

https://amazon.com/author/oldcenturybooks

Copyright © 2020 by Old Century Books.

All rights reserved.

The Fell Types are digitally reproduced by Igino Marini. www.iginomarini.com

This book belongs to the Magazine Illustrations Series. You may use the designs and illustrations for graphics and crafts applications, free and without special permission.

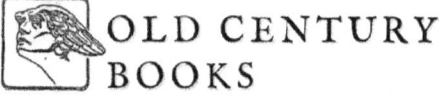

Contents

Introduction	4
Women	7
Men	23
Groups & Scenes	43
Animals	90
Miscellaneous	97
References	113

INTRODUCTION

From cave art to the development of artificial intelligence, techniques that allow the reproduction of images have evolved from primitive mechanisms to intricate processes involving zeros and ones.

Nowadays, it is possible to reproduce images massively with unsurpassed fidelity. But this was not always the case. During the course of the 19th century, various printing techniques were employed. They were as laborious as they were ingenious. Techniques such as woodcutting, where the artist draws on a block of wood and the carver is responsible for following the lines of the drawing with millimetric precision. Then, transfers the illustration to the paper once the wood is inked and pressed.

Woodcutting, along with other techniques such as lithography, was used in the periodicals of the 19th century. Some publications are remembered today for the quality of the artists who illustrated the most relevant news of their time.

However, most of these illustrations remain, at best, in archives that no one visits. They are hidden, waiting to be rescued through digitalization.

This book provides artists with 100 illustrations grouped in different themes. The images were processed with an Ink Sketch effect to highlight the lines and offer less saturated drawings.

The illustrations that are part of this book are practically unknown because it is a local publication of a nascent republic in the 19th century: **Caras y Caretas**.

Caras y Caretas was a weekly magazine published between 1890 and 1897 in Montevideo, Uruguay.

It was founded by the Spanish journalist Eustaquio Pellicer (Burgos, September 3, 1859 - Buenos Aires, December 23, 1937), living in Uruguay, and the French illustrator Charles Schütz. In the pages of Caras y Caretas, we find varied themes. From satirical humor ridiculing political characters to theater criticism, literature and news.

During the seven years of the publication, several cartoonists left their mark on the magazine, such as Juan Bellver (who signed under the pseudonym Juan Sanuy), Aurelio Giménez Pastor, better known as Wimplane II, Eduardo Sojo (Democritus), and Manuel Mayol (Heraclitus).

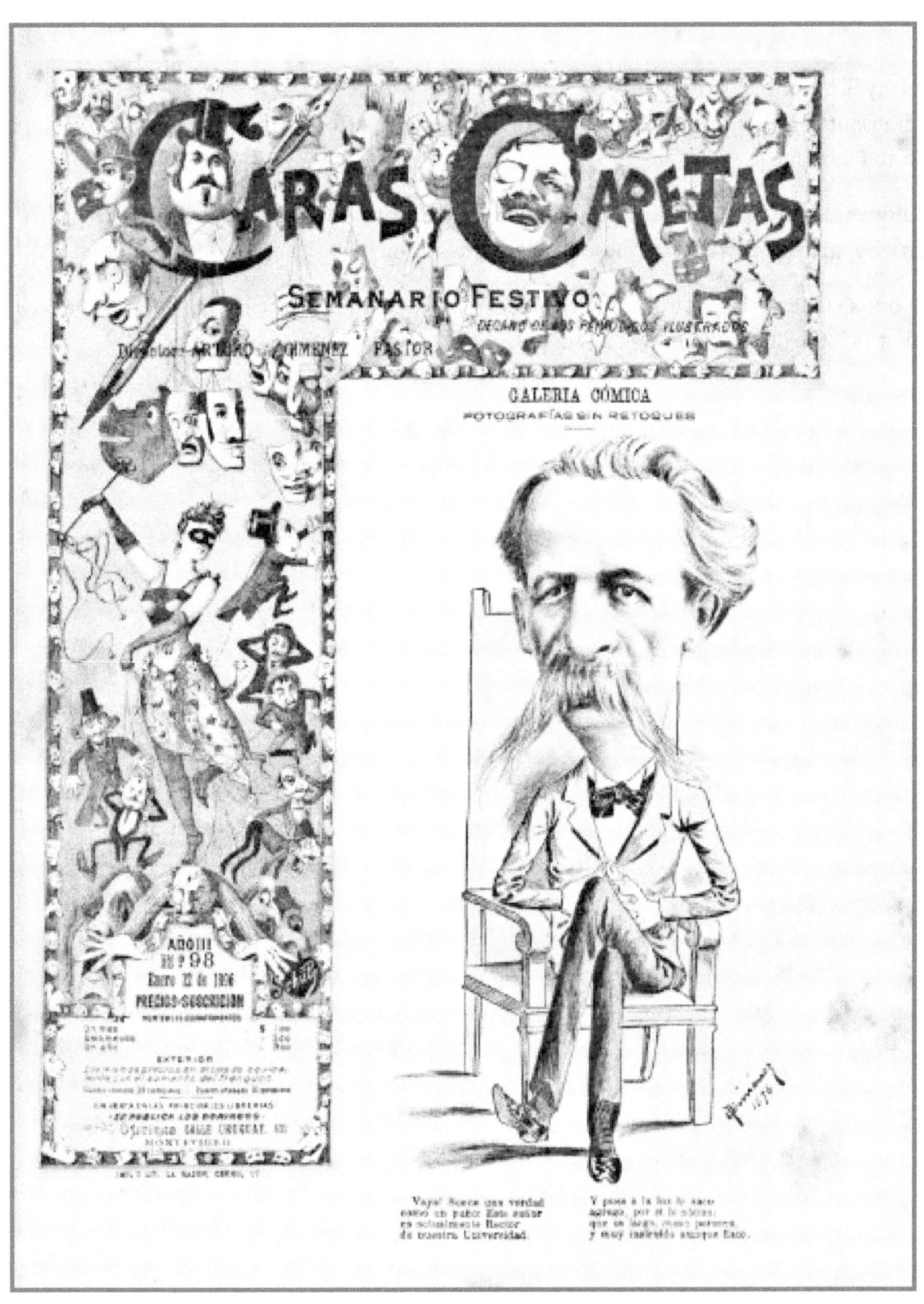

Cover of **Caras y Caretas**. N° 98. January 1896.

In many illustrations, expressivity prevails over correction. However, expressivity is responsible for transmitting energy, movement and life, achieving an effect that transcends the frontier of time and its context.

We hope that the reader will find in this work a source of inspiration that will encourage his creativity, giving "new life" to these timeless illustrations.

The book comes with a download link. It provides access to both the images and the magazines from which the illustrations were obtained.

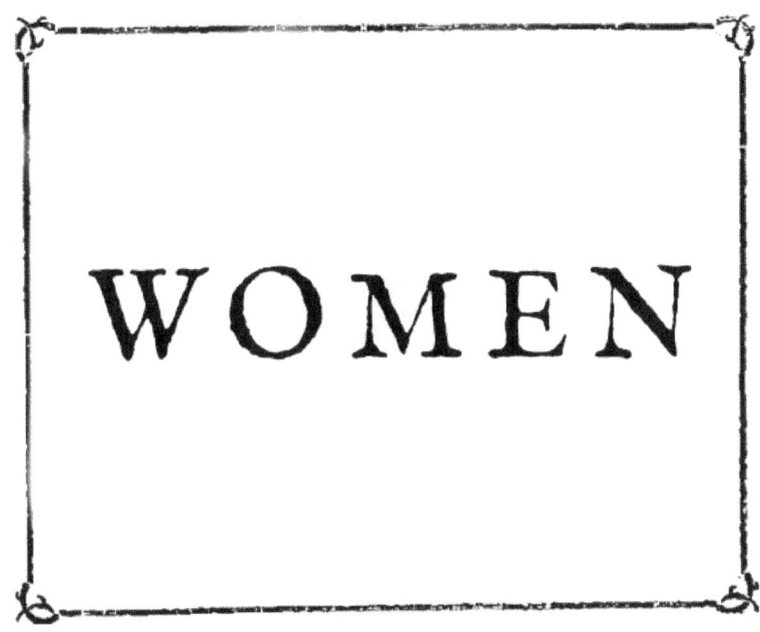

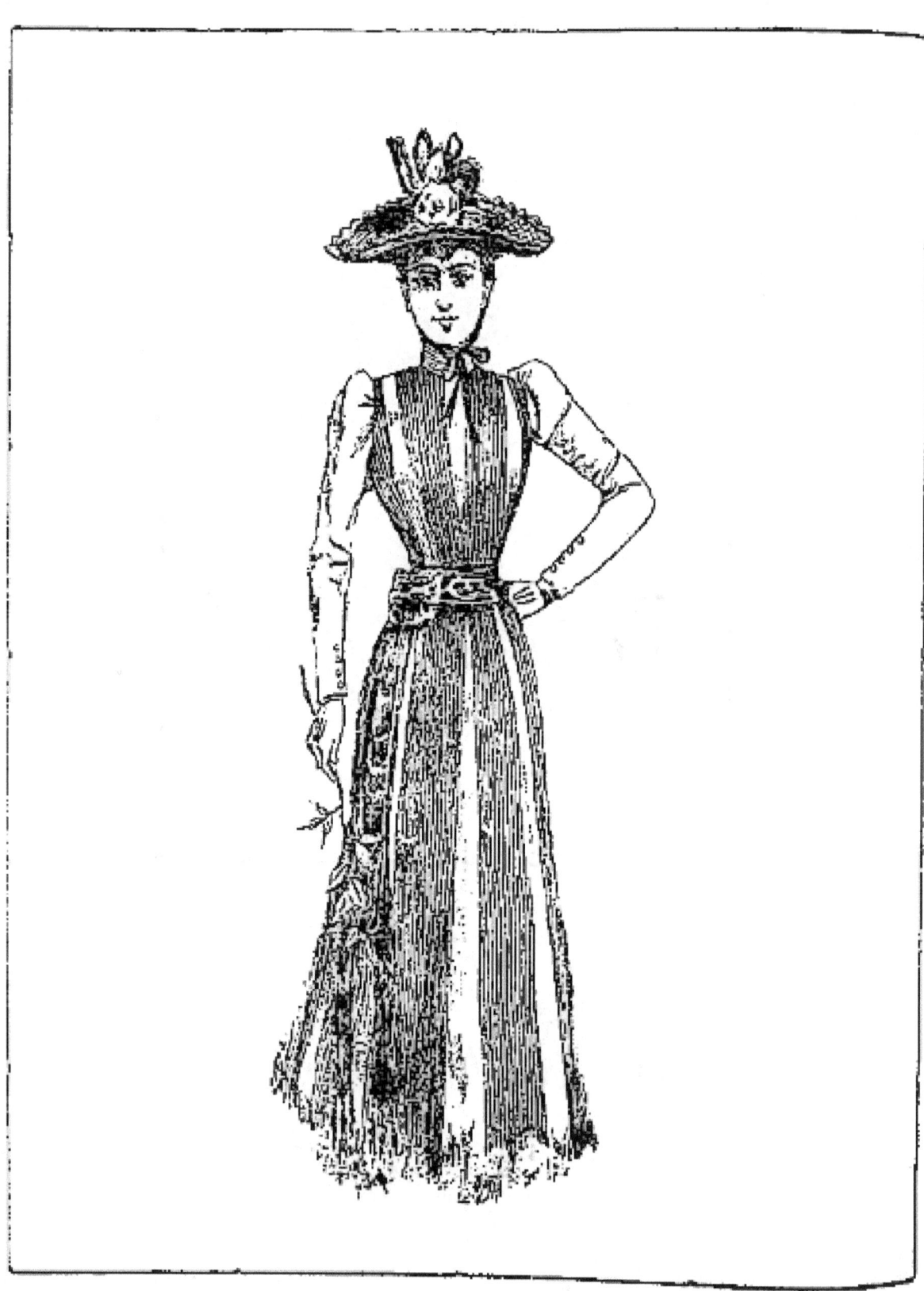

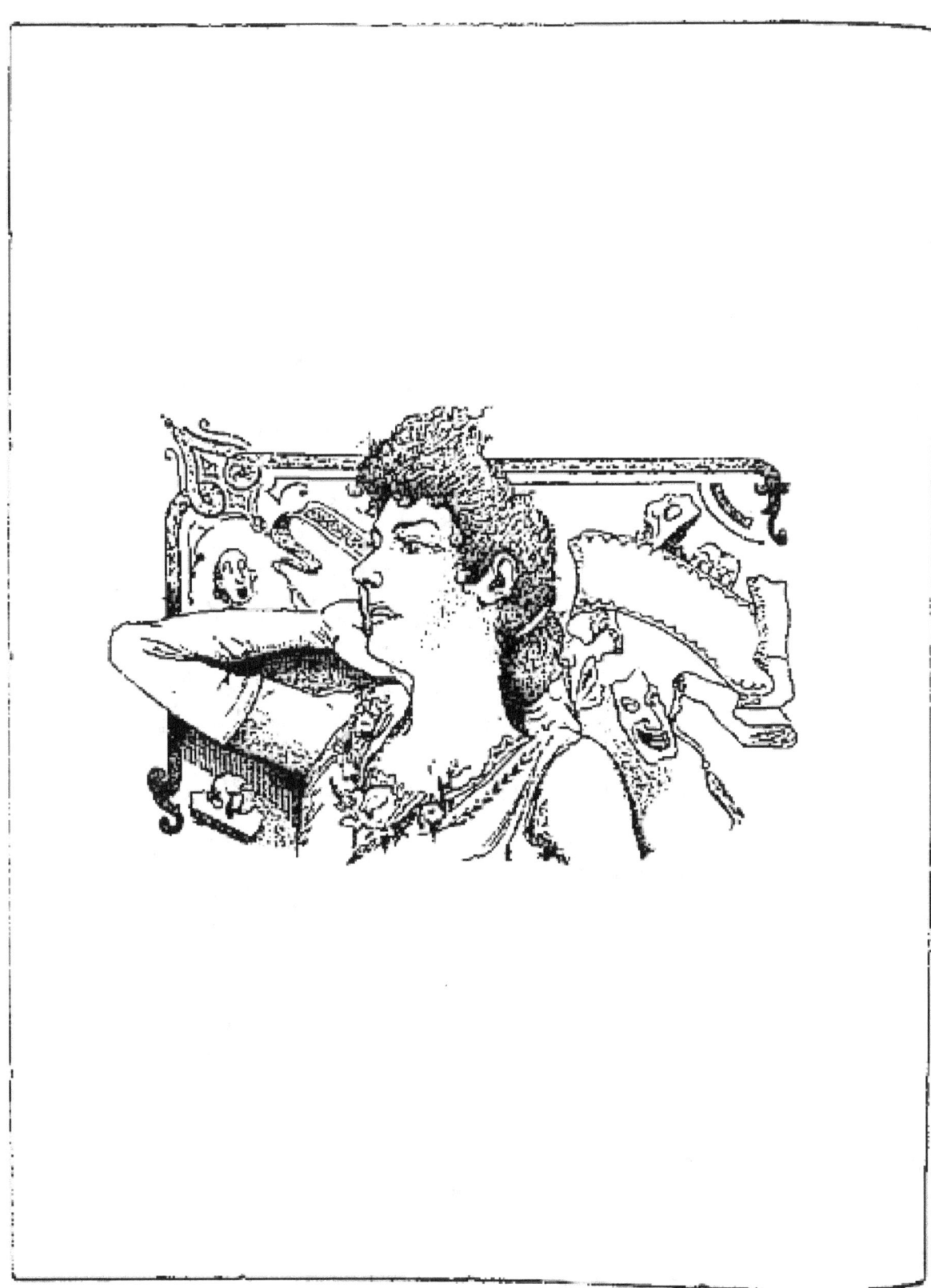

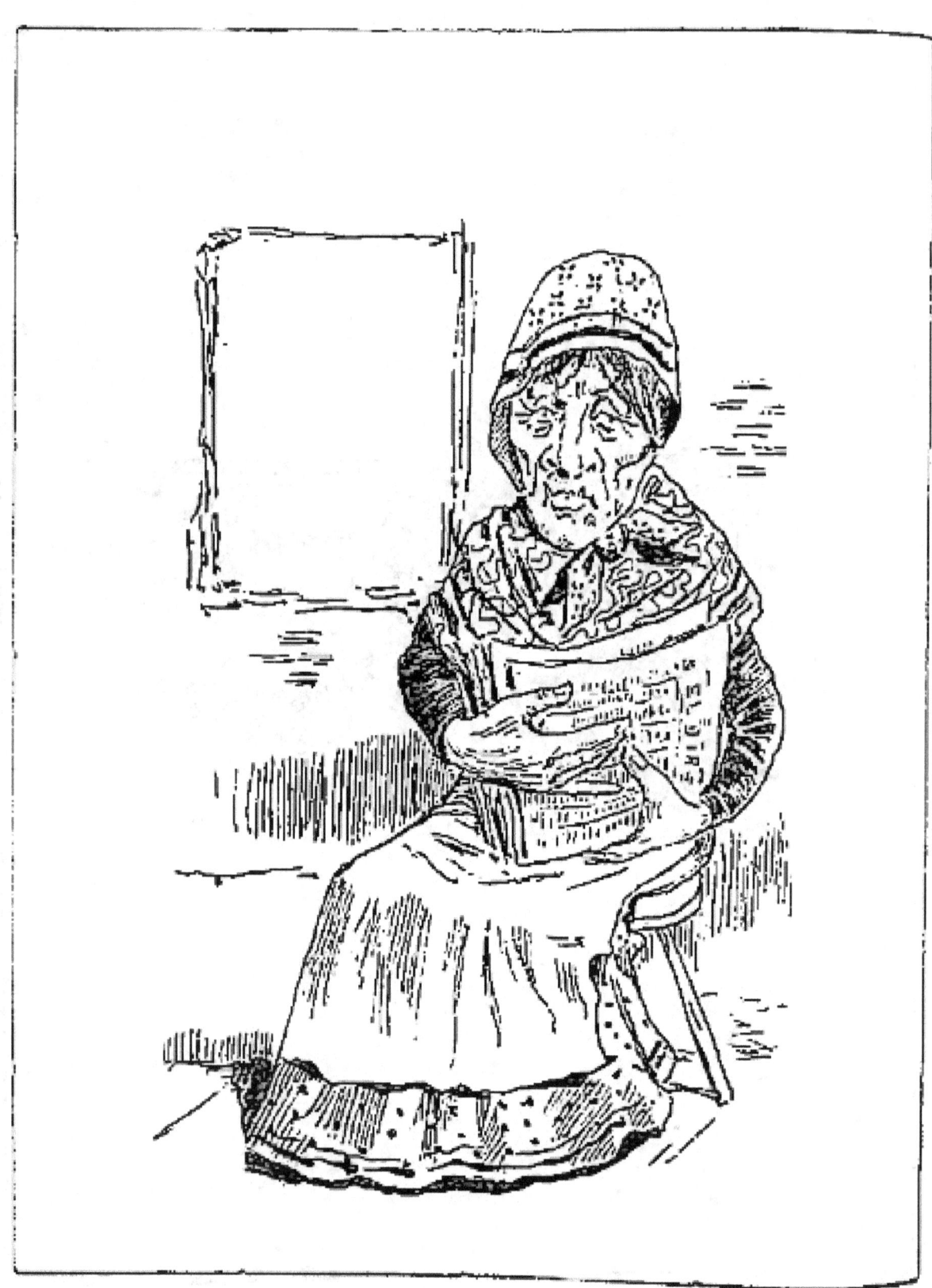

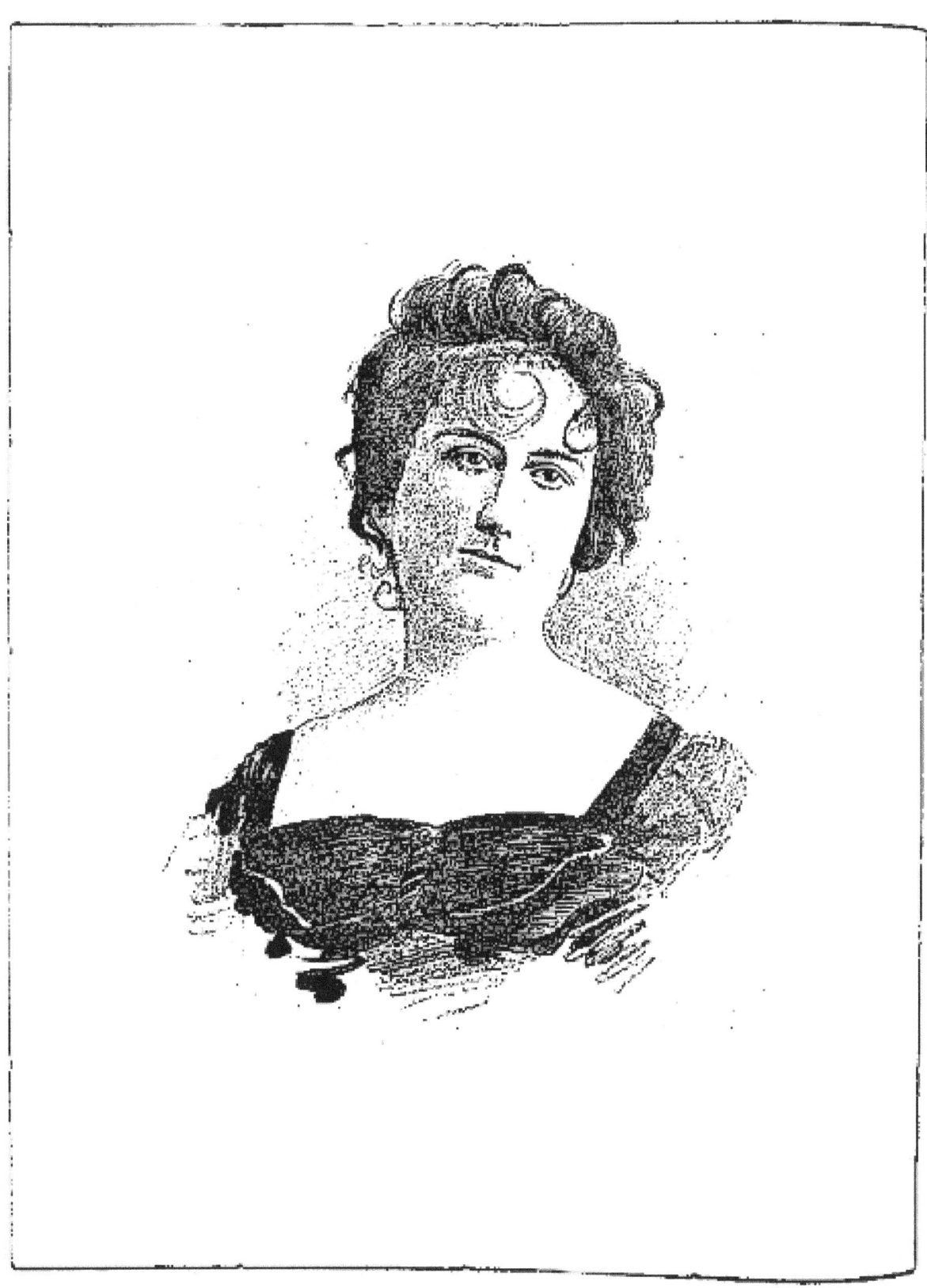

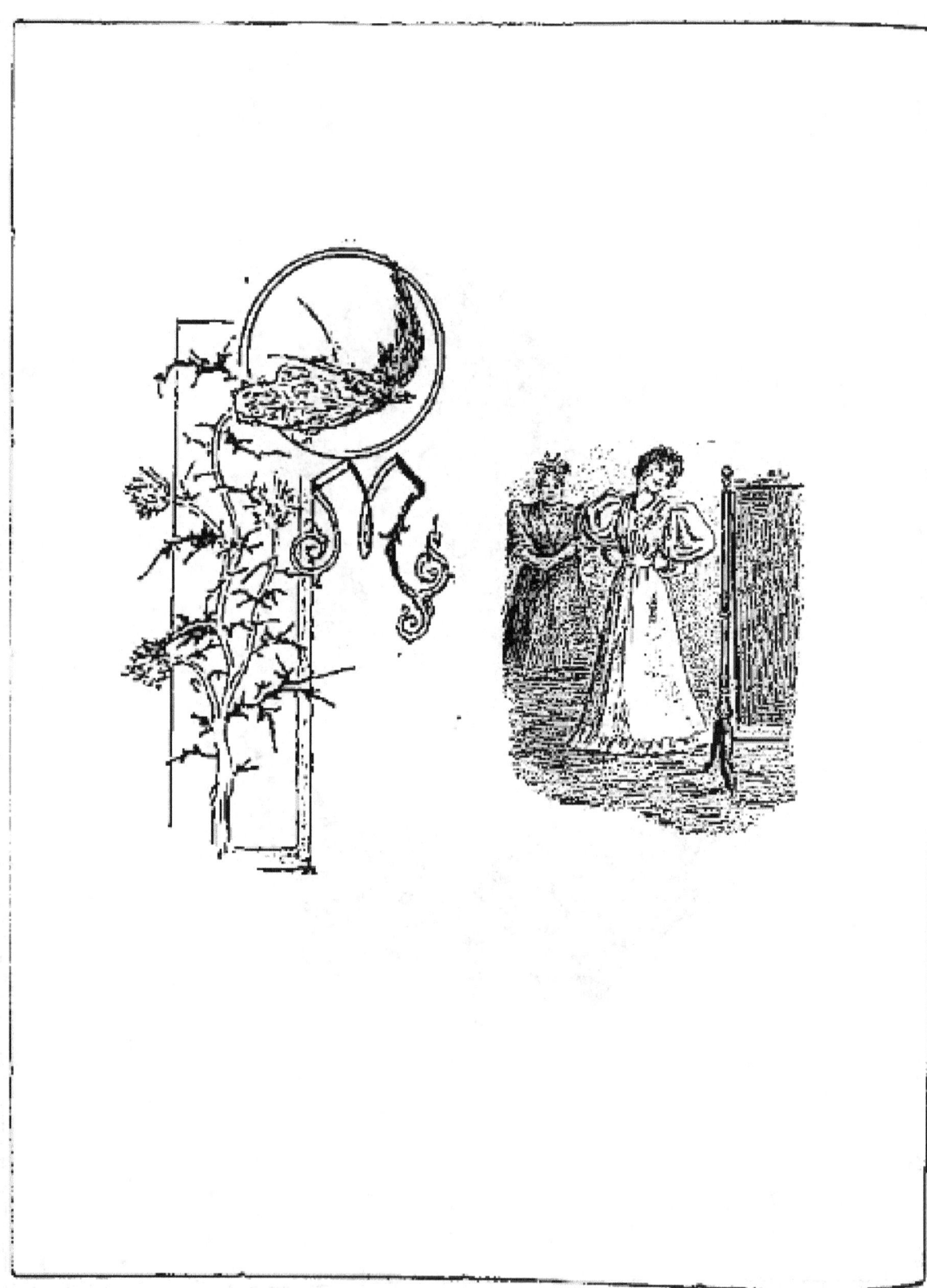

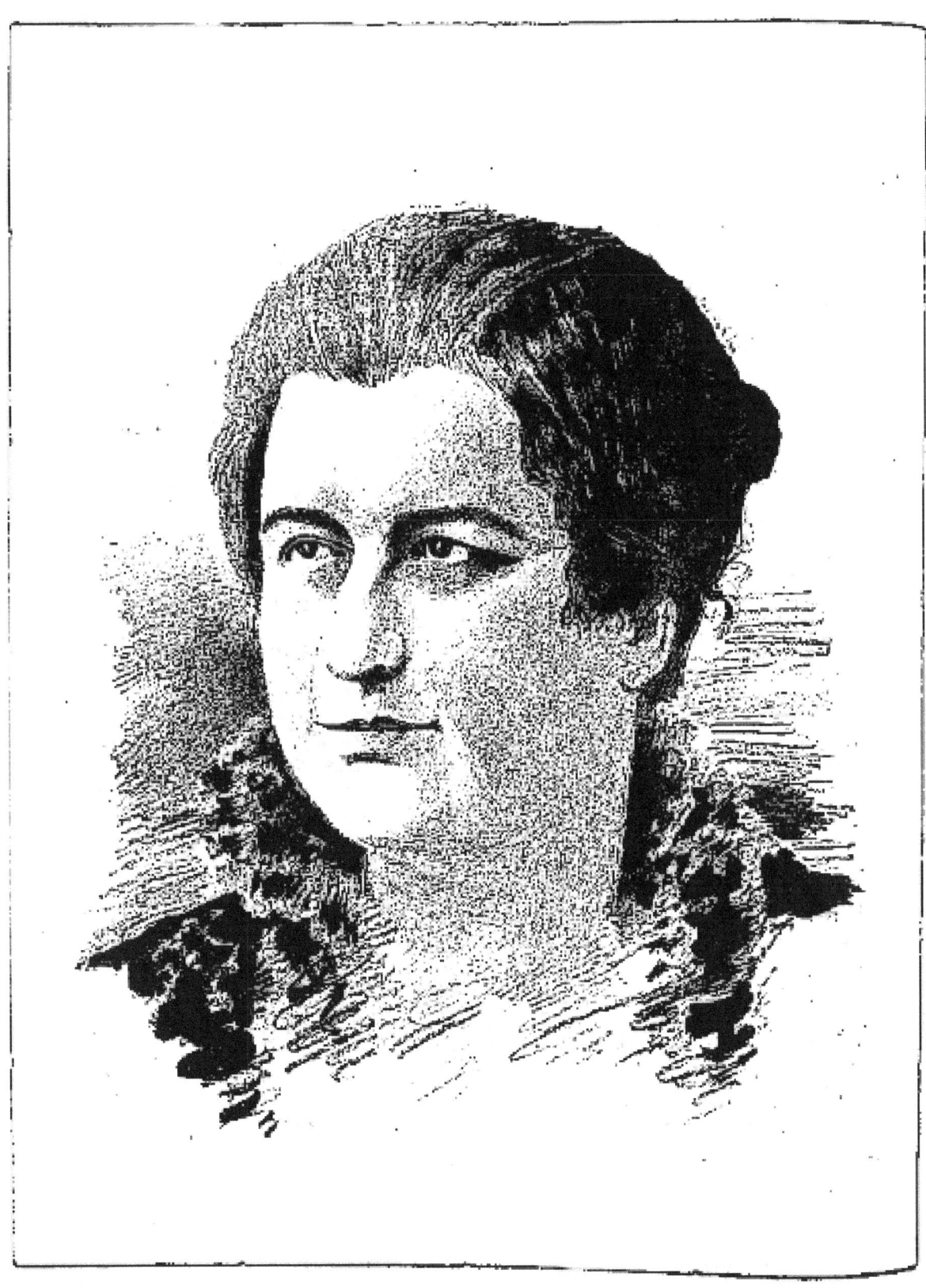

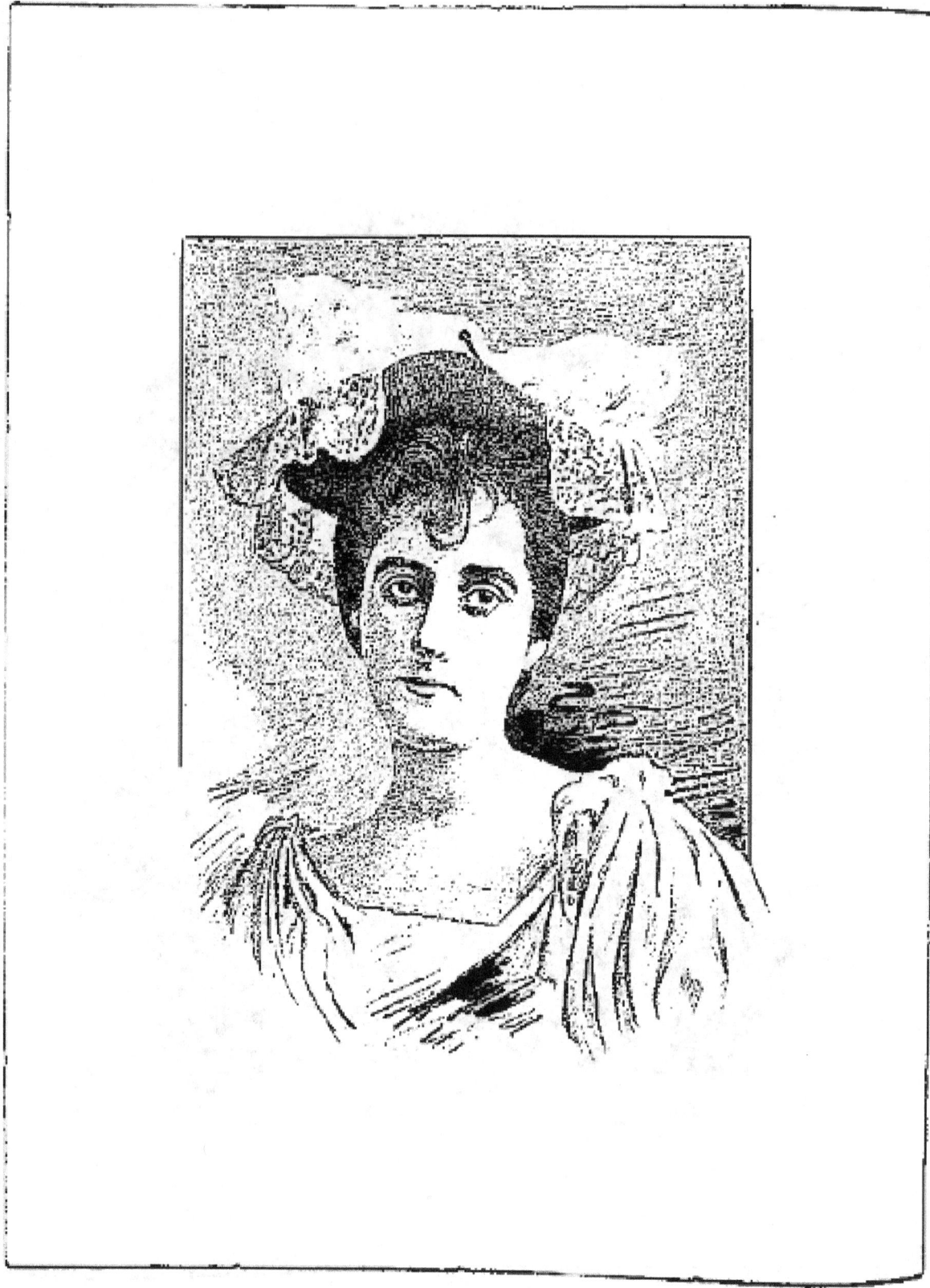

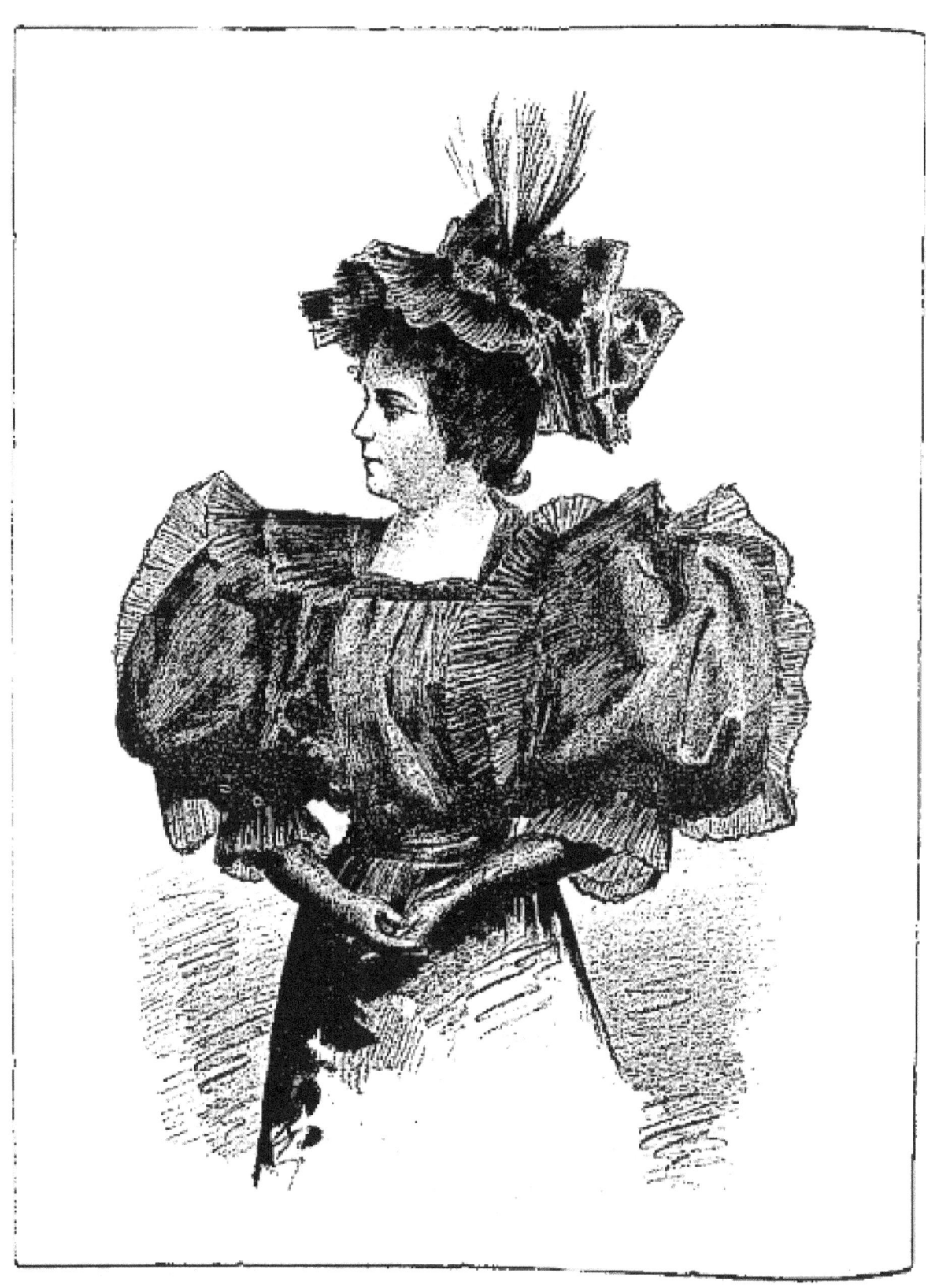

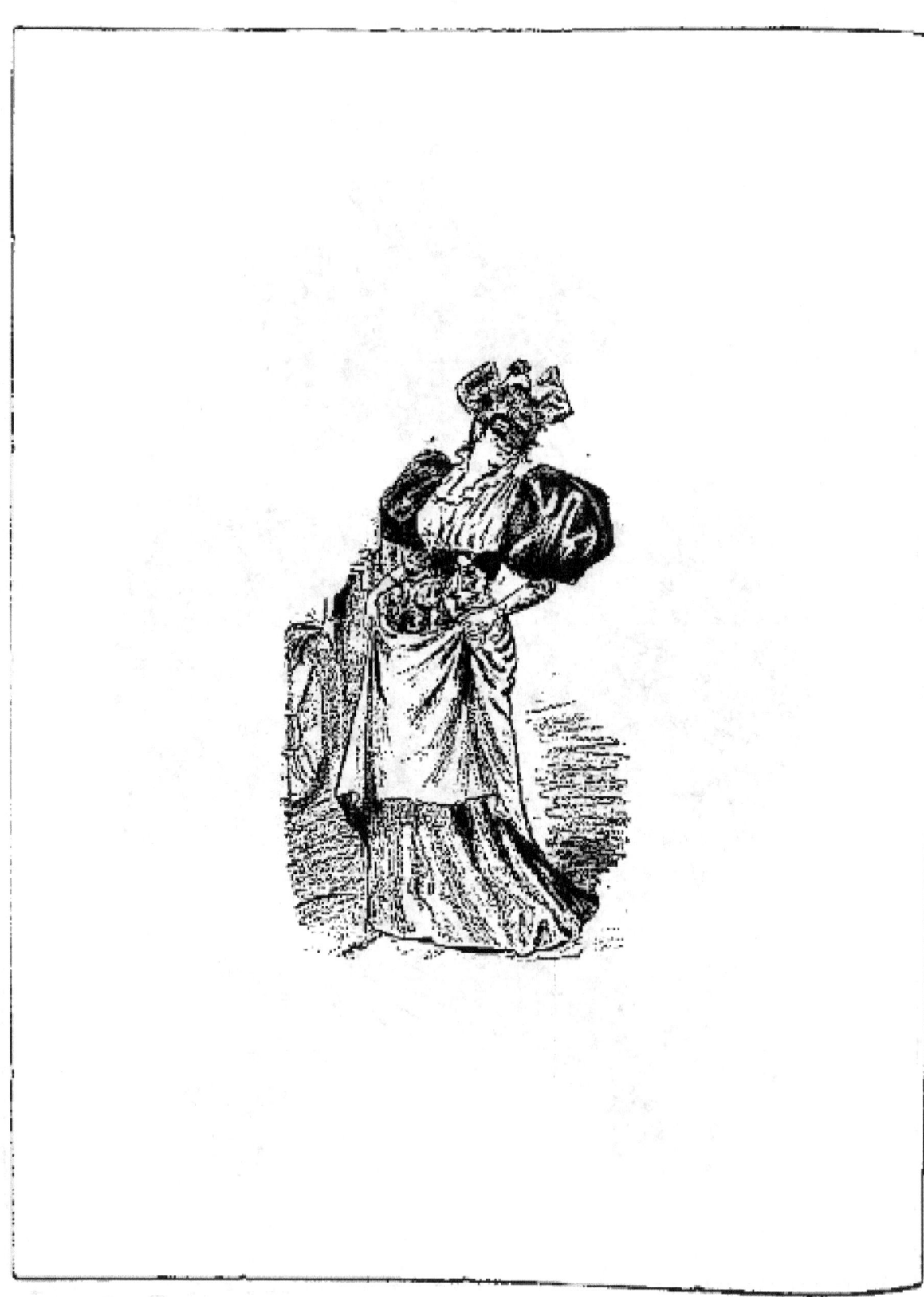

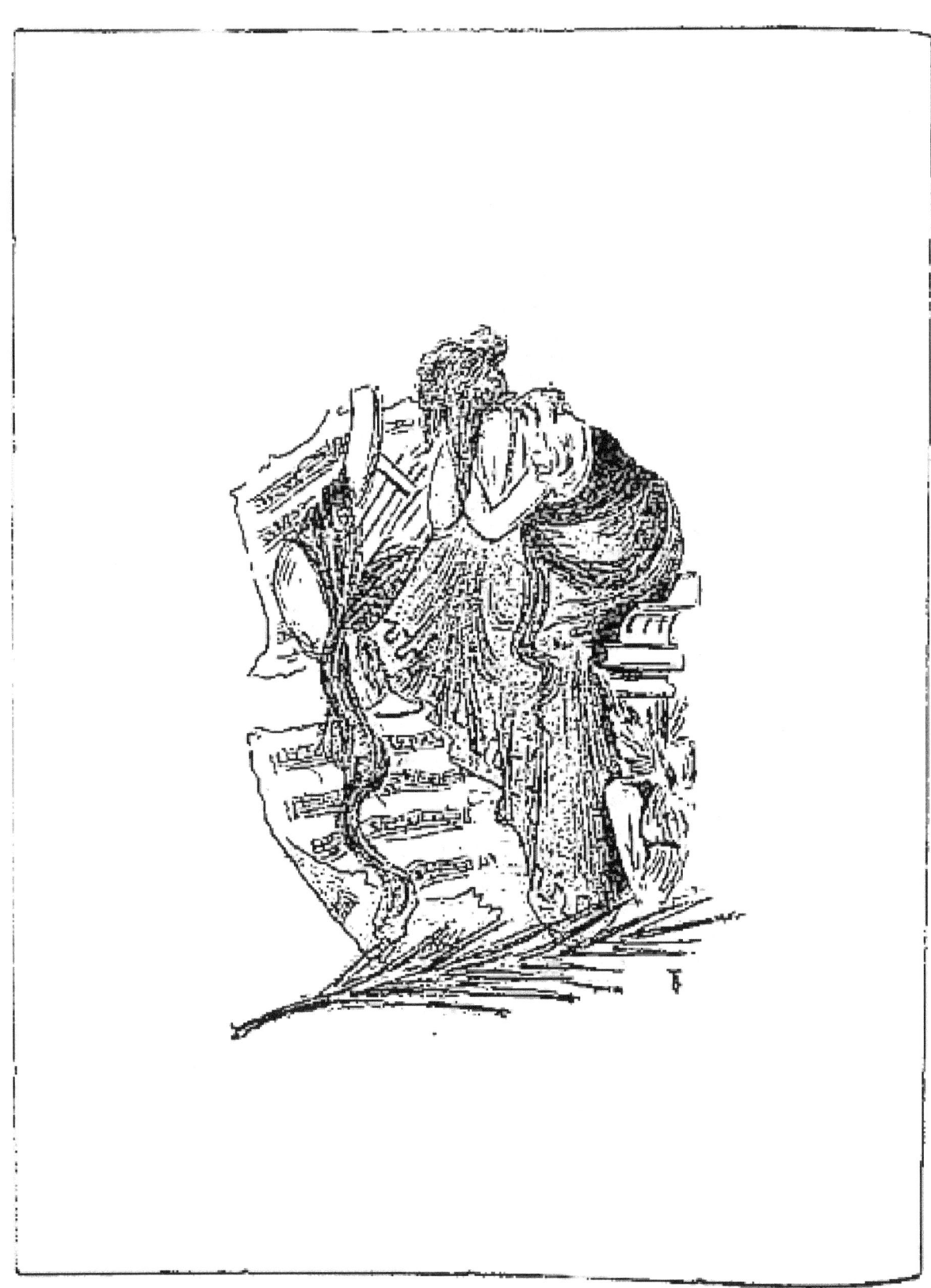

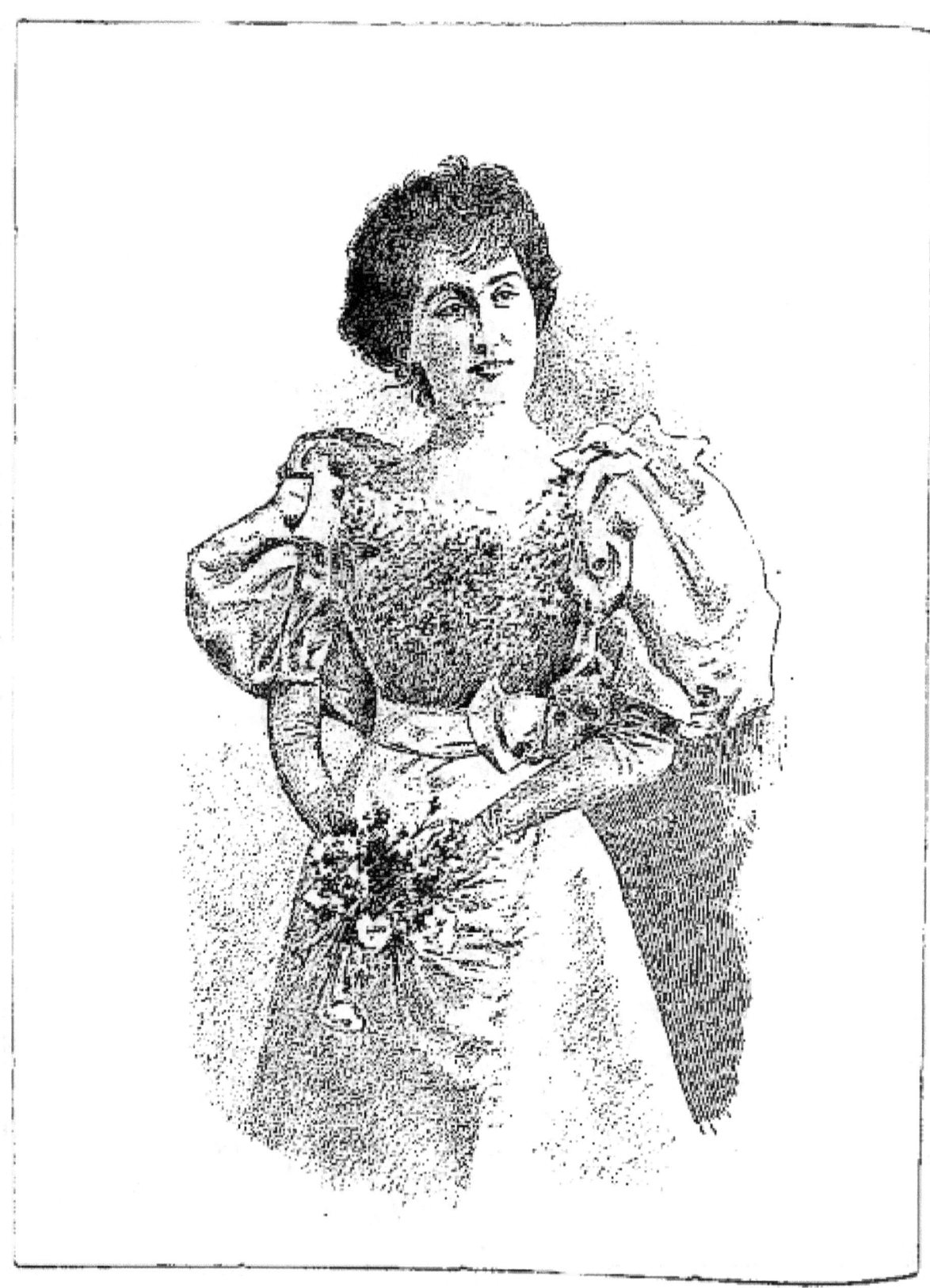

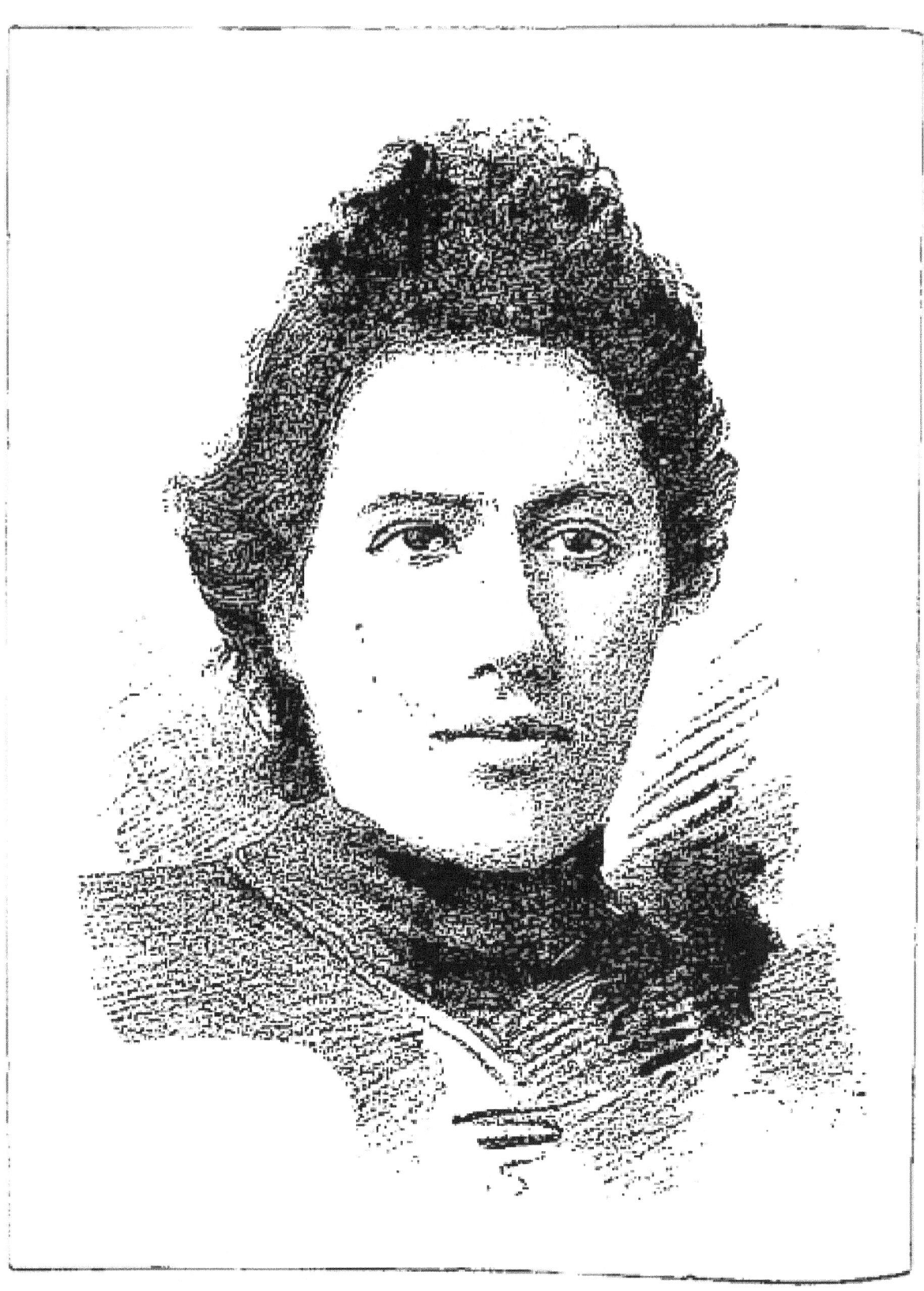

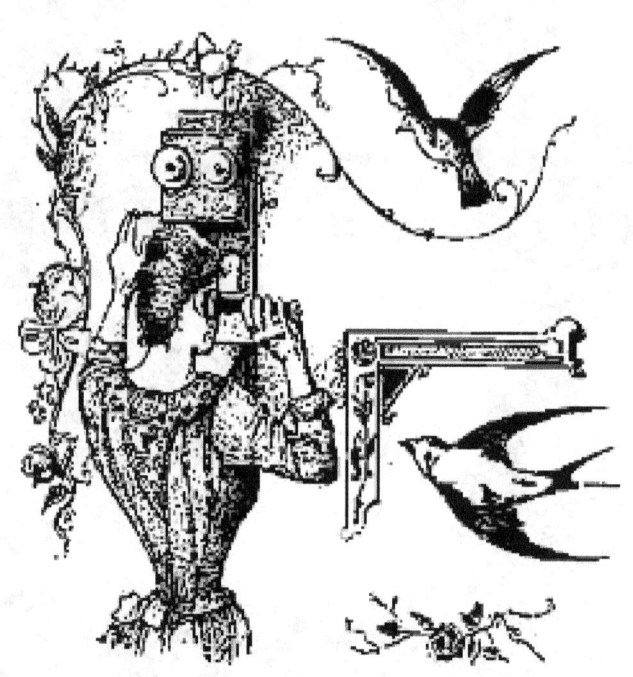

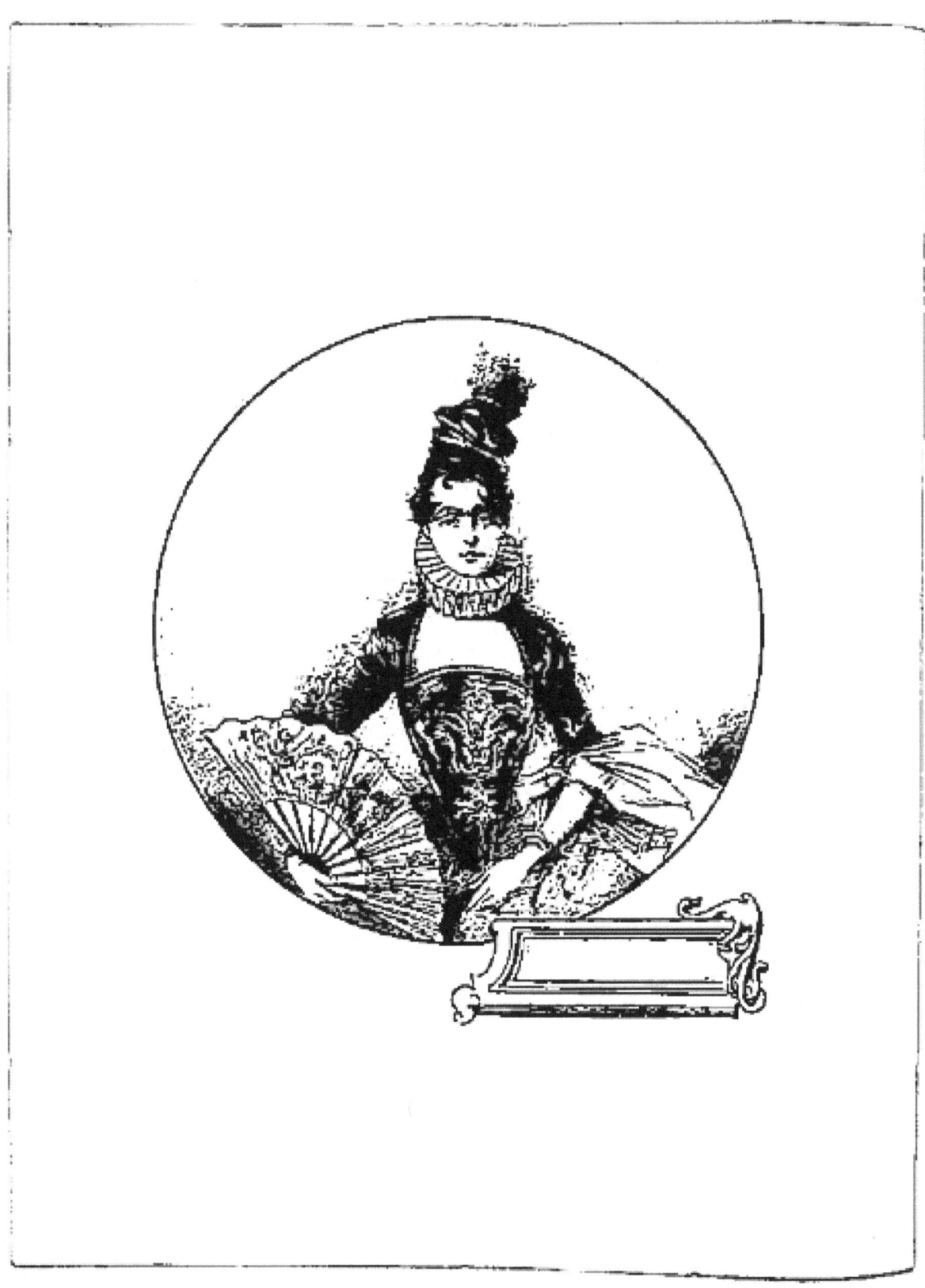

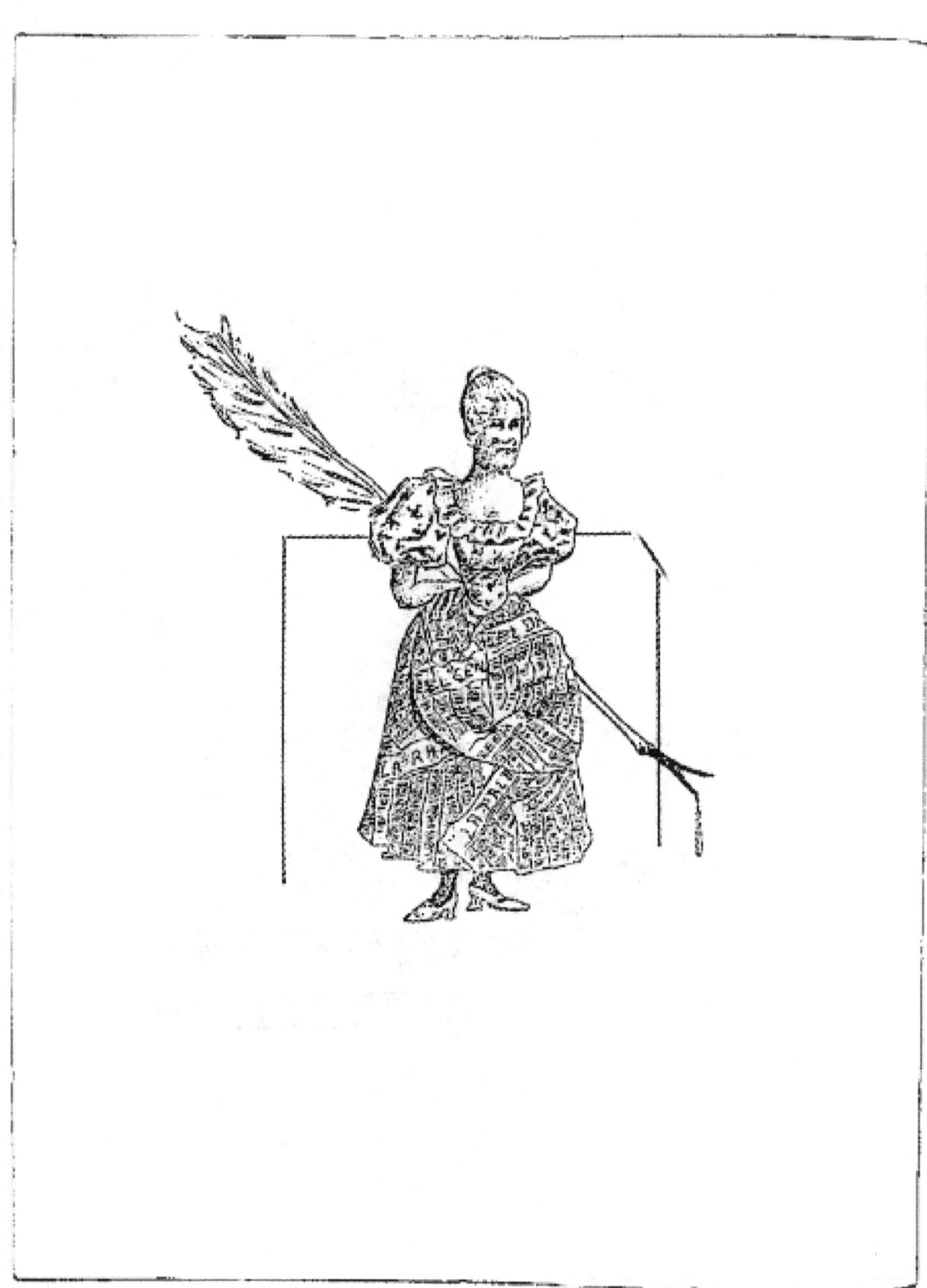

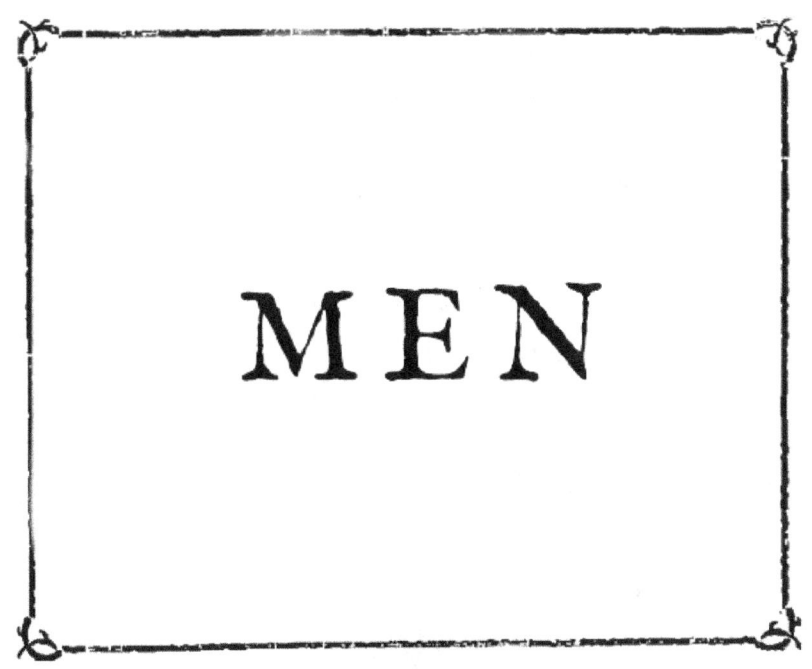

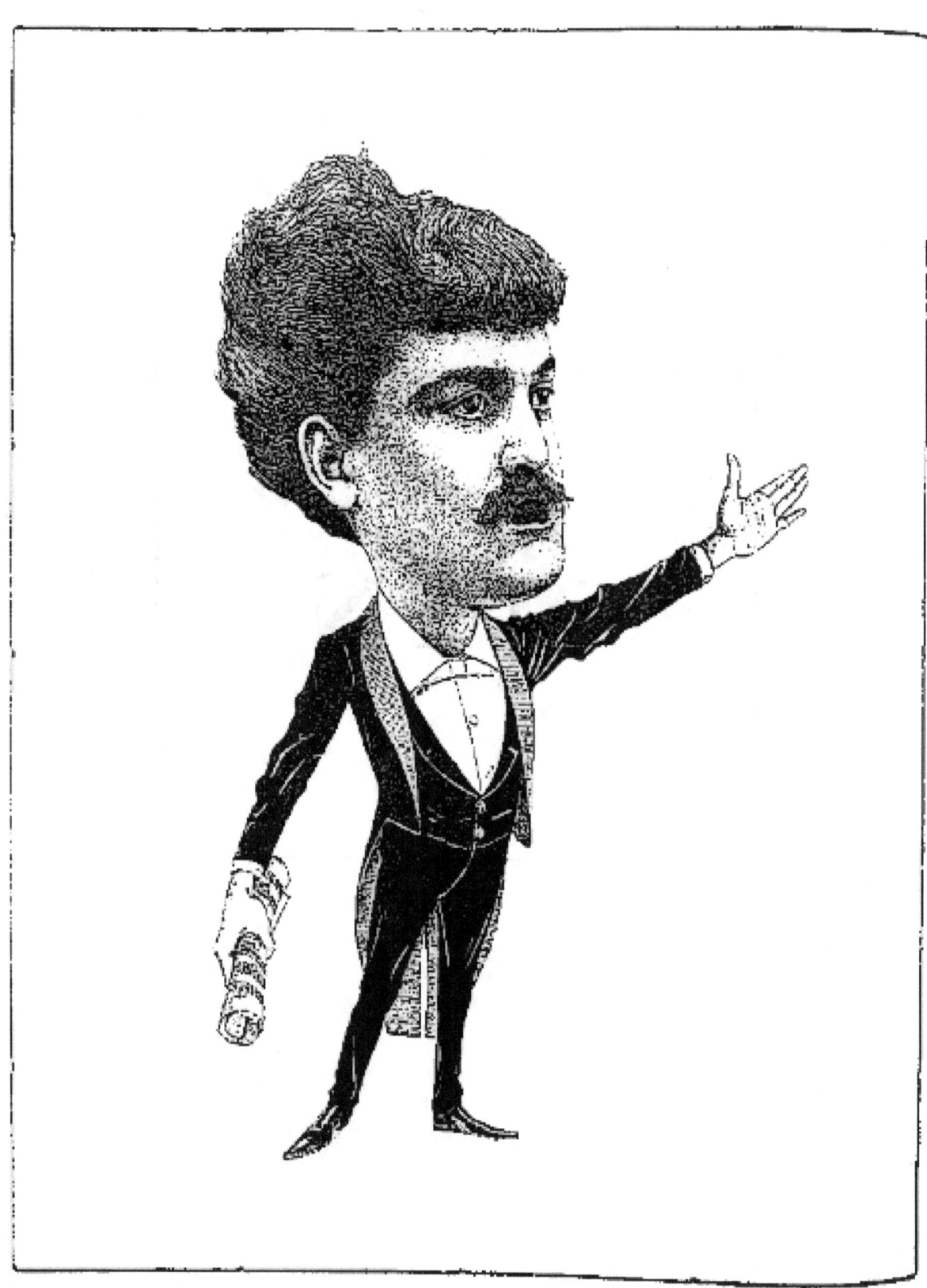

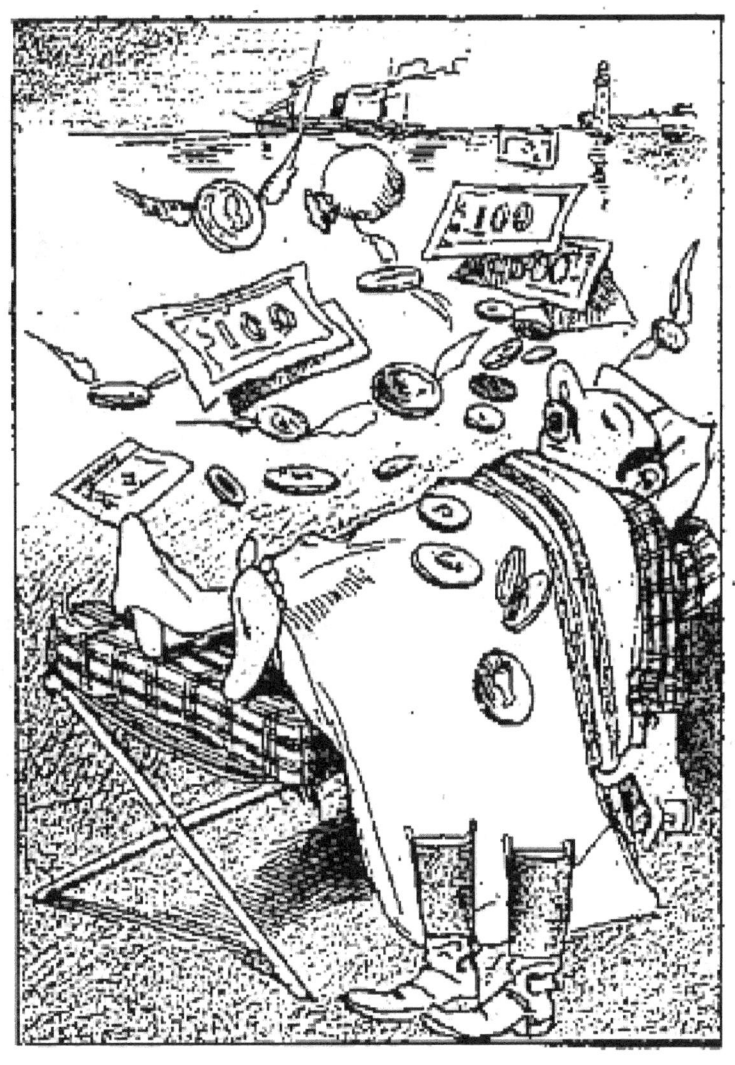

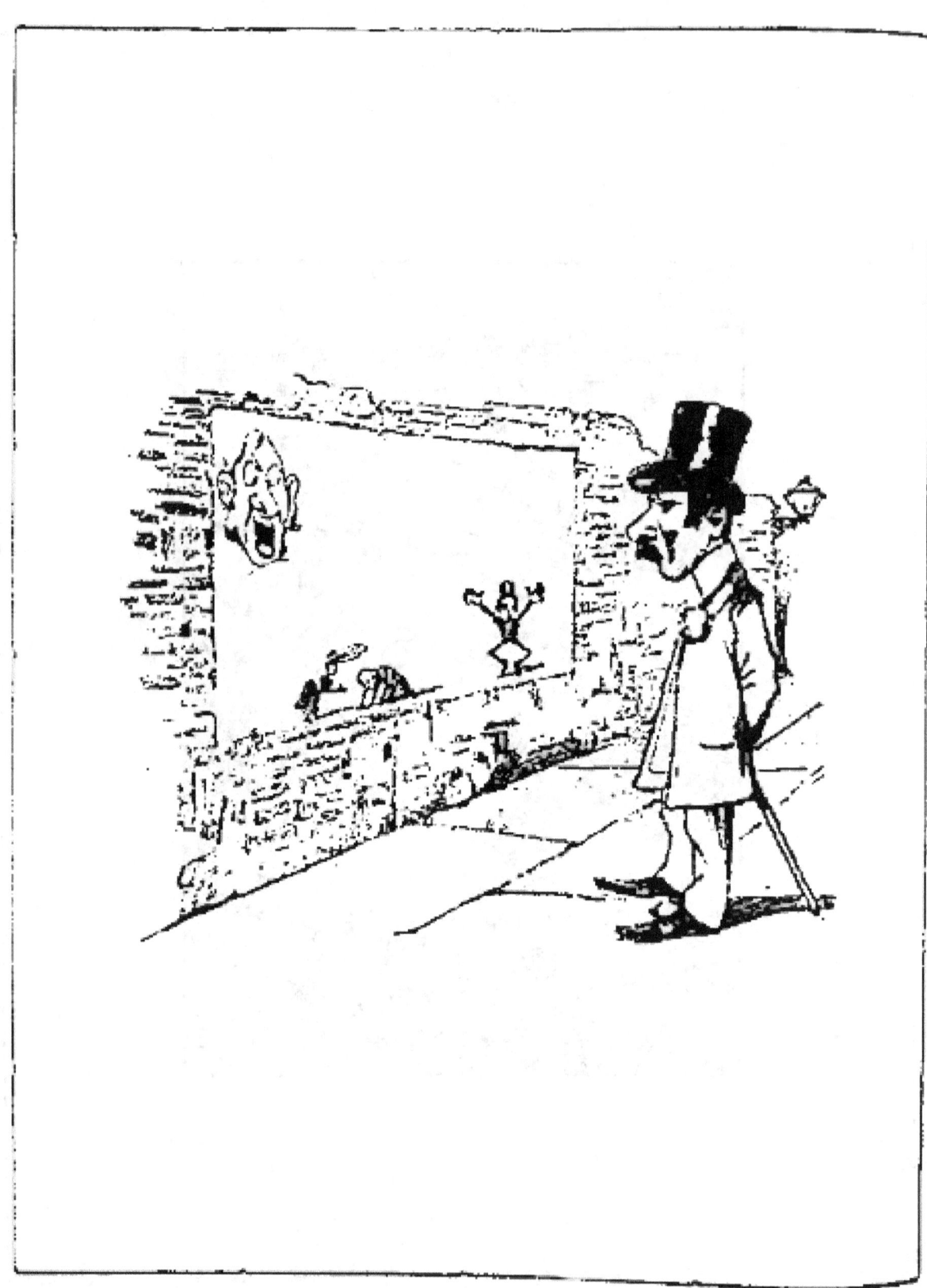

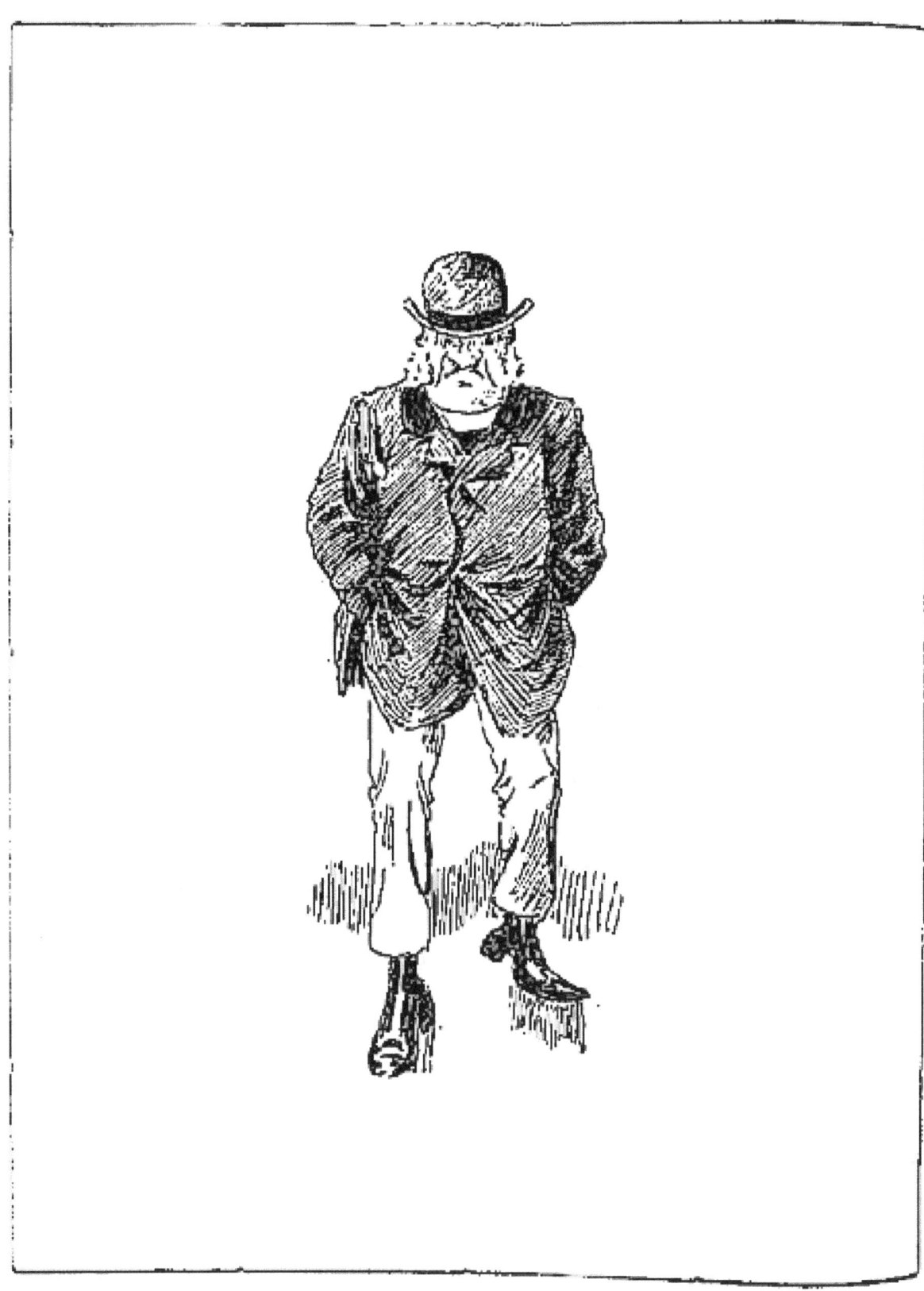

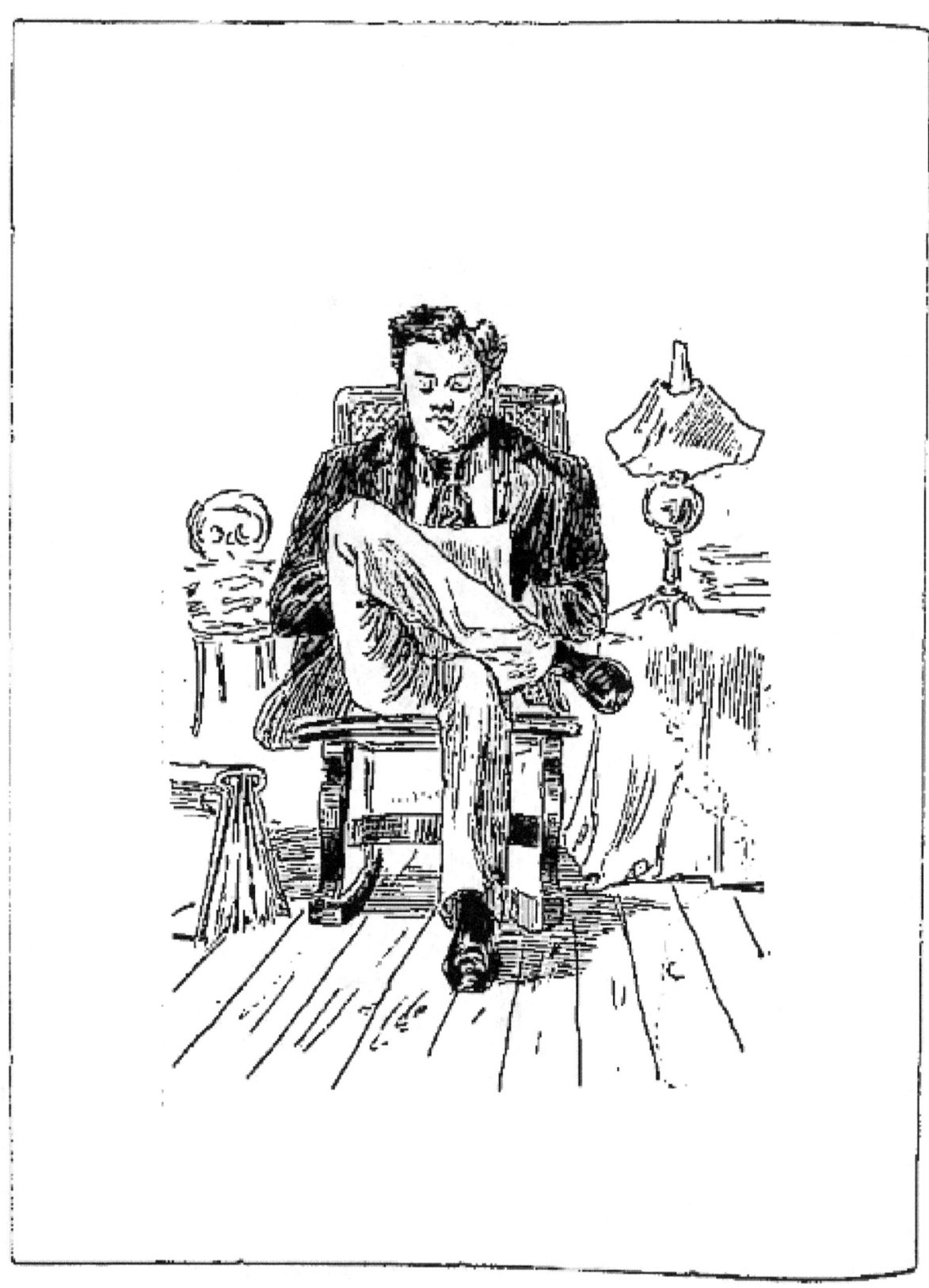

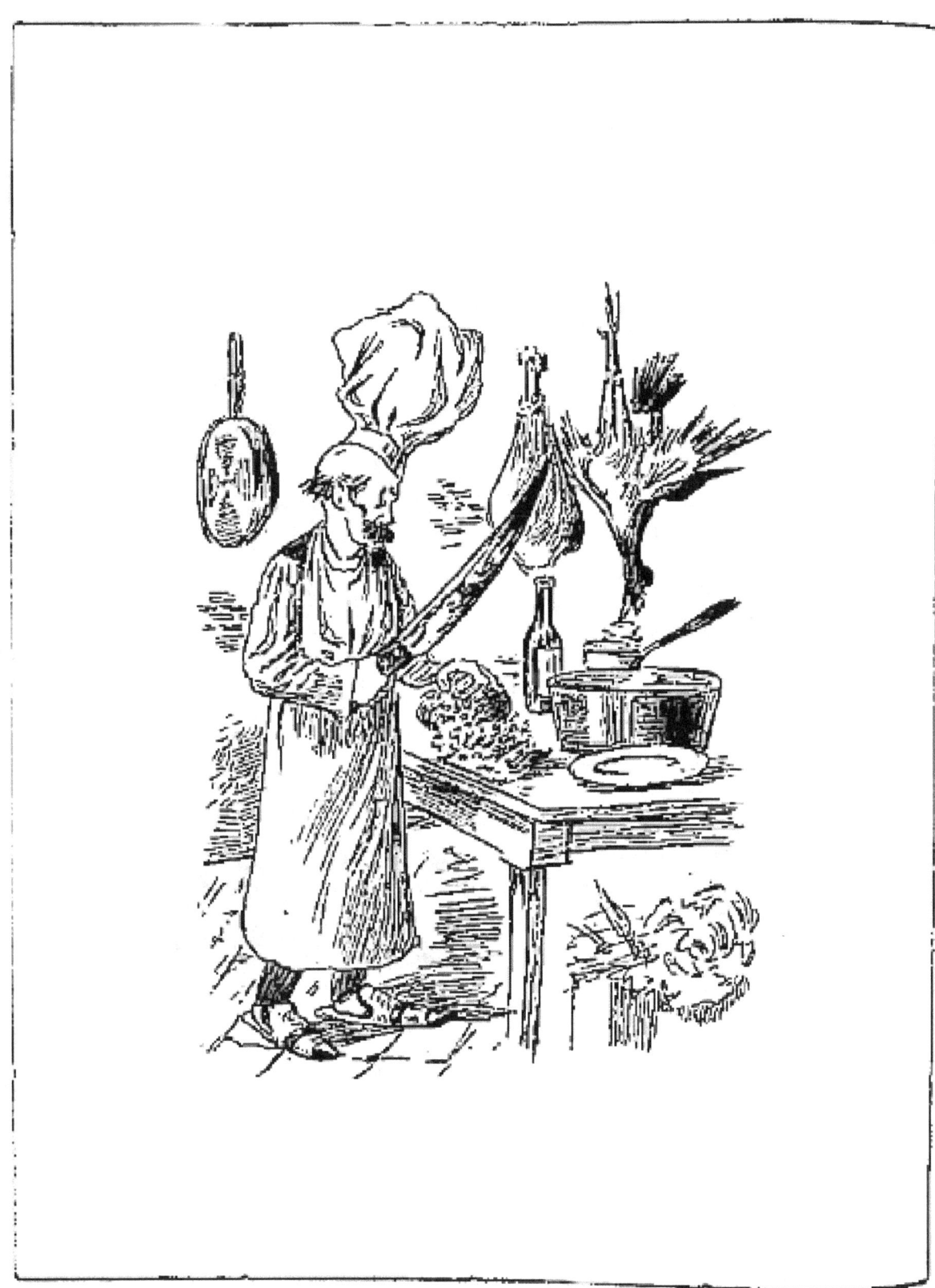

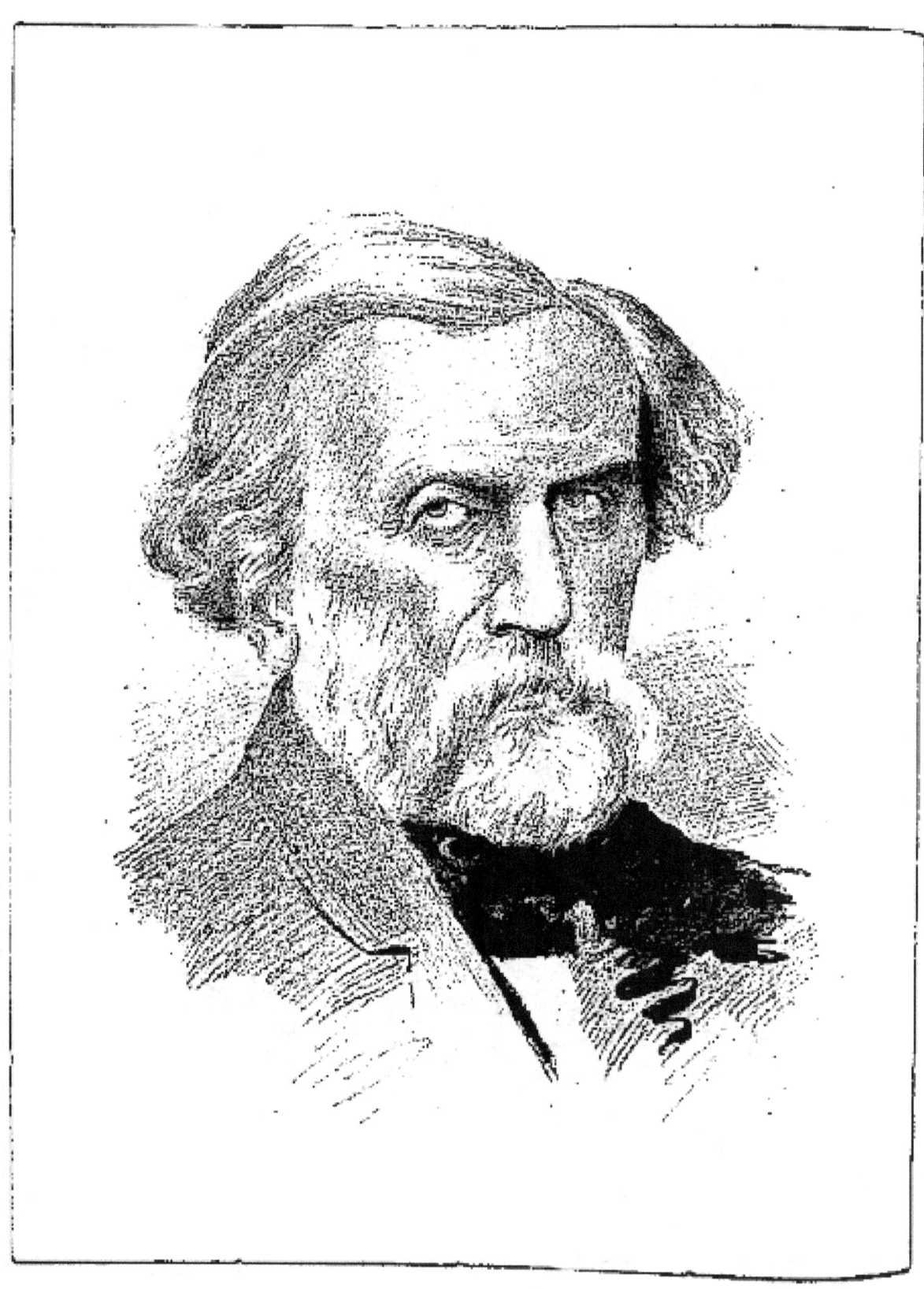

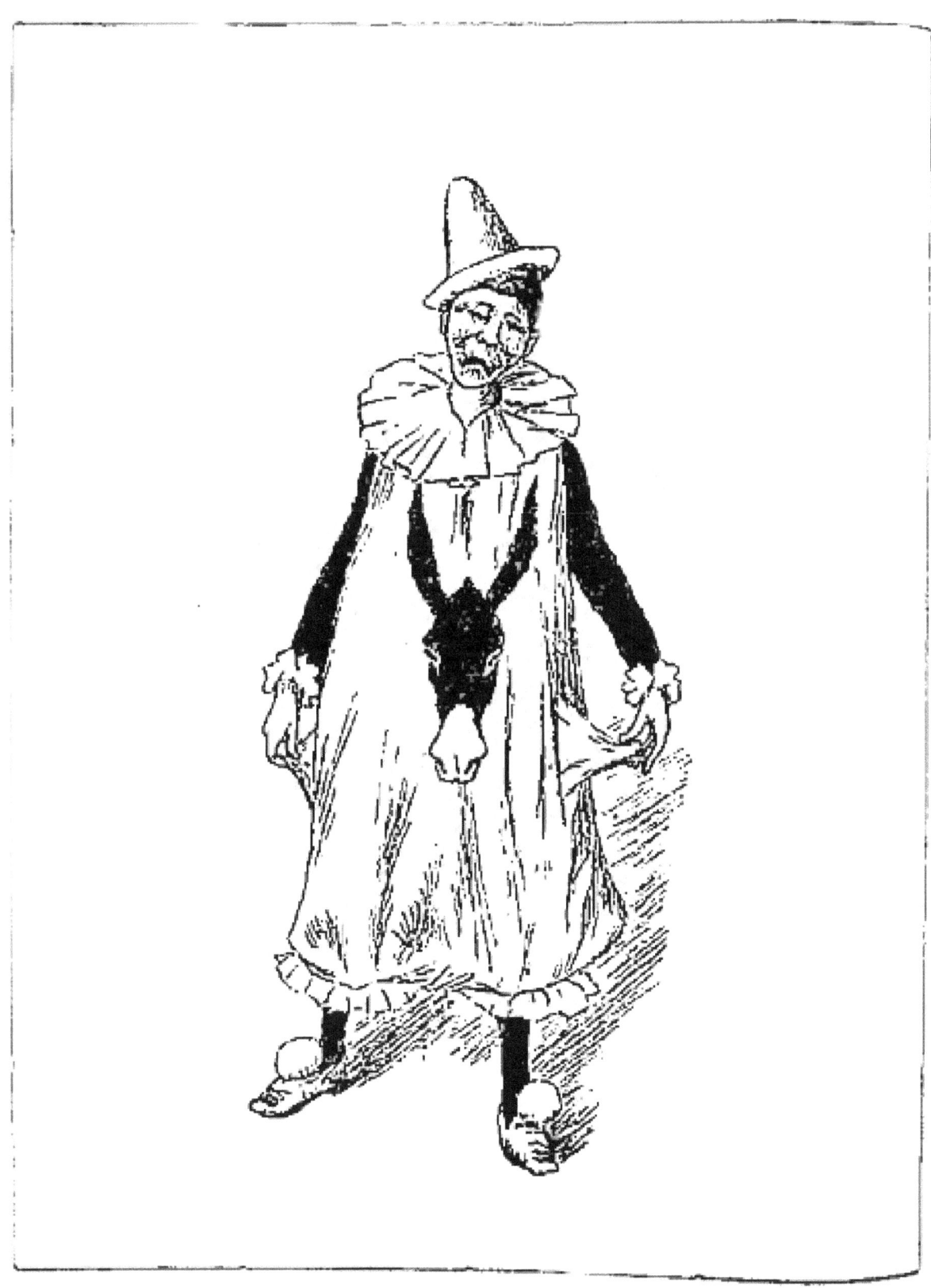

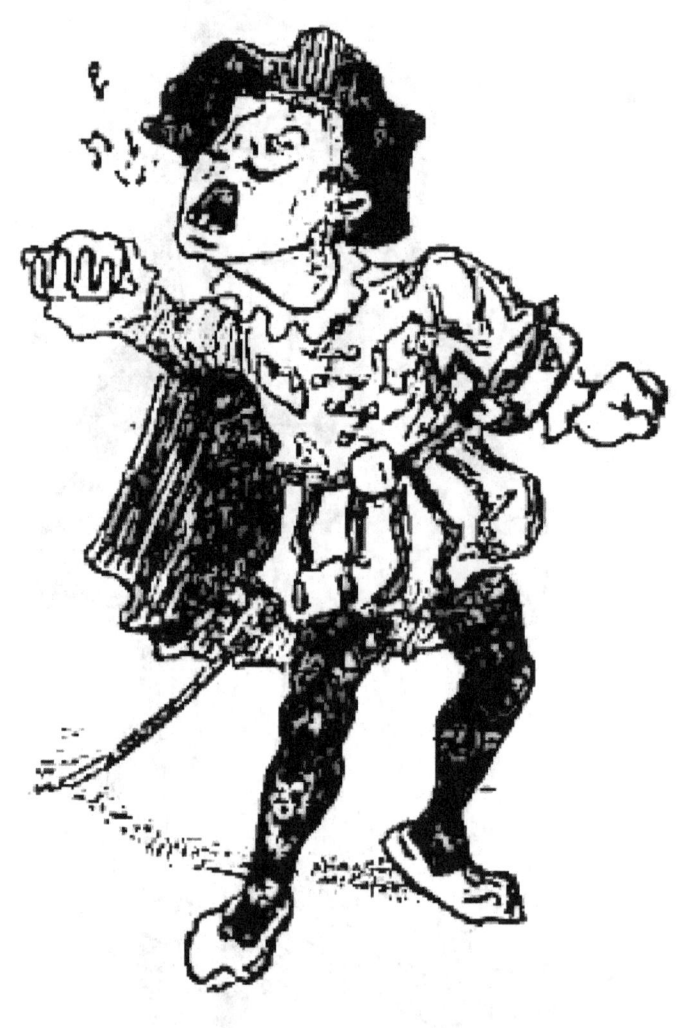

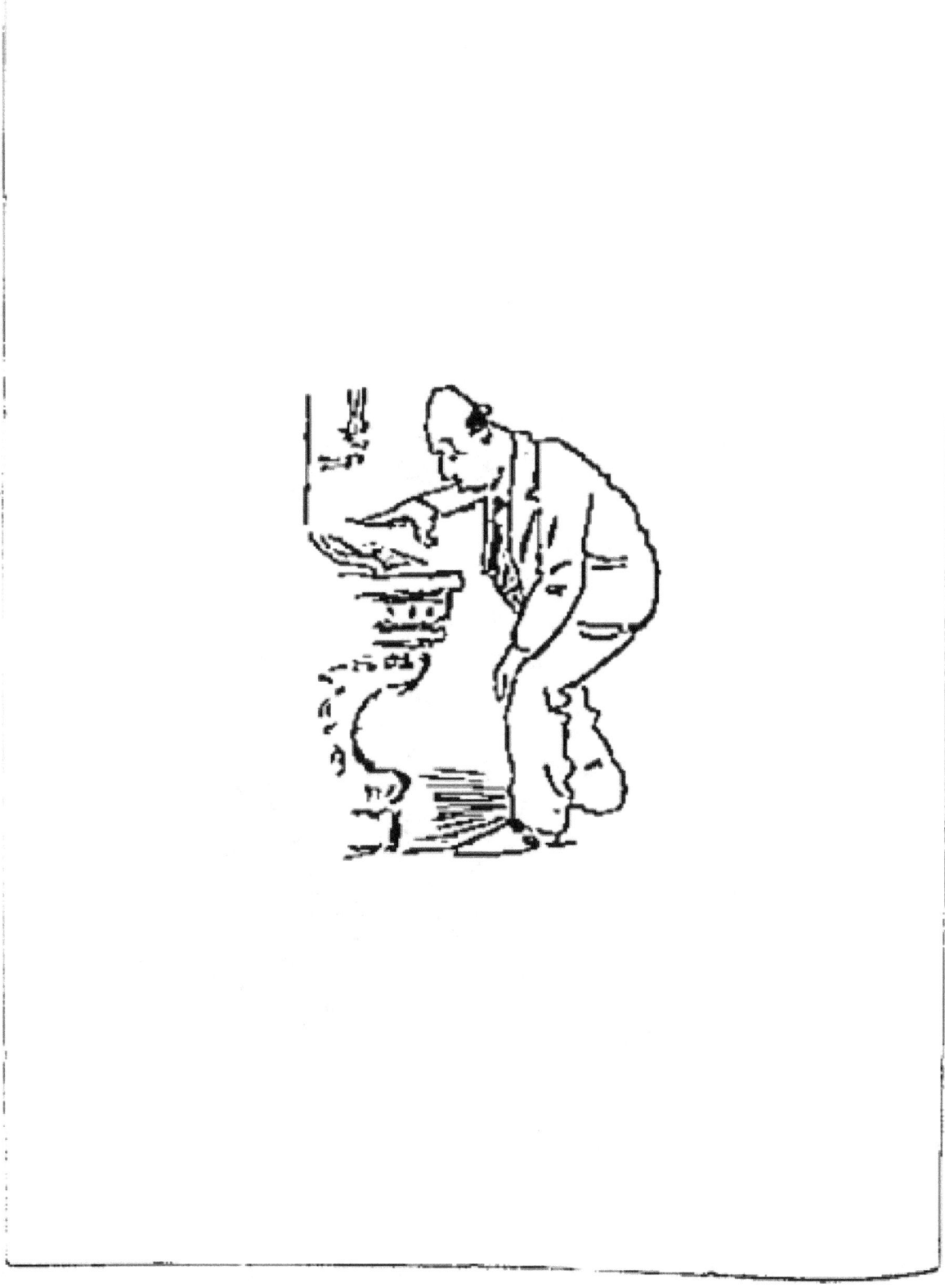

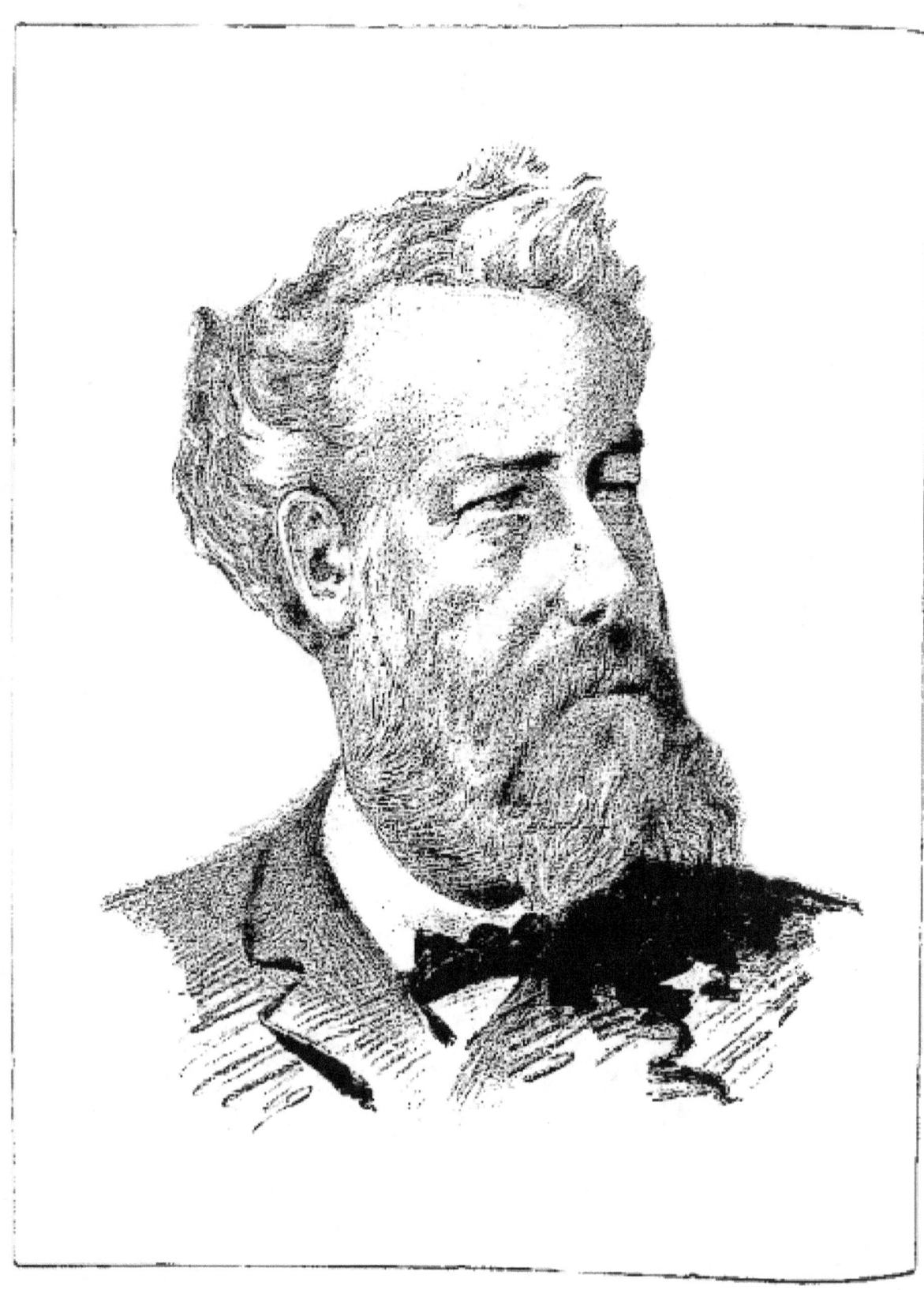

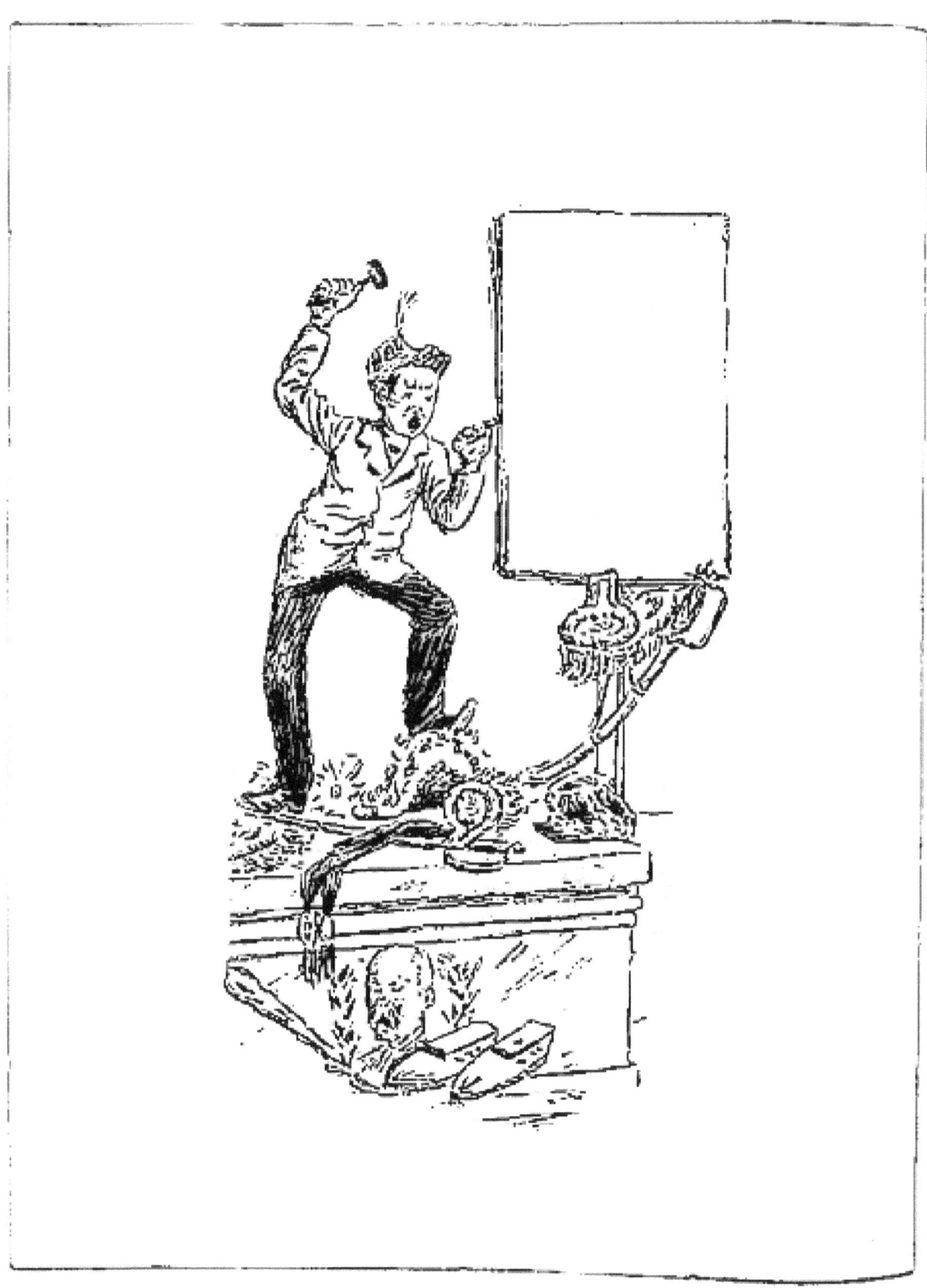

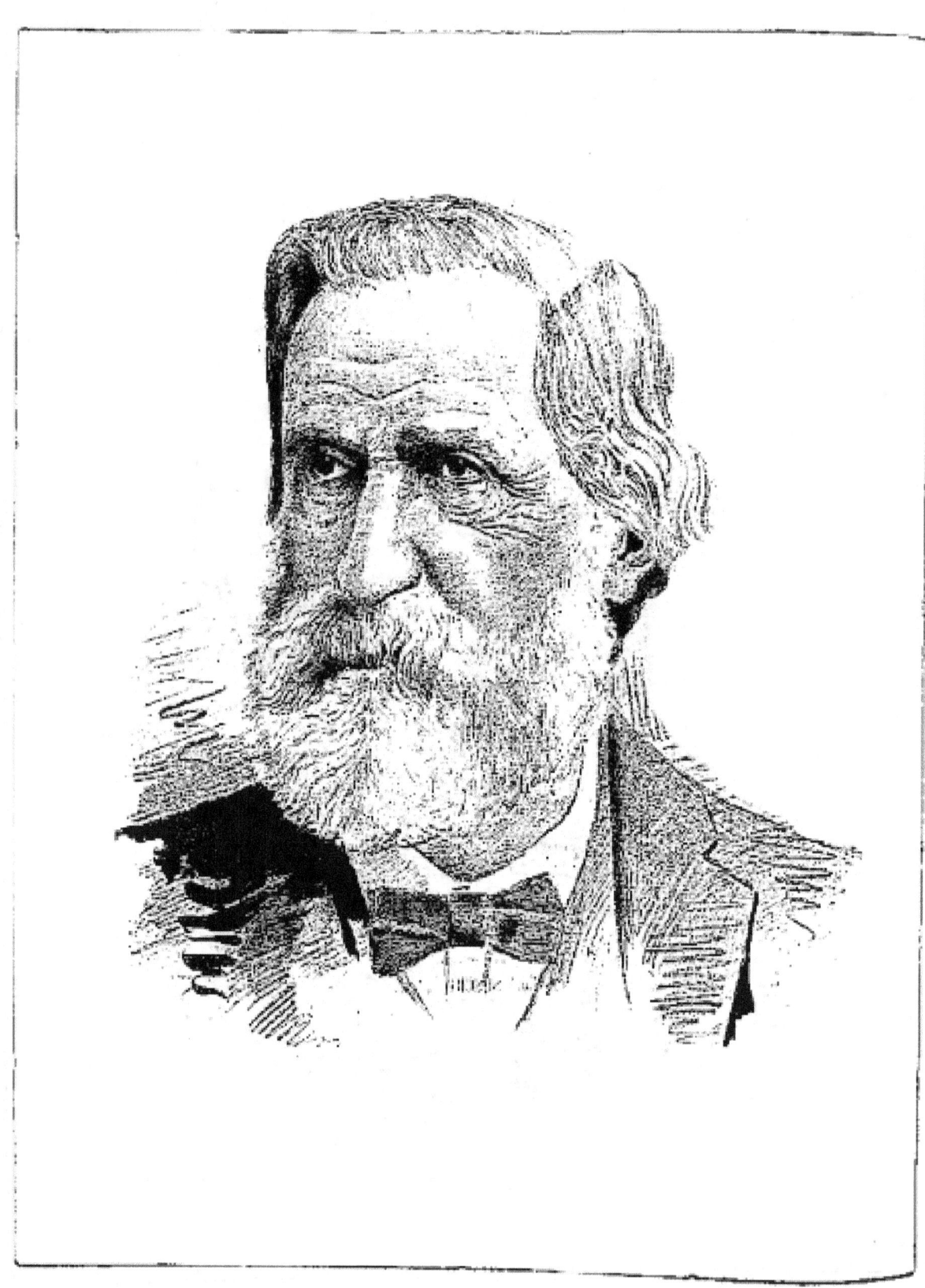

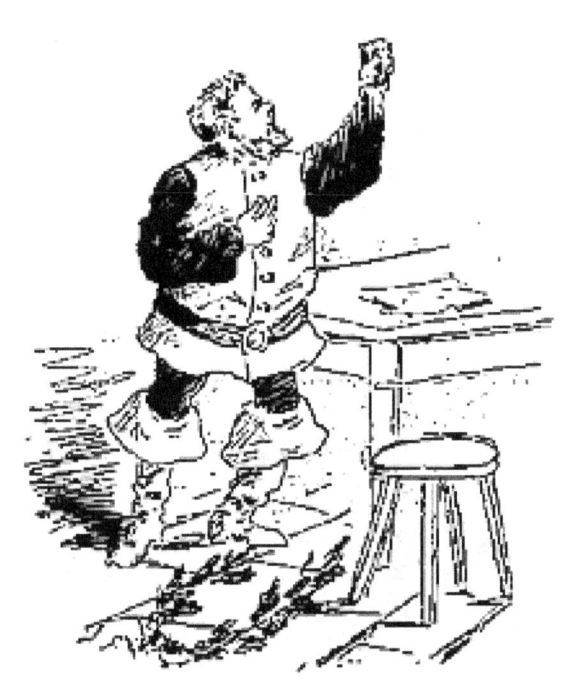

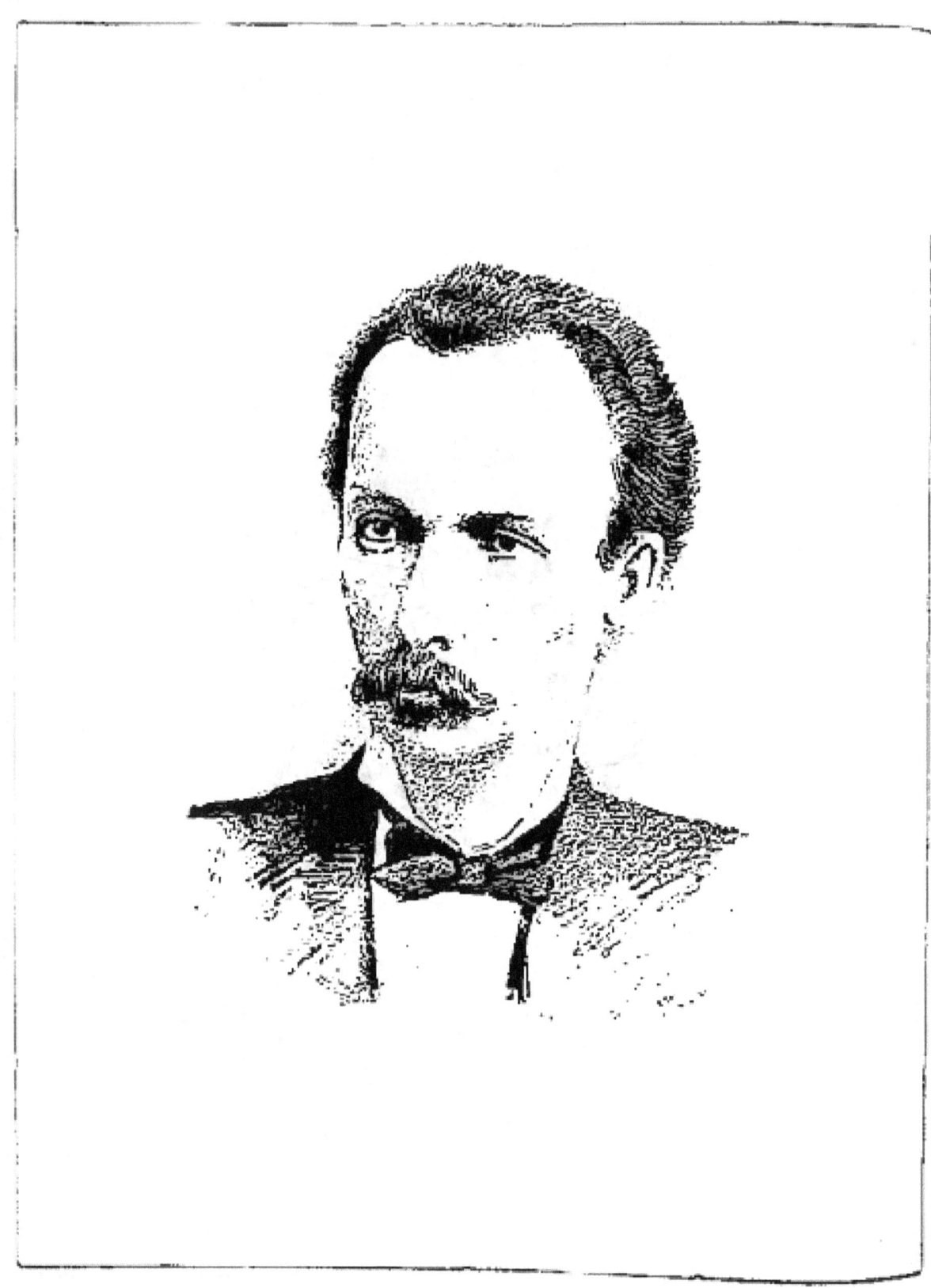

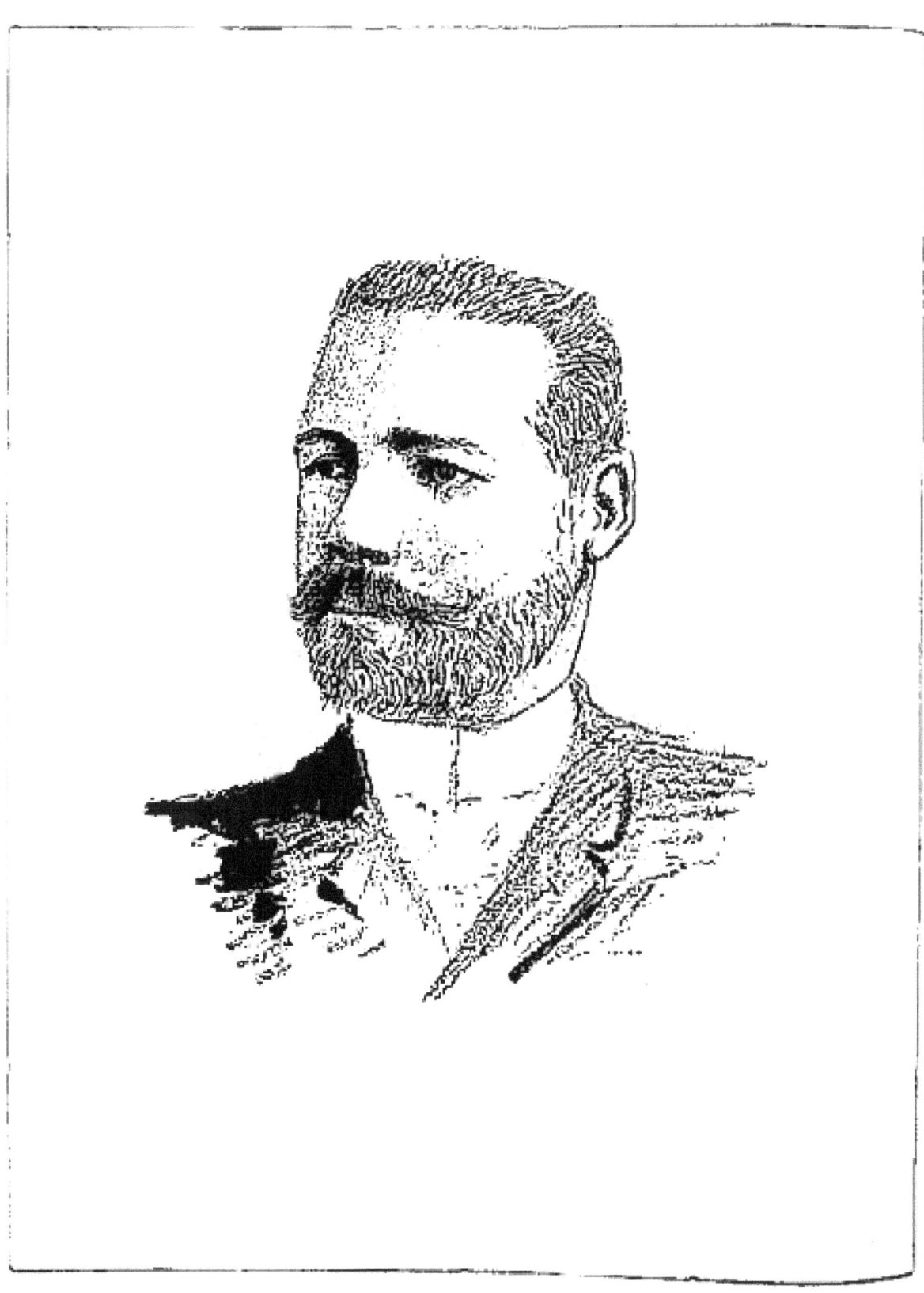

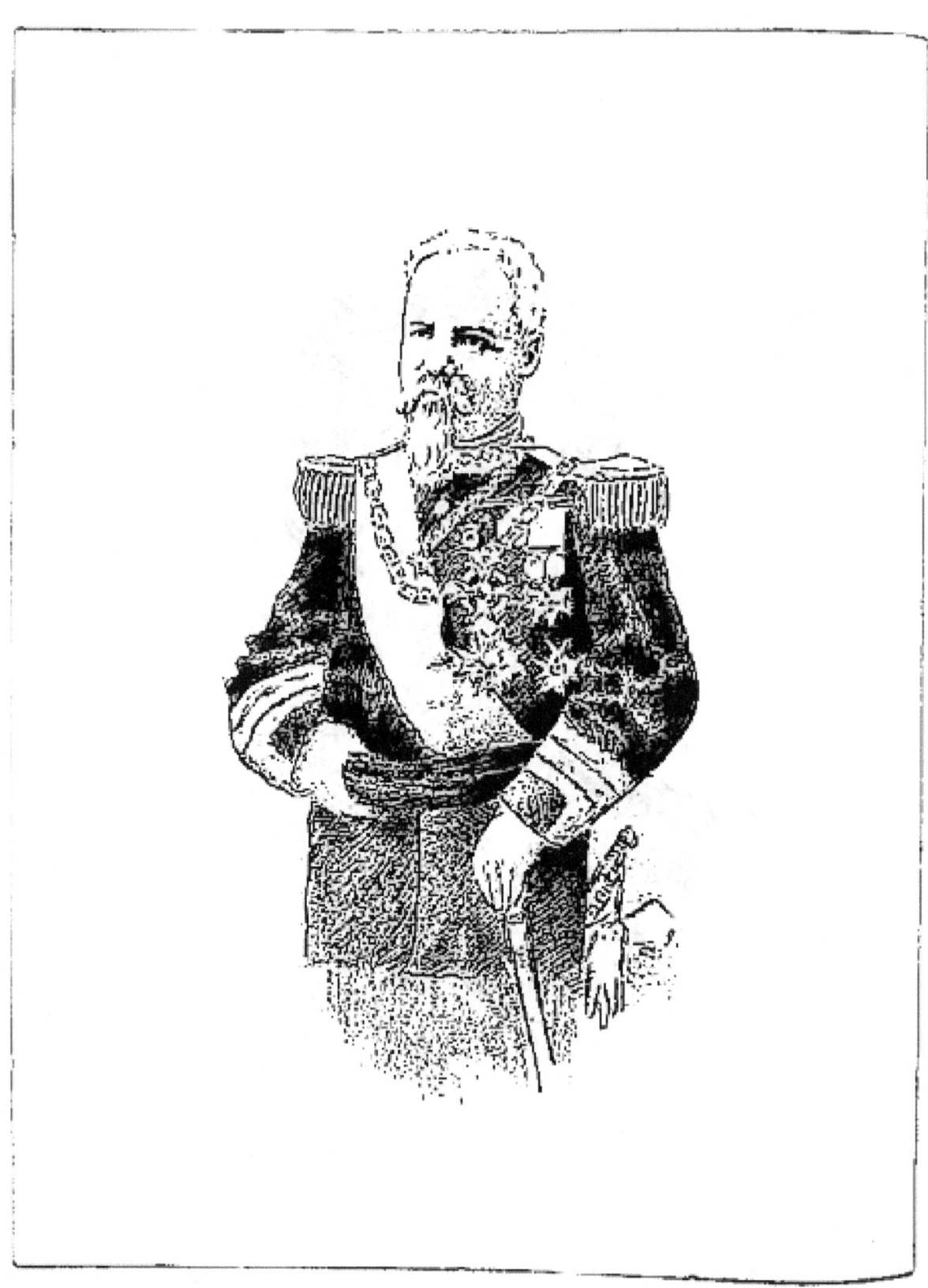

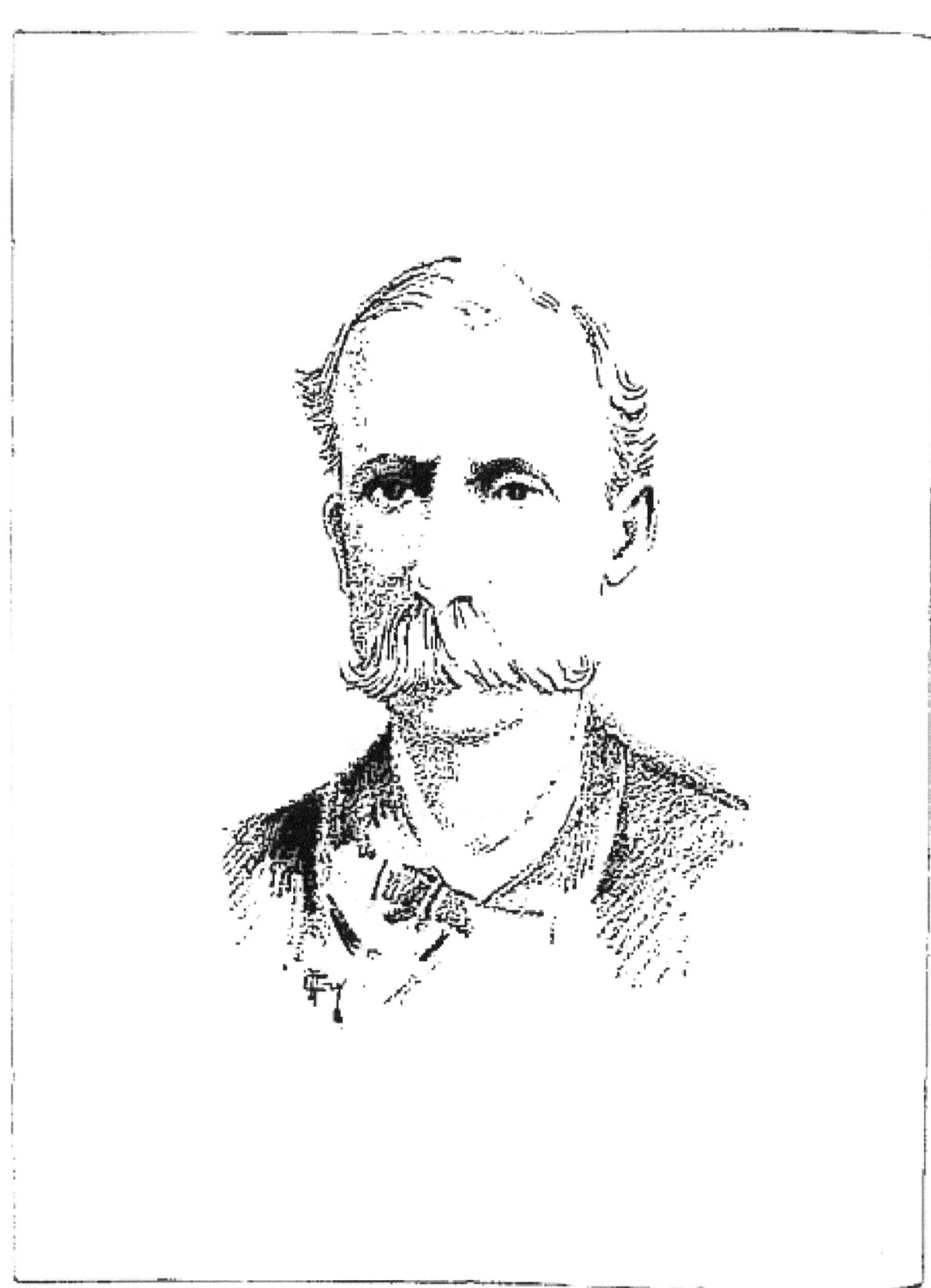

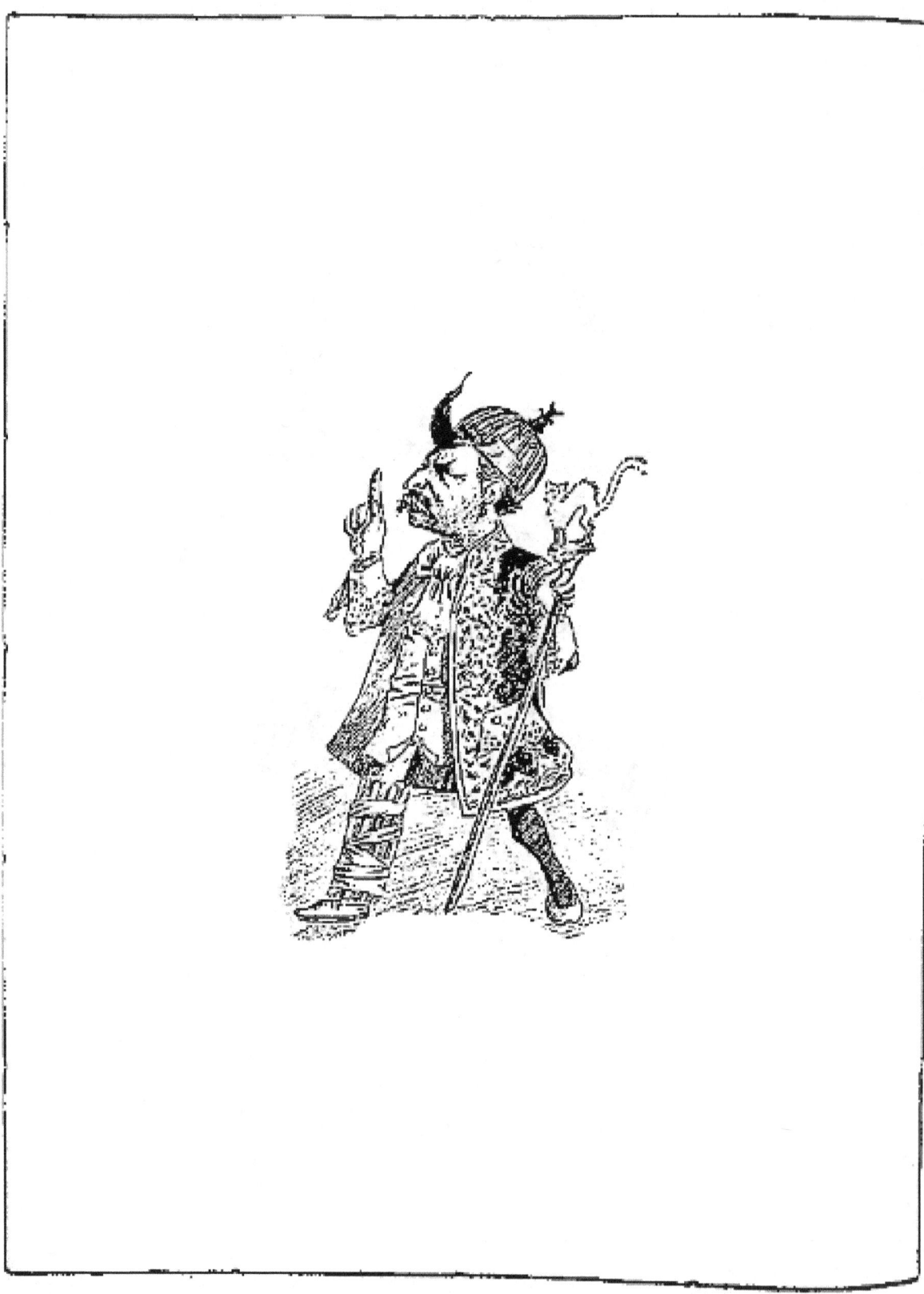

GROUPS & SCENES

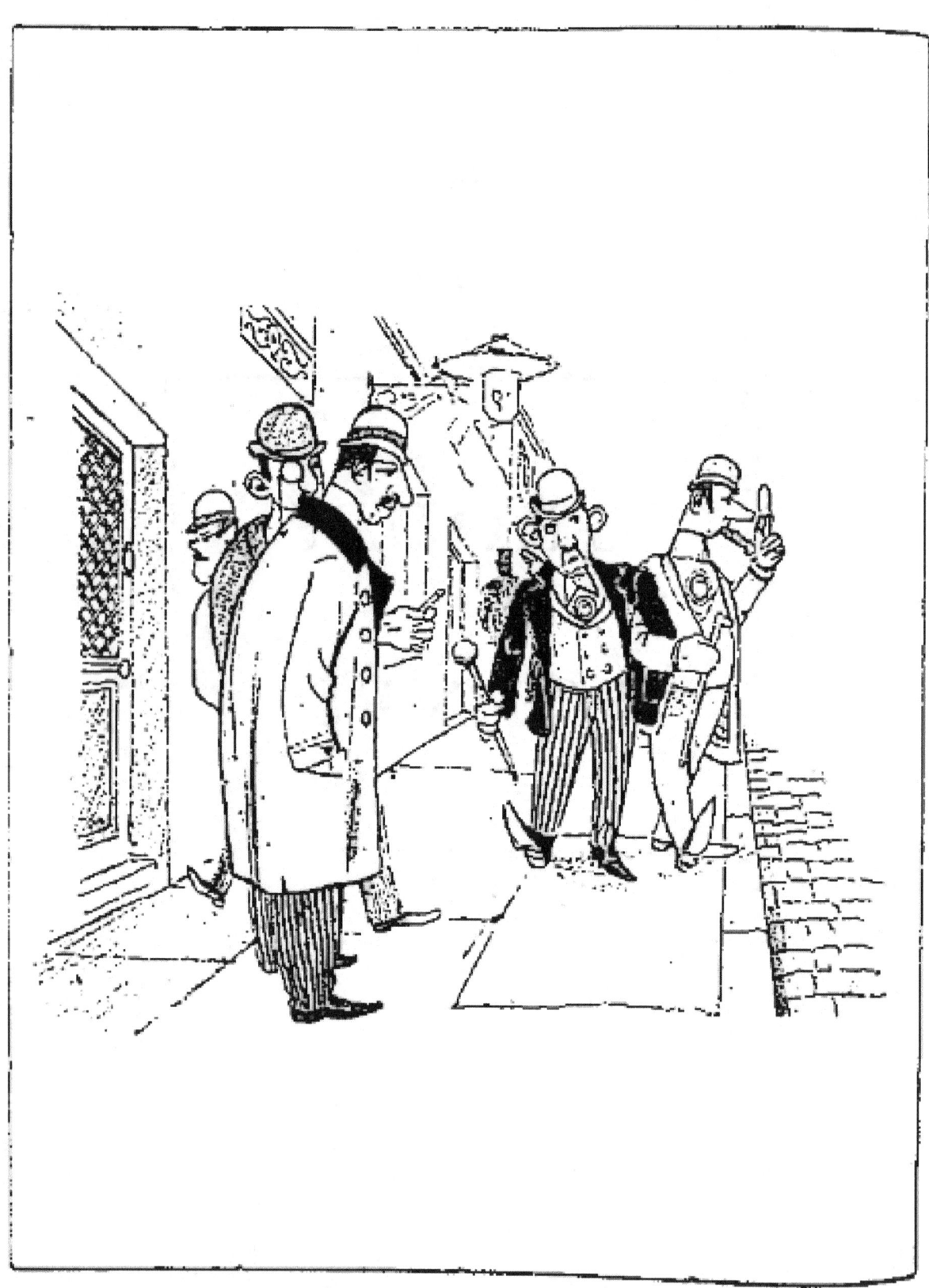

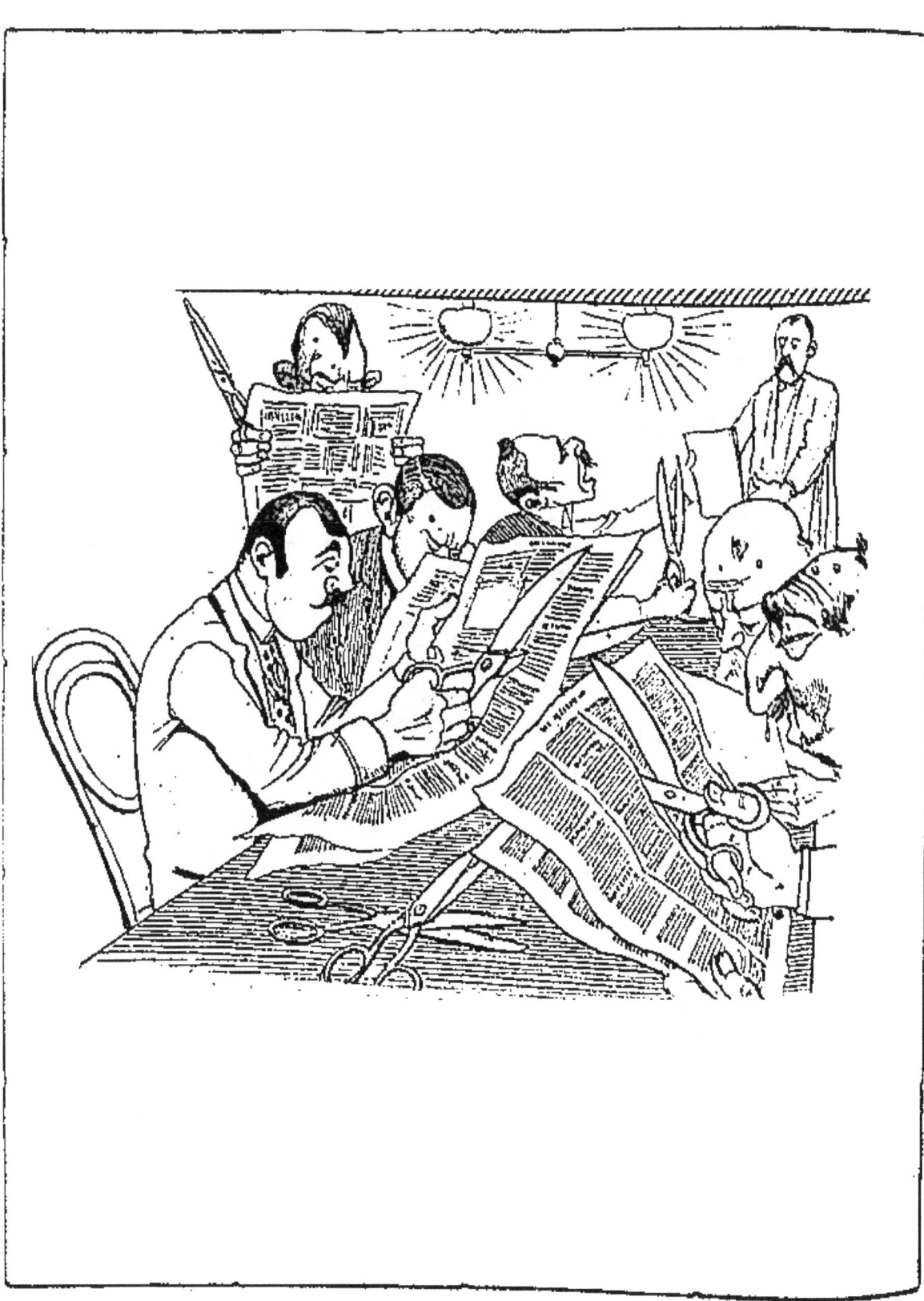

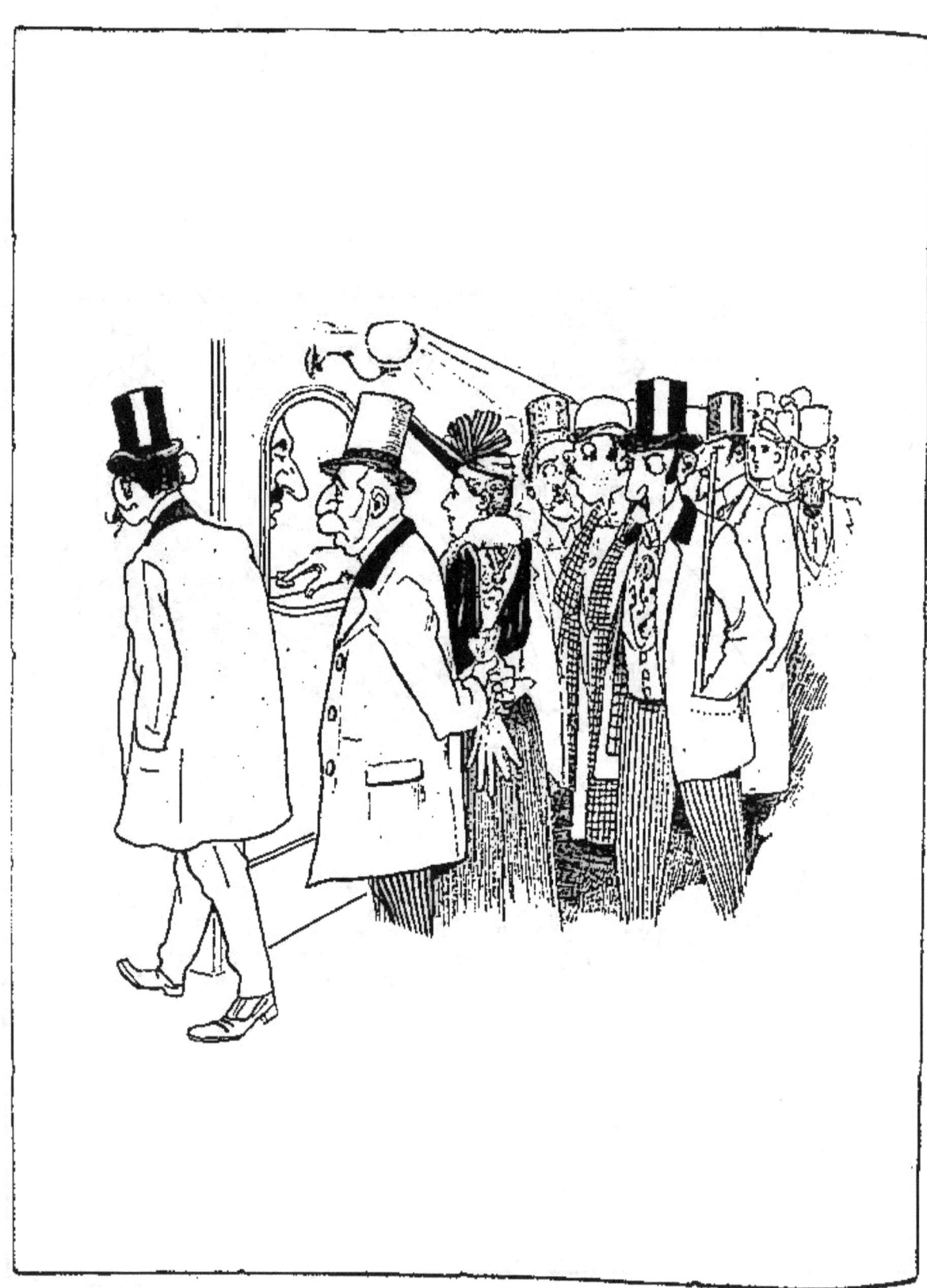

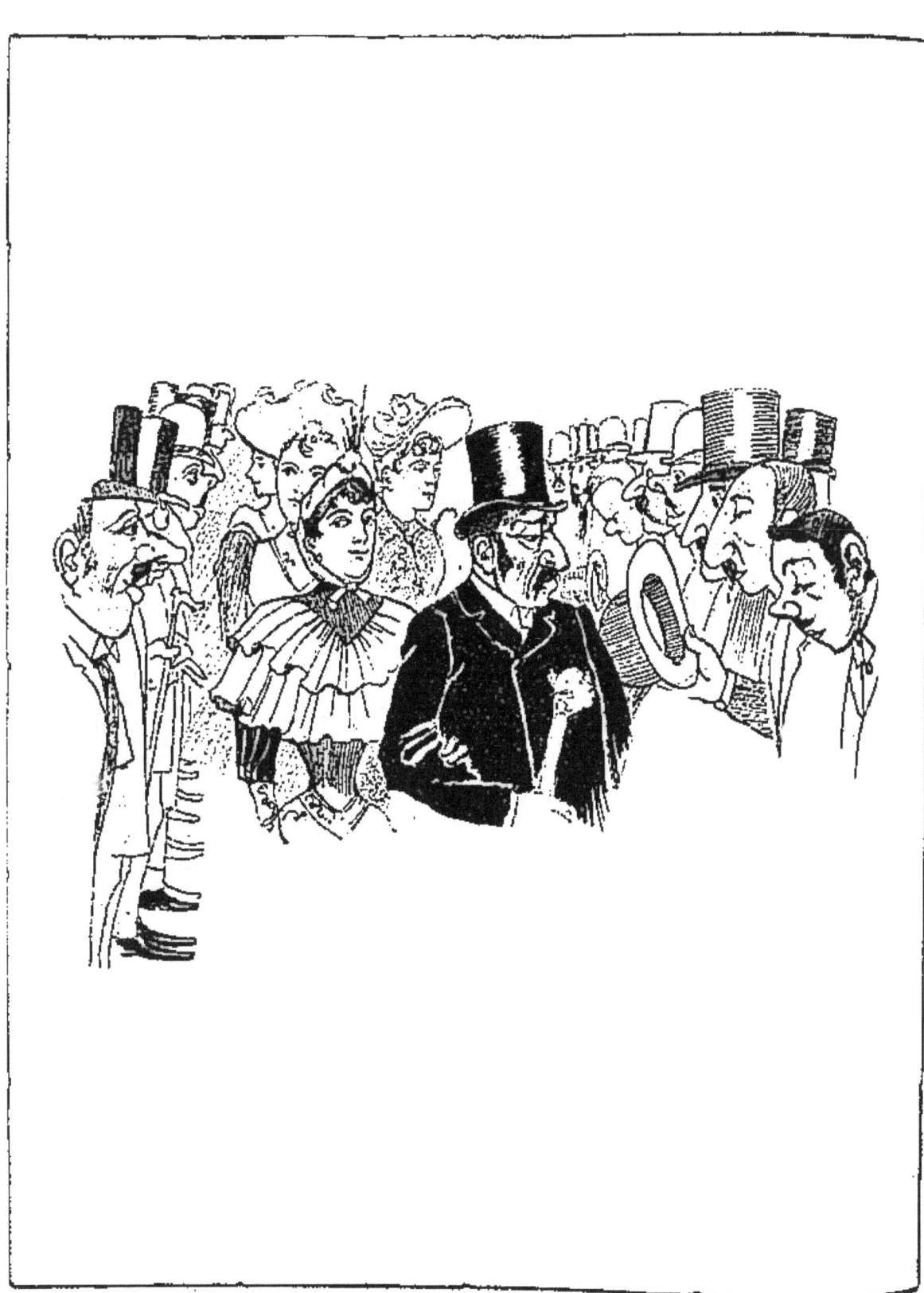

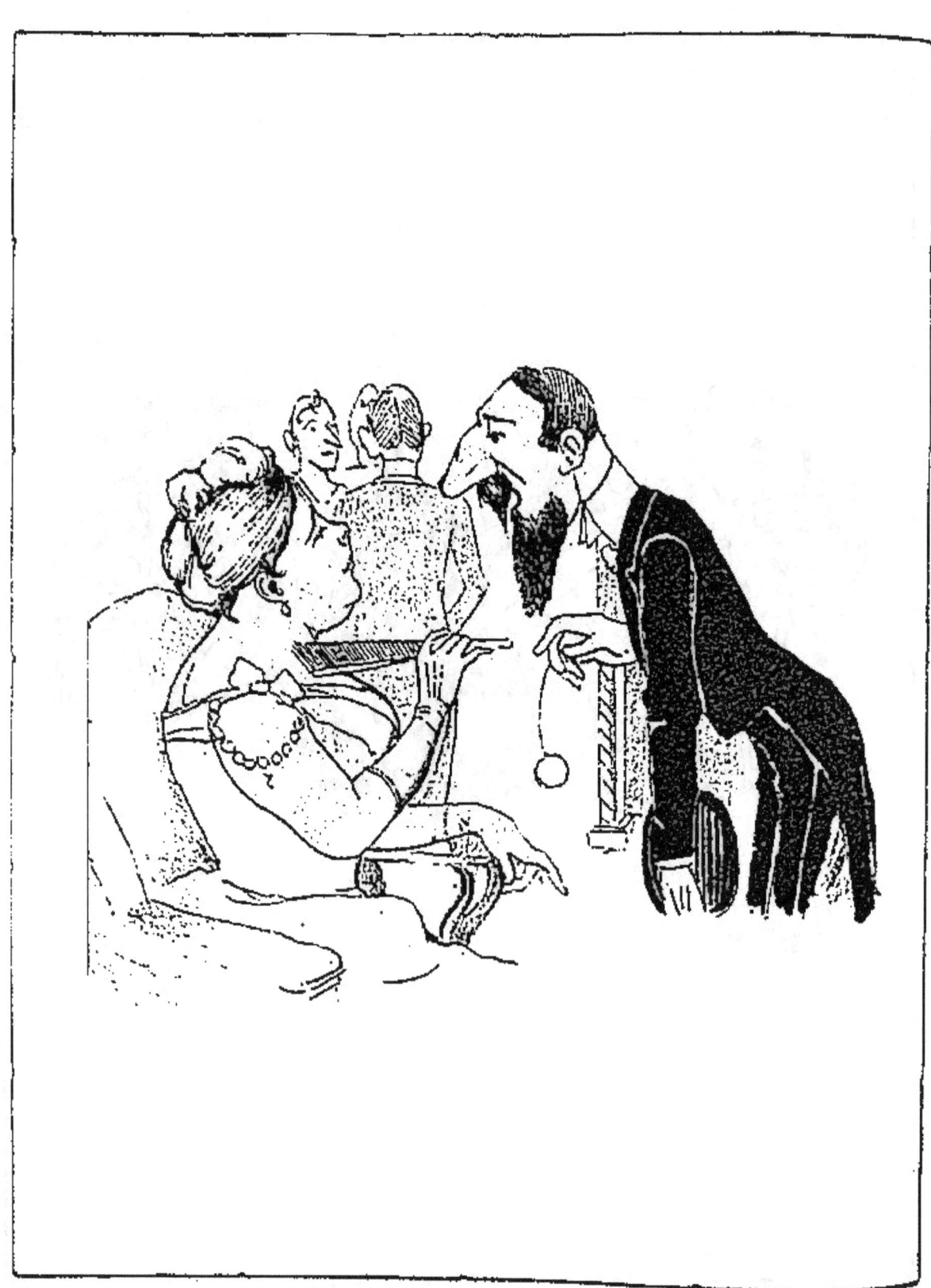

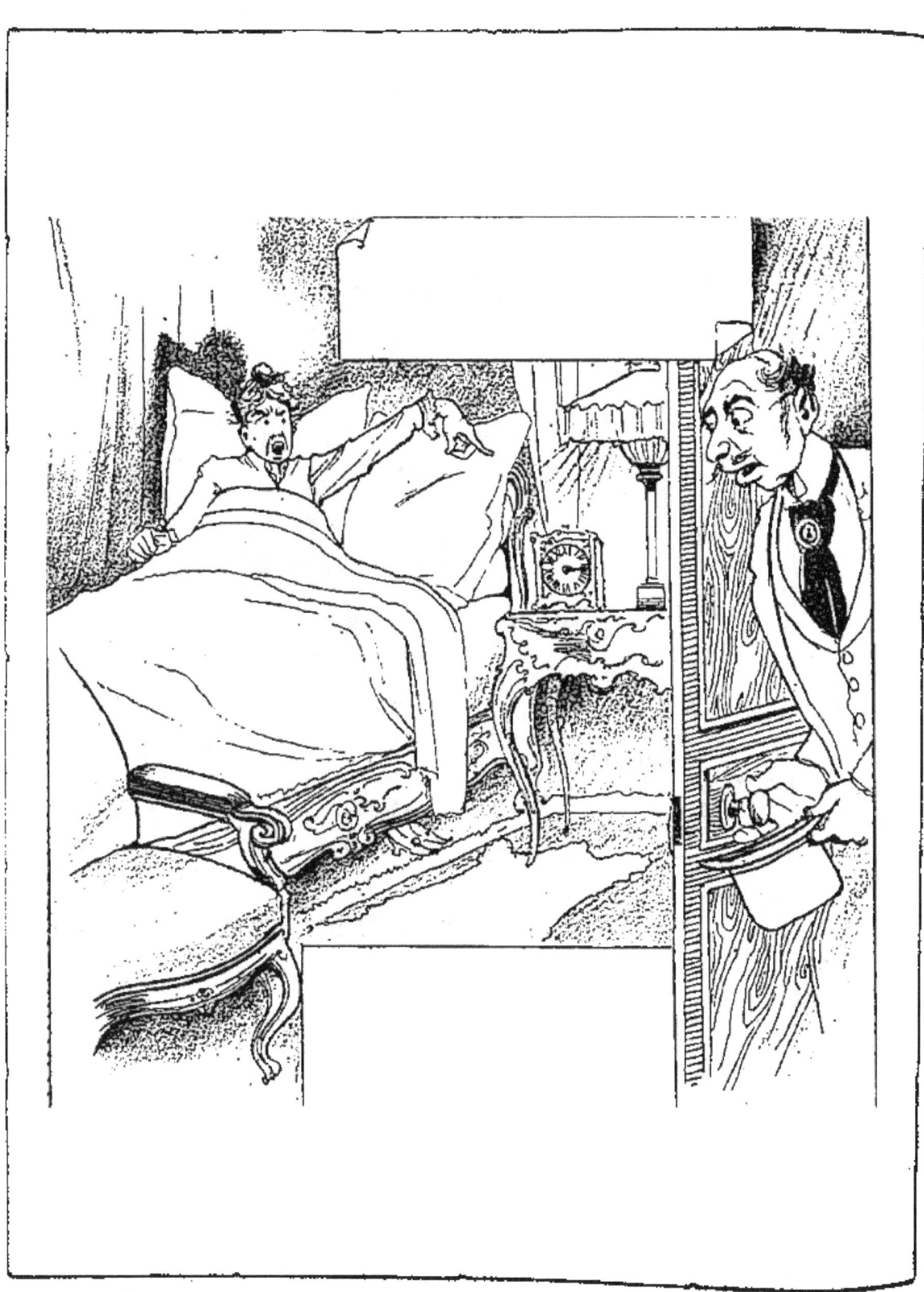

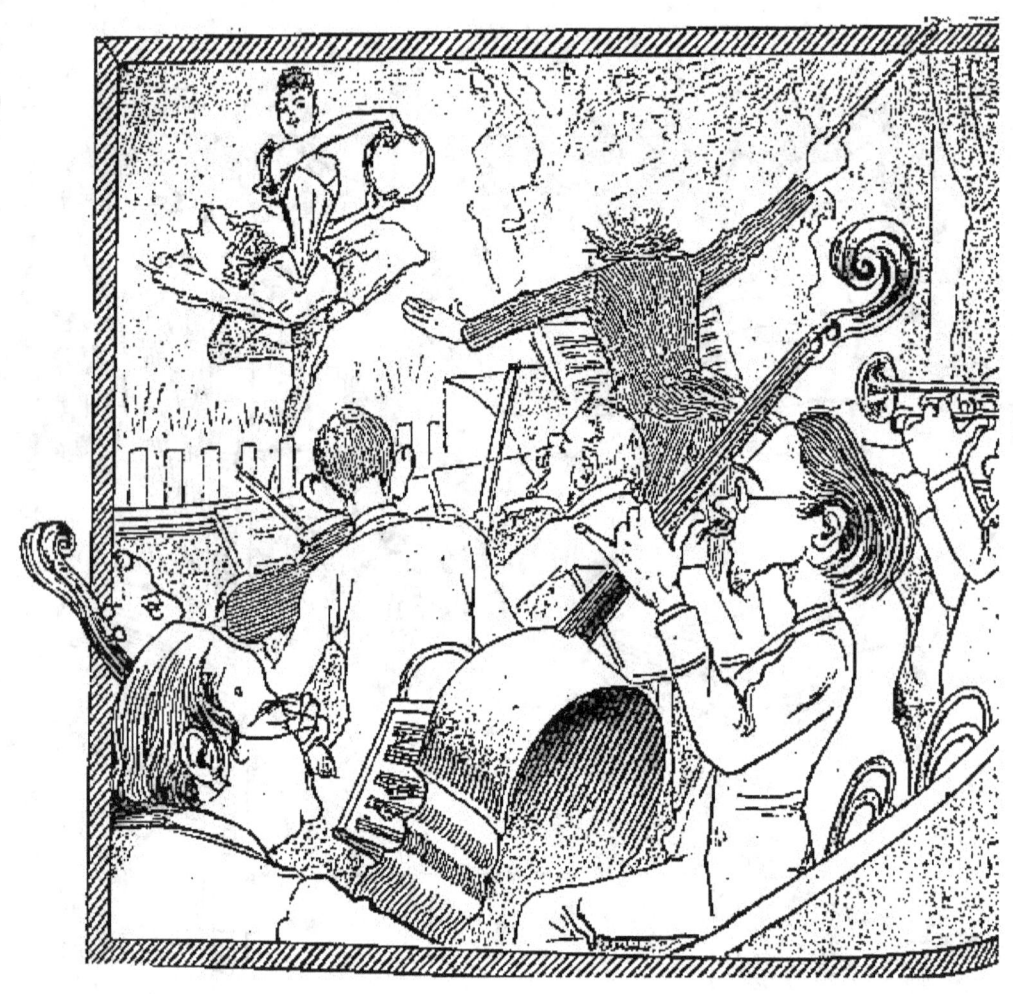

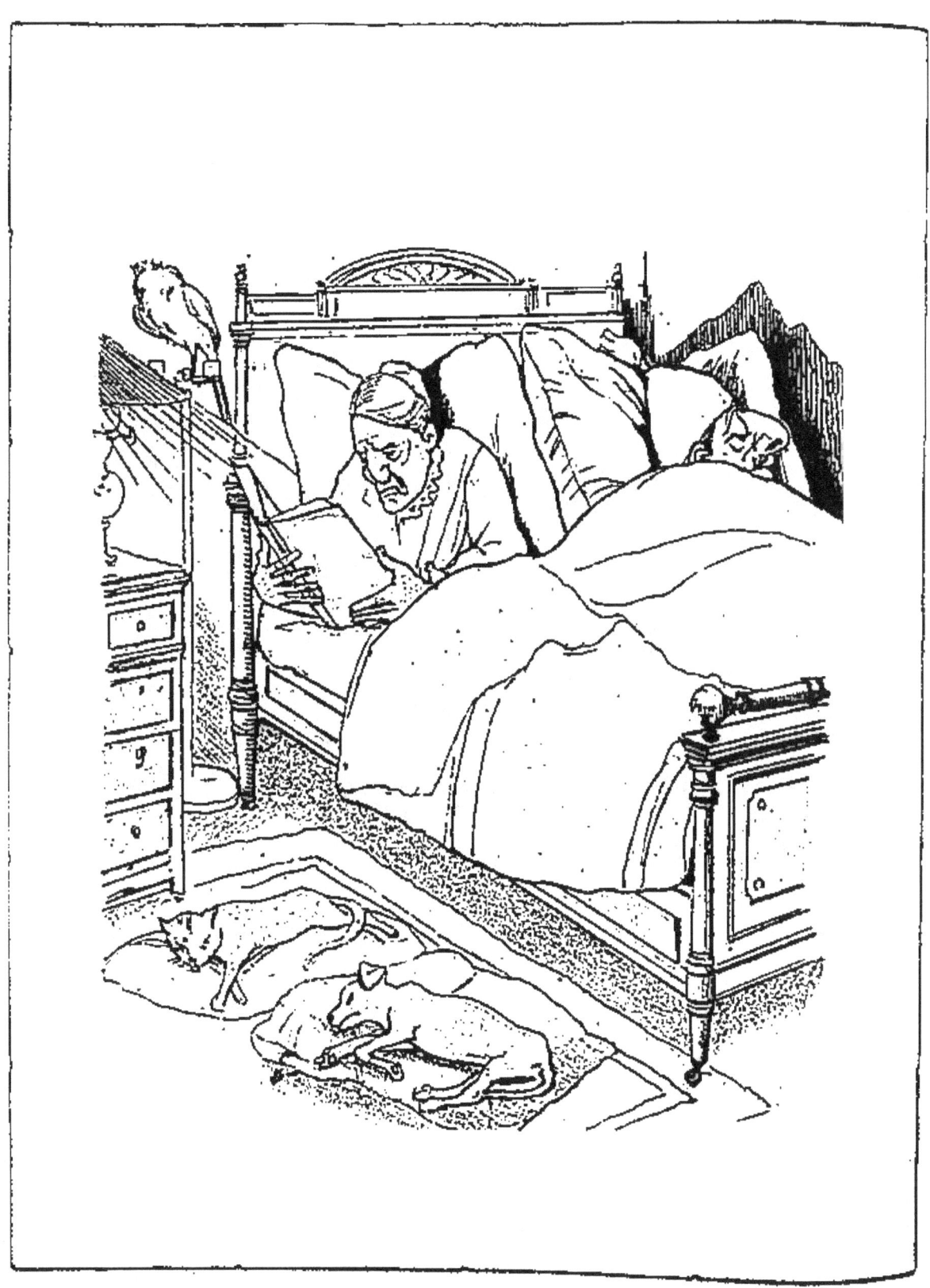

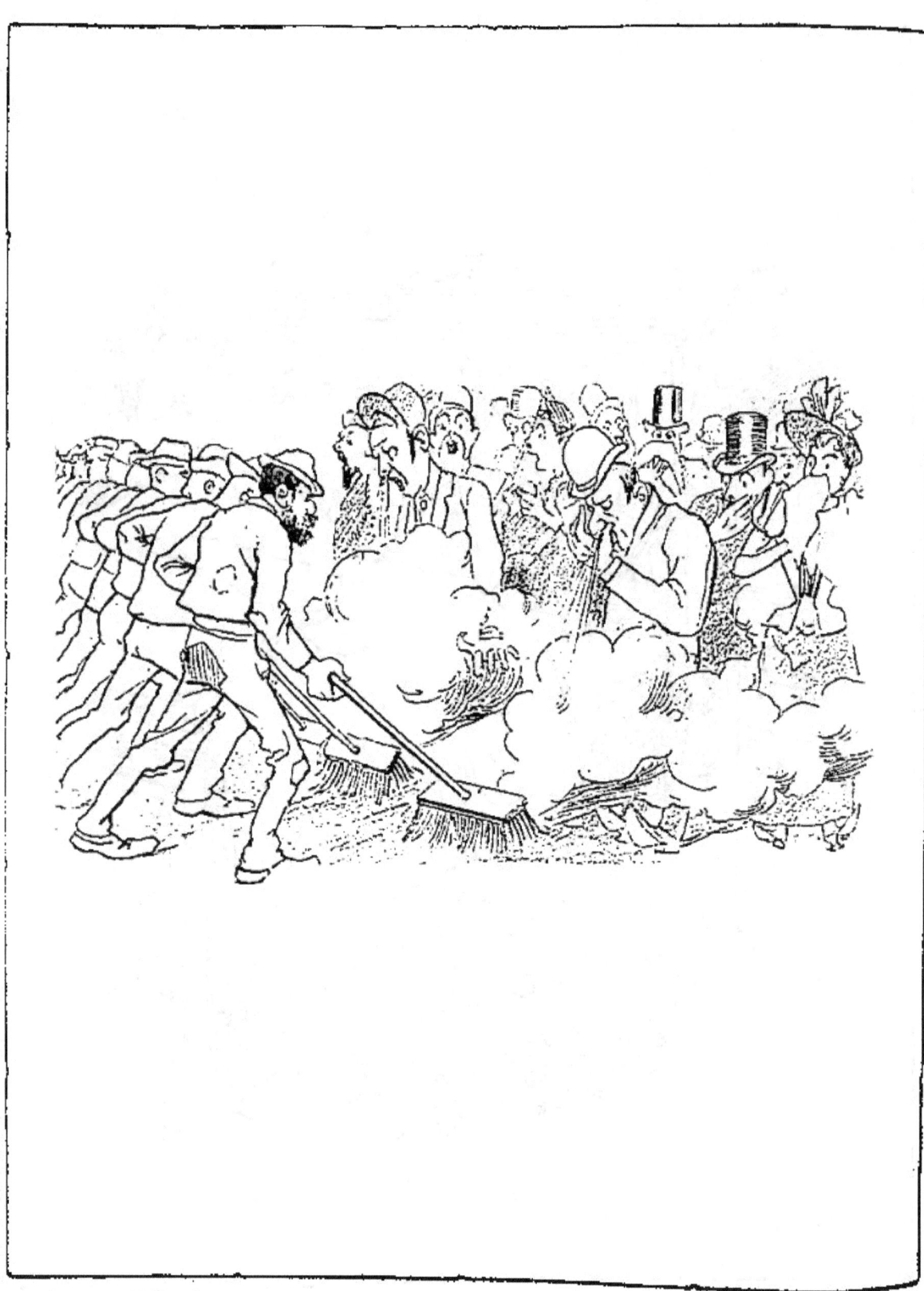

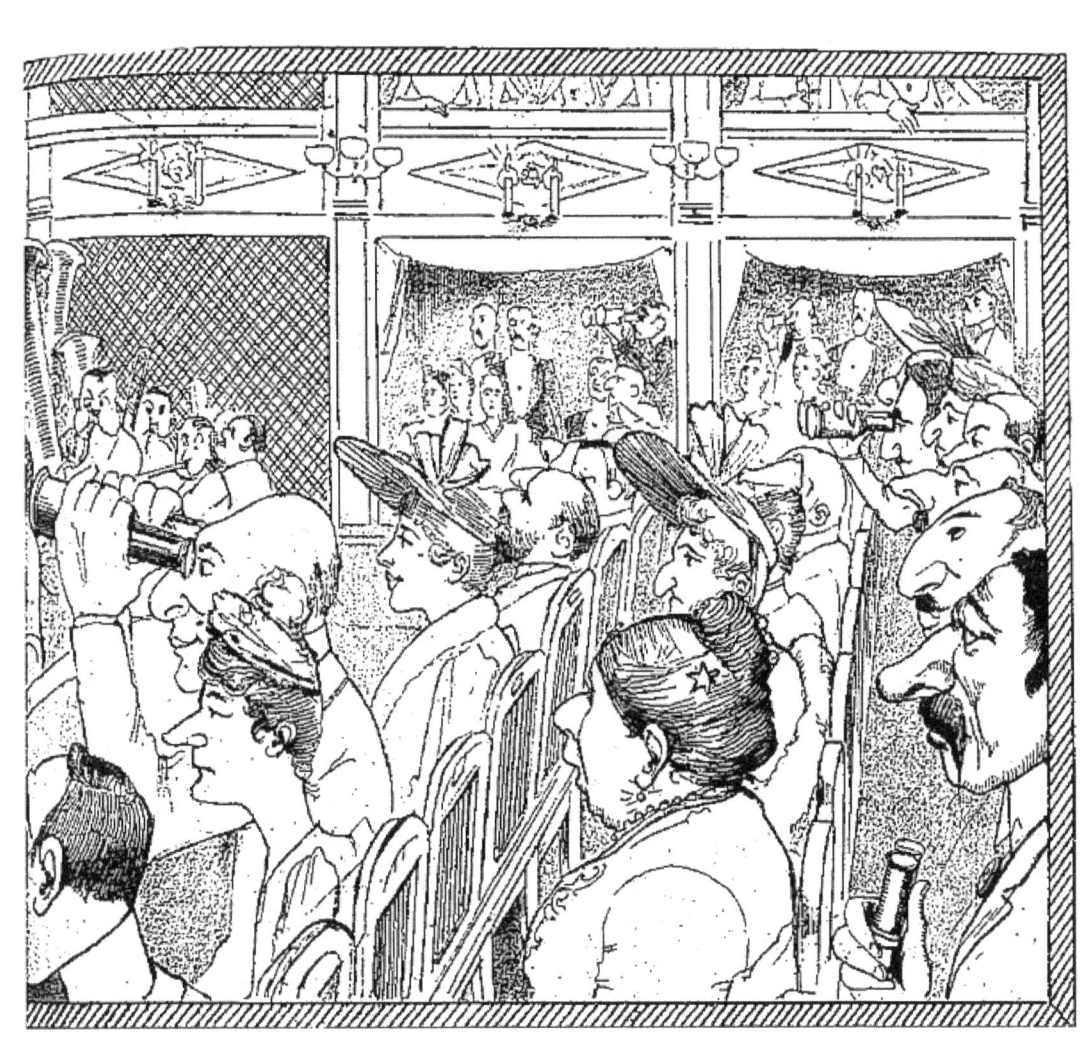

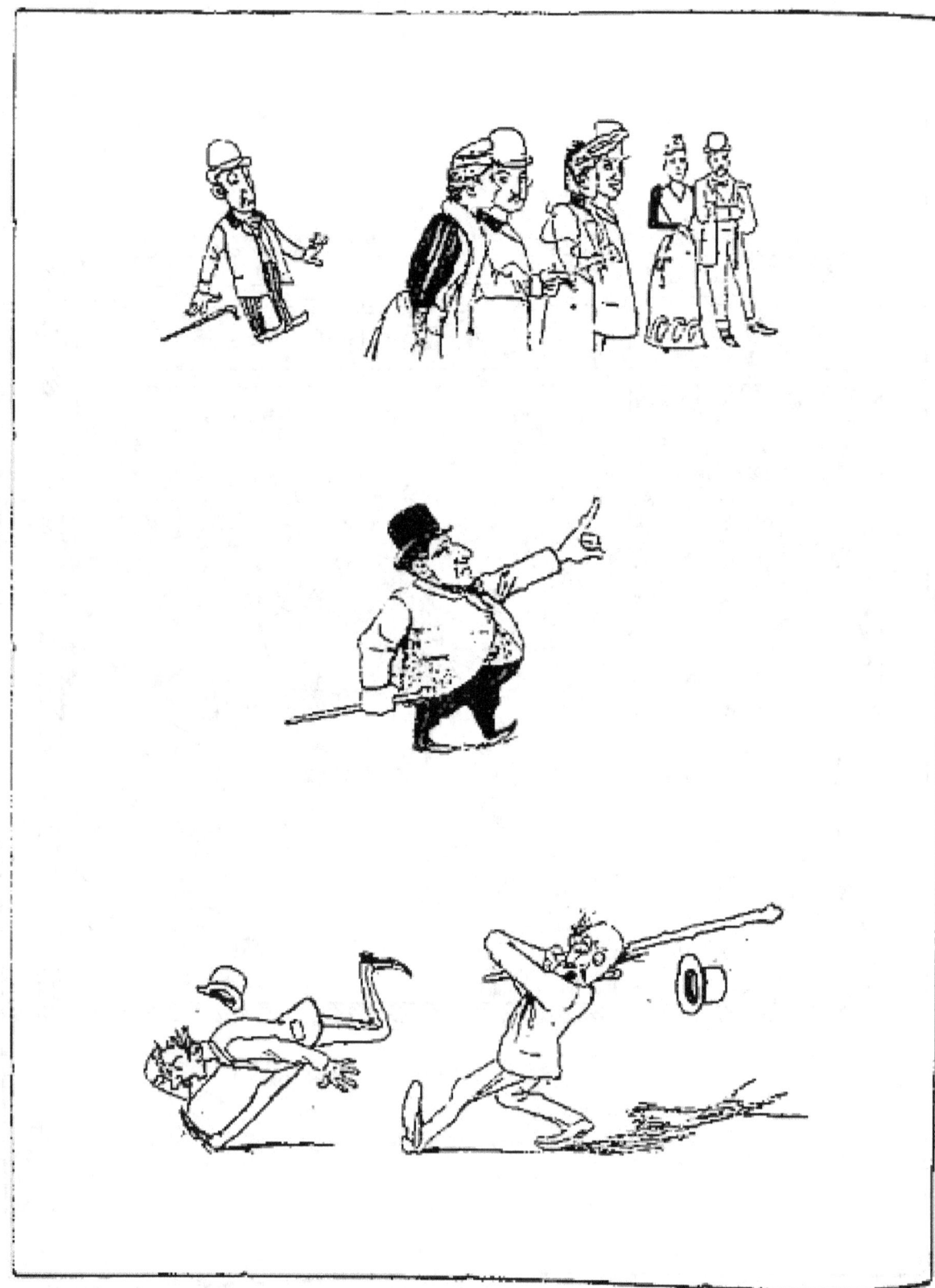

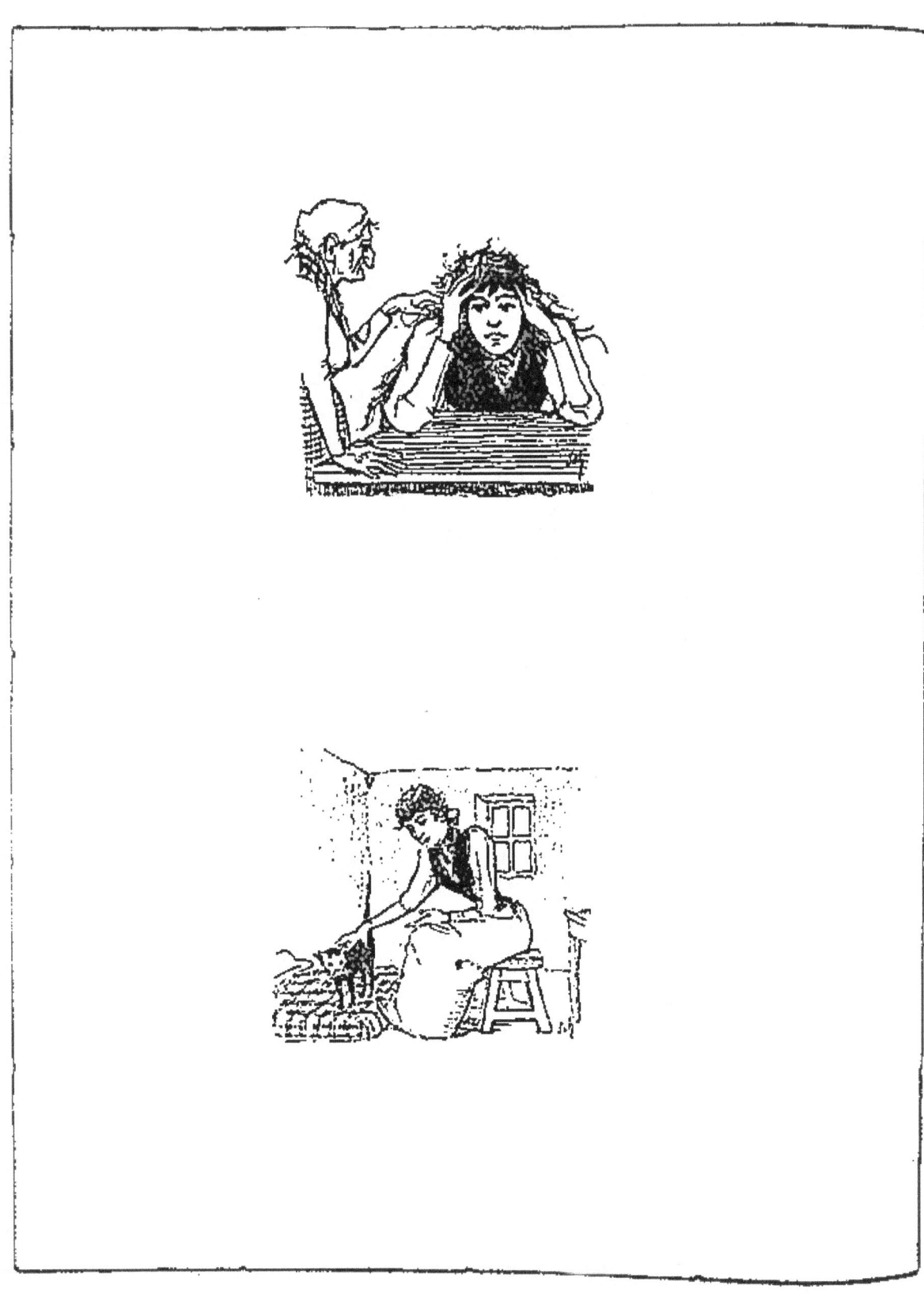

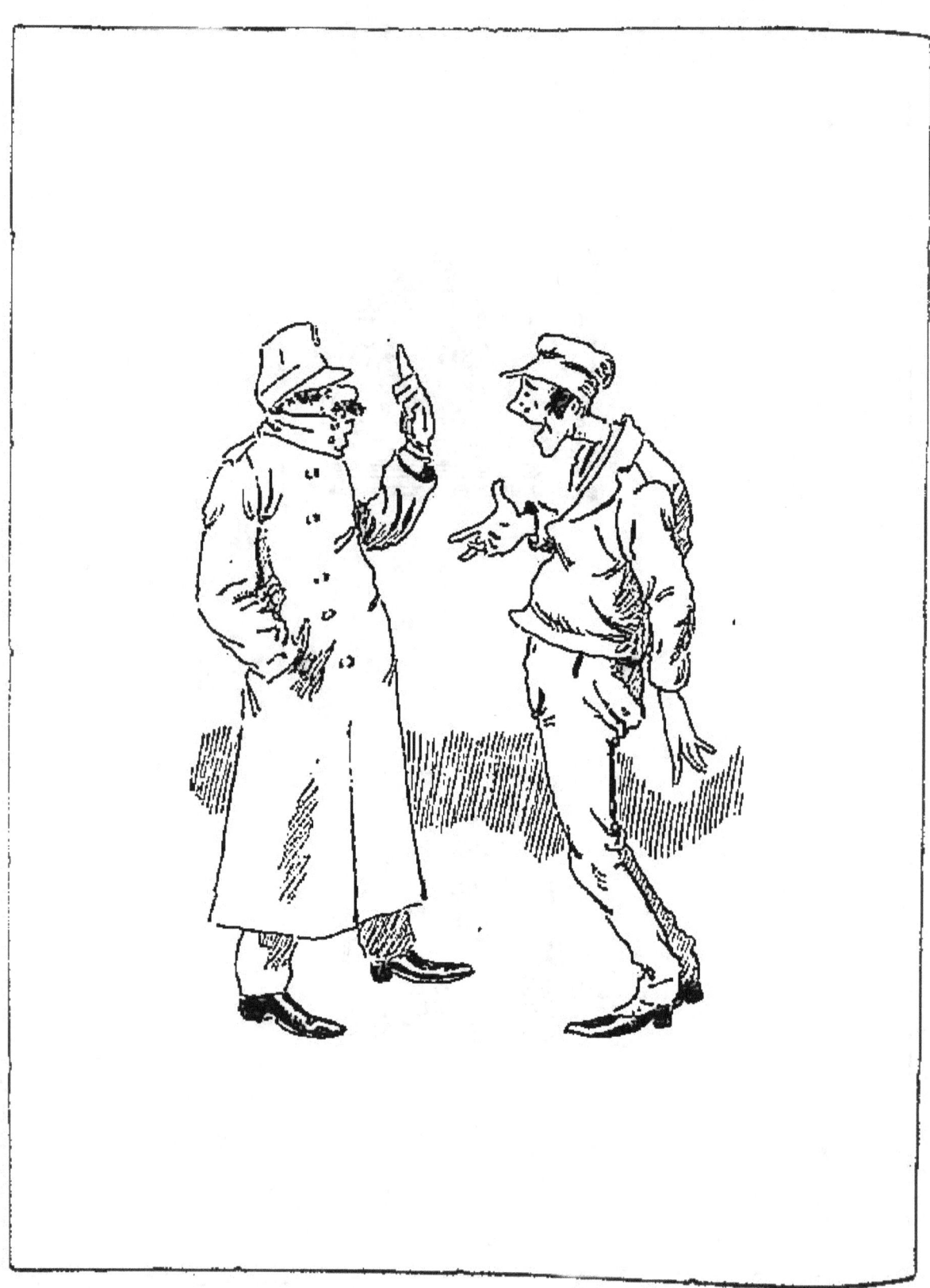

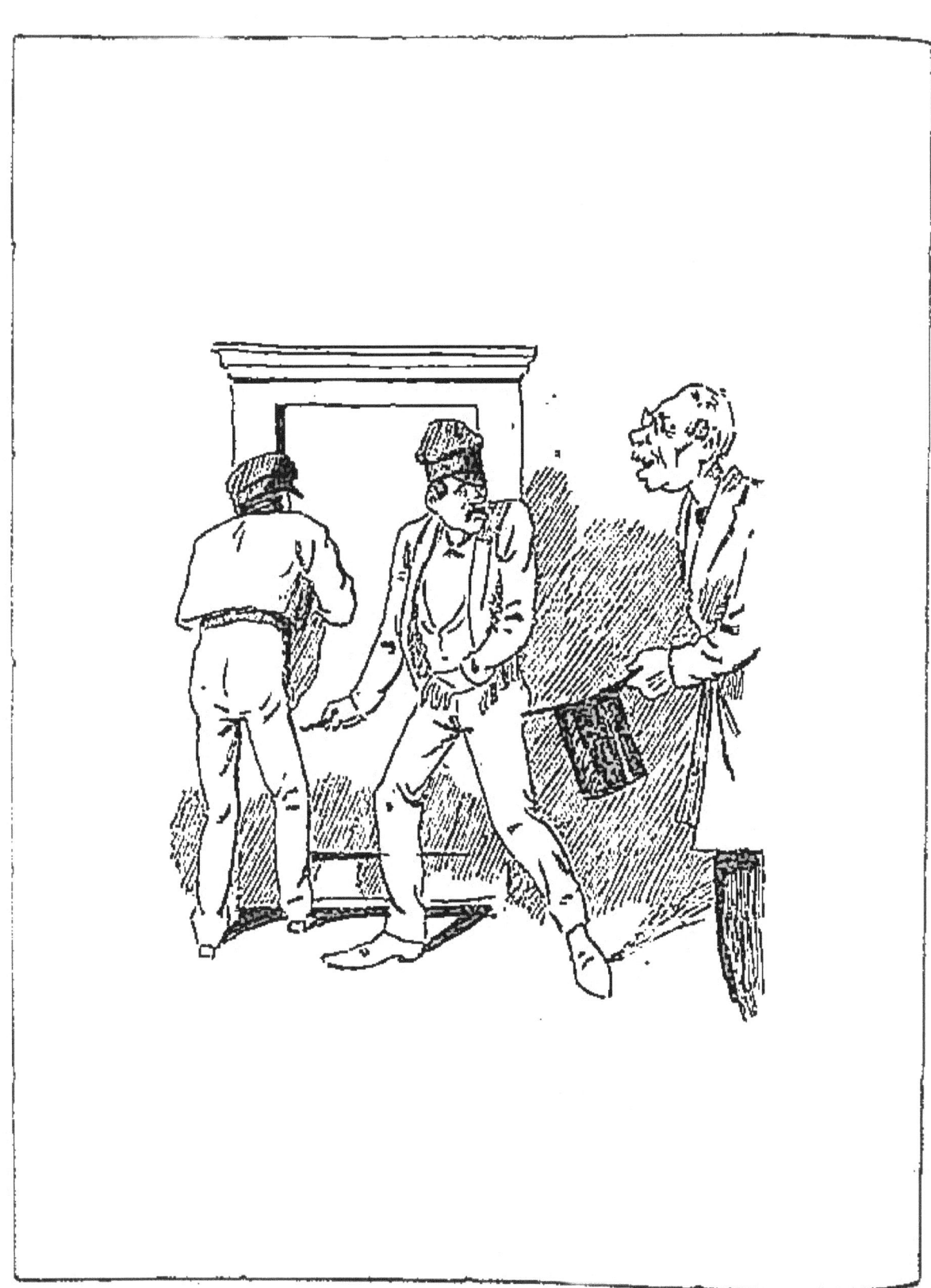

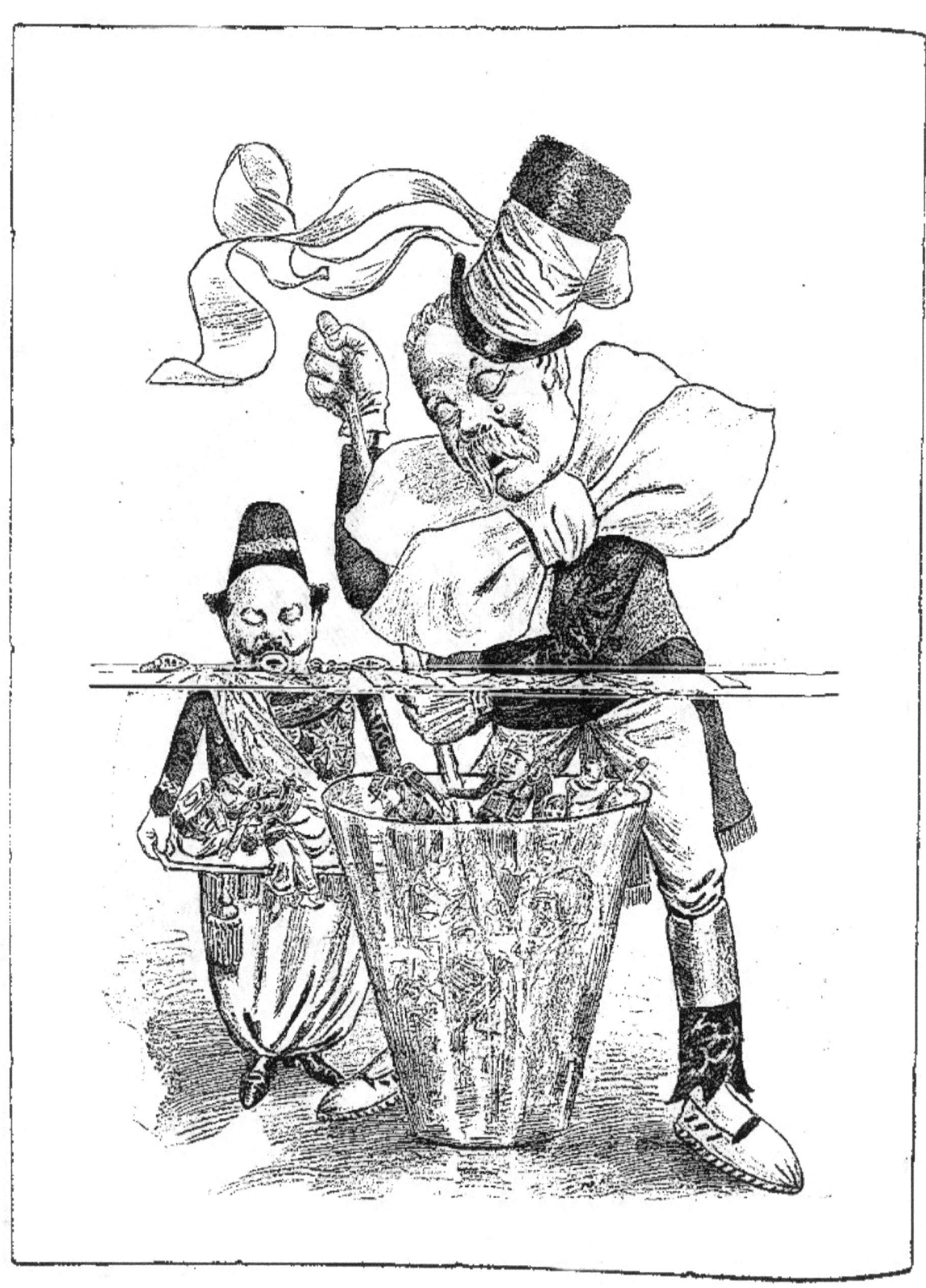

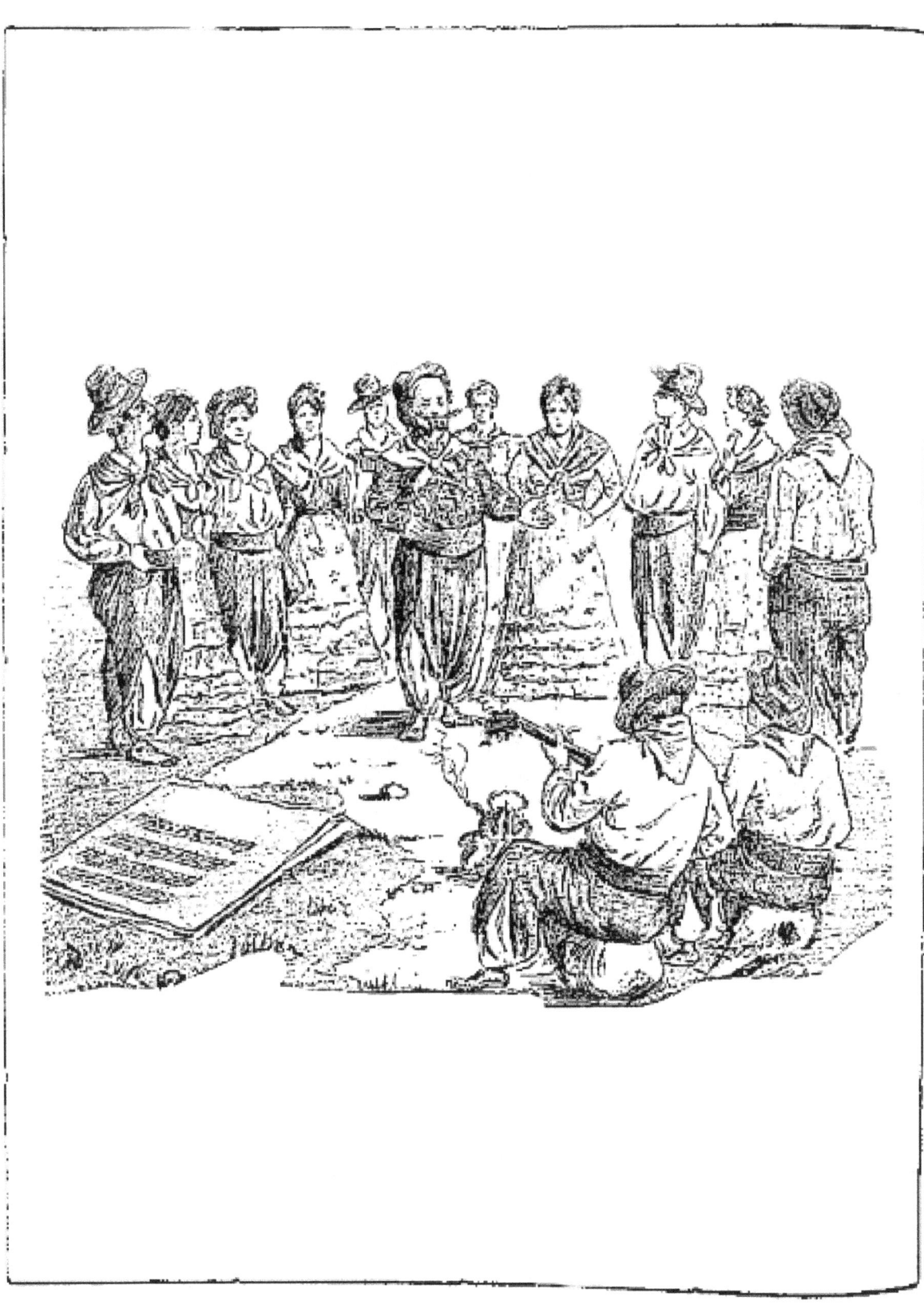

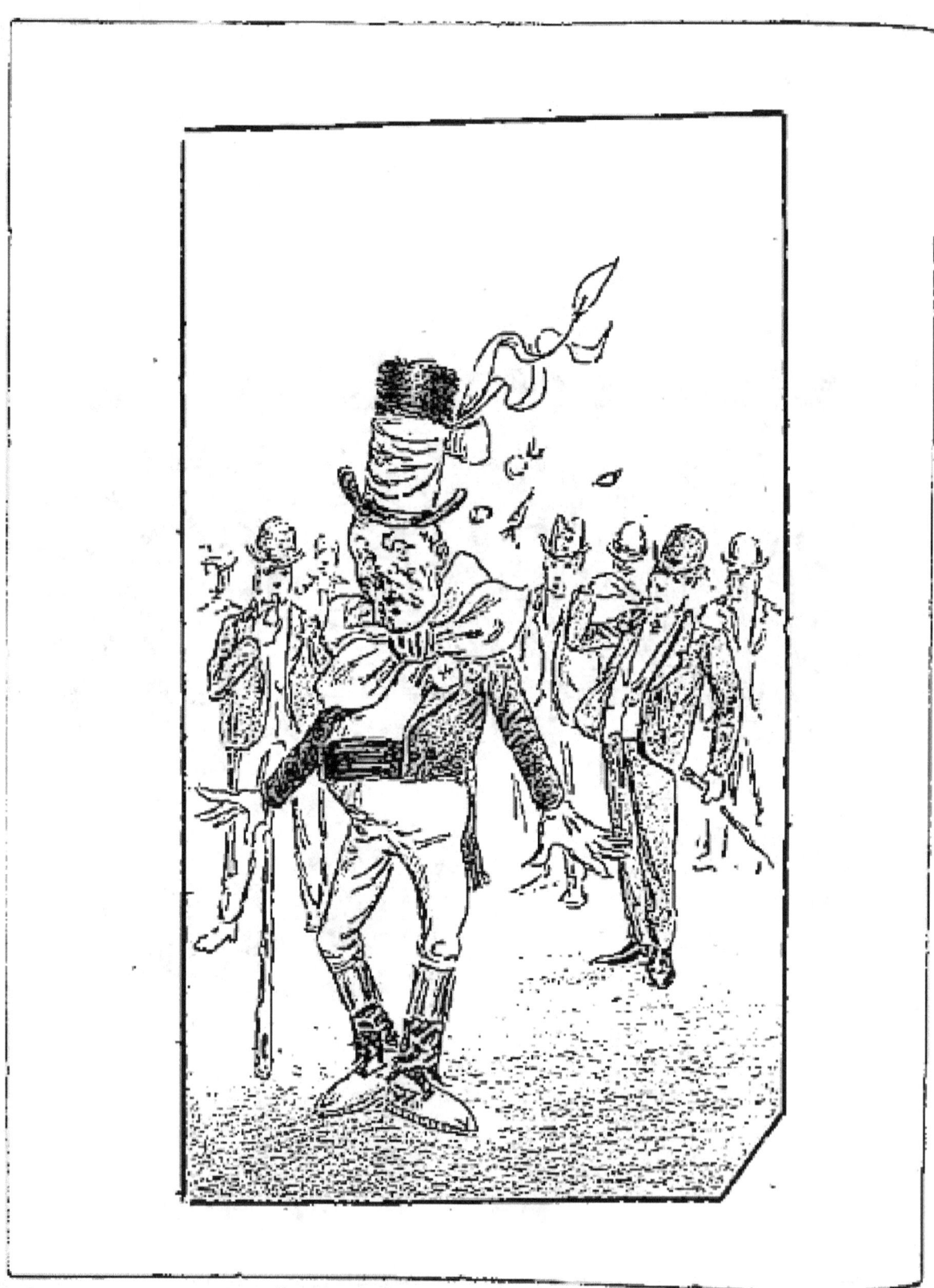

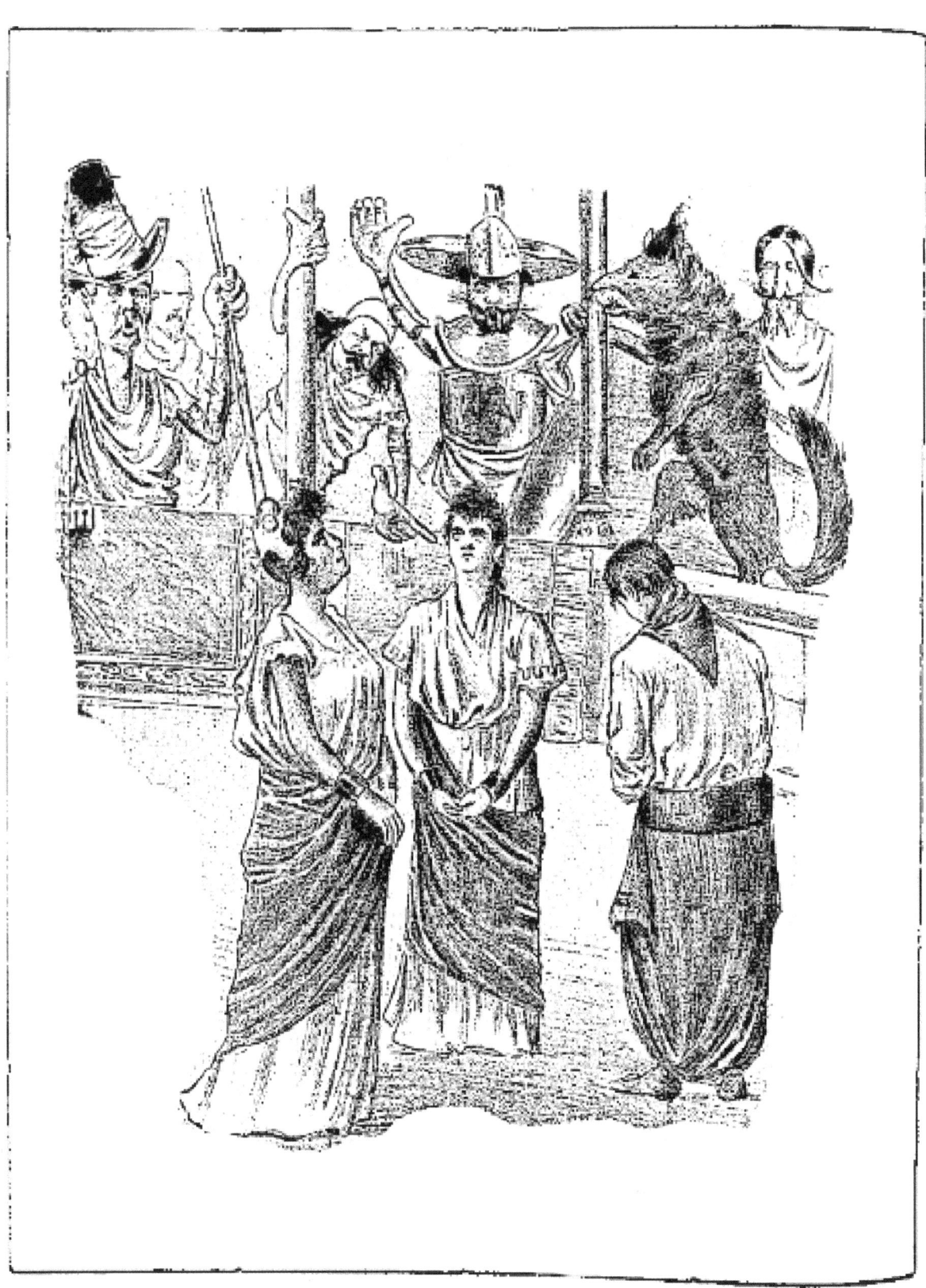

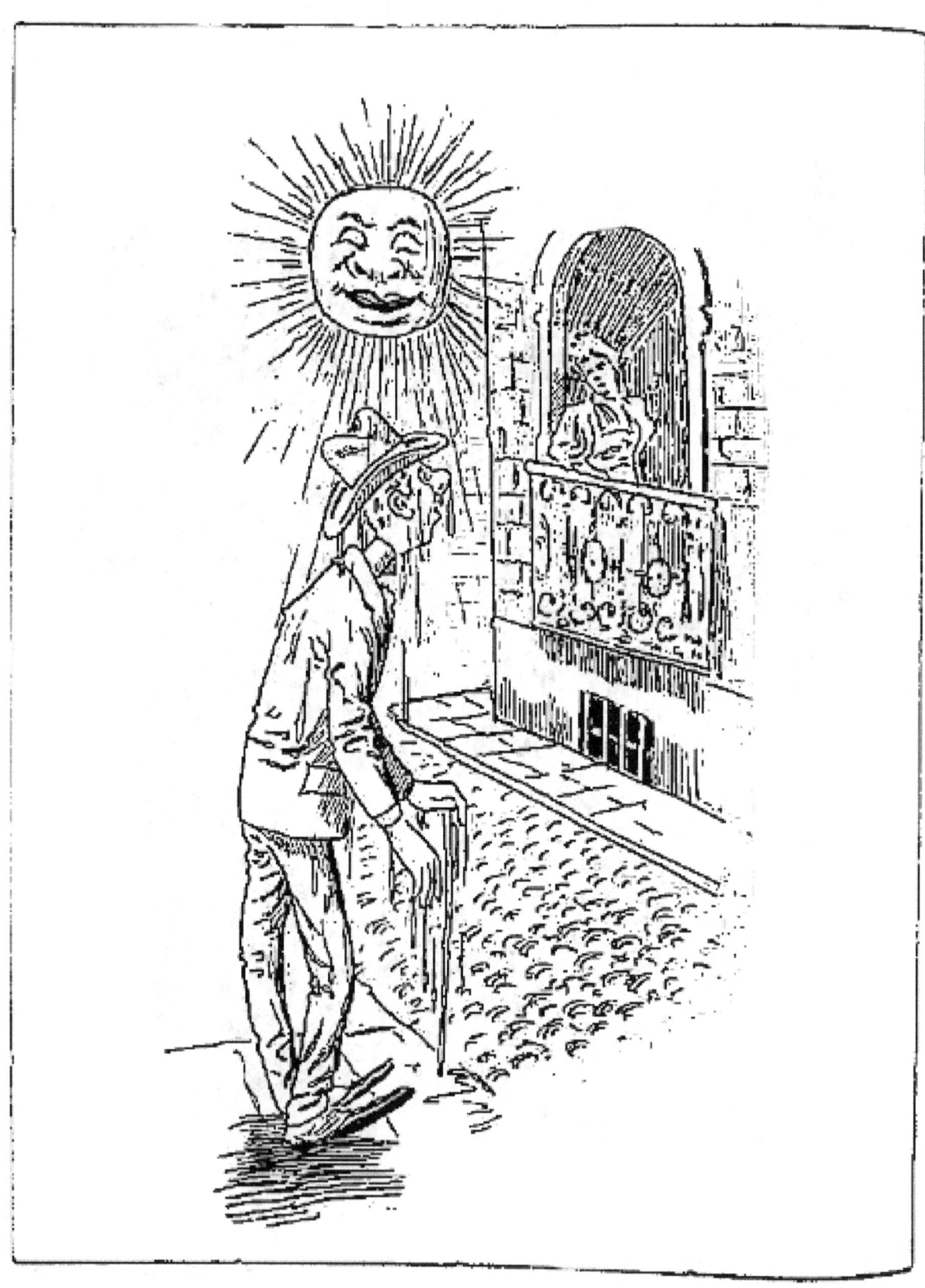

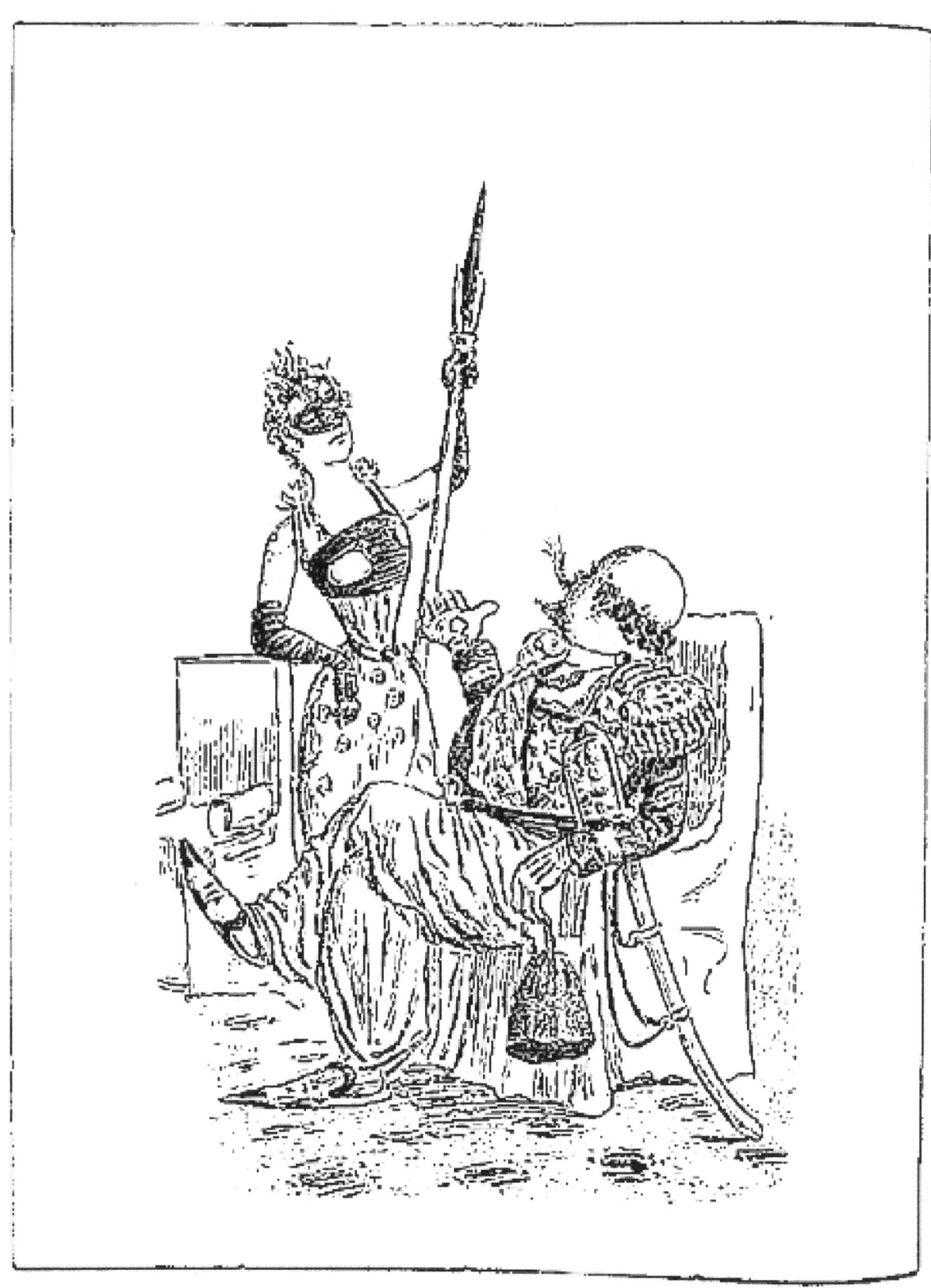

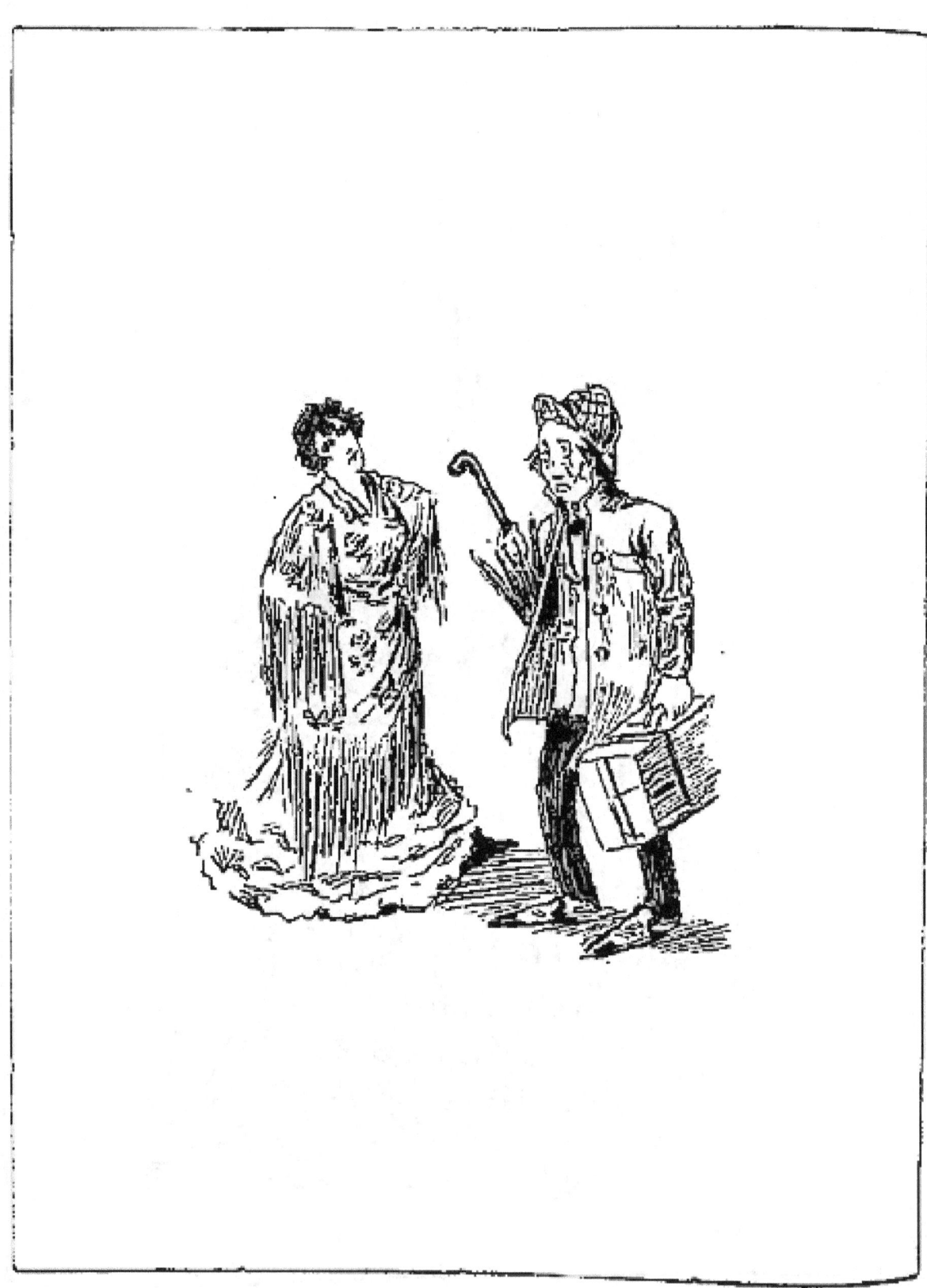

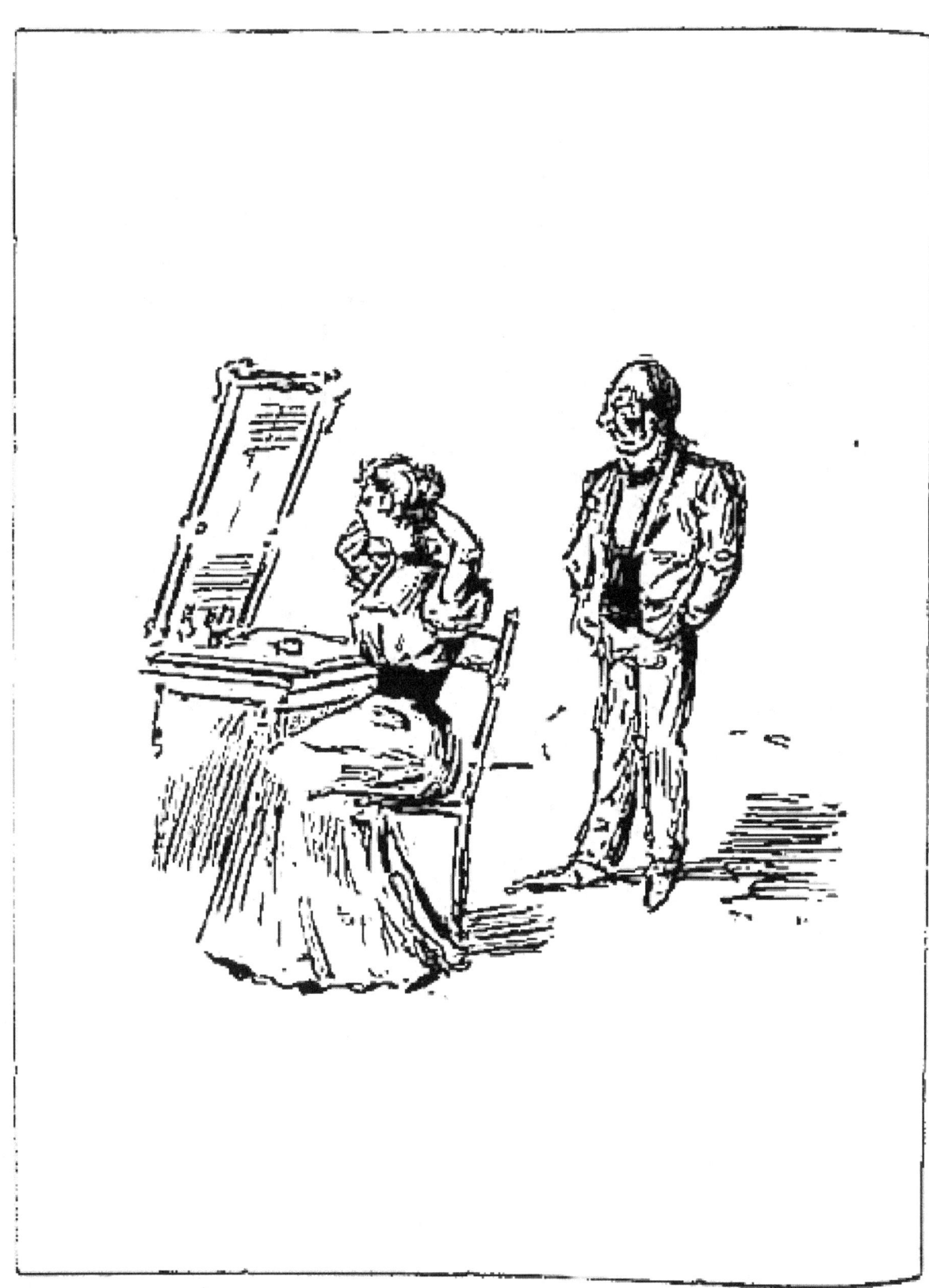

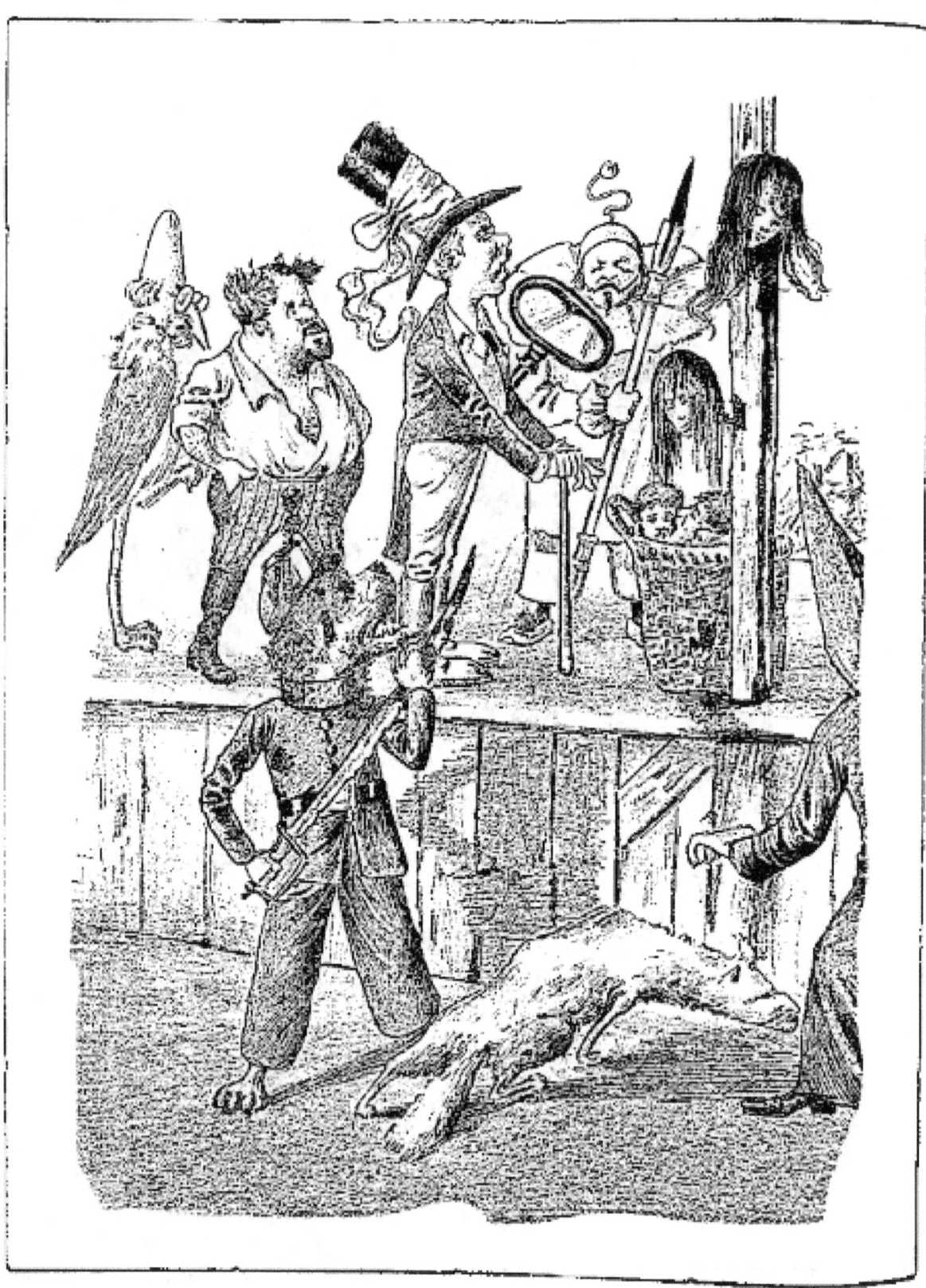

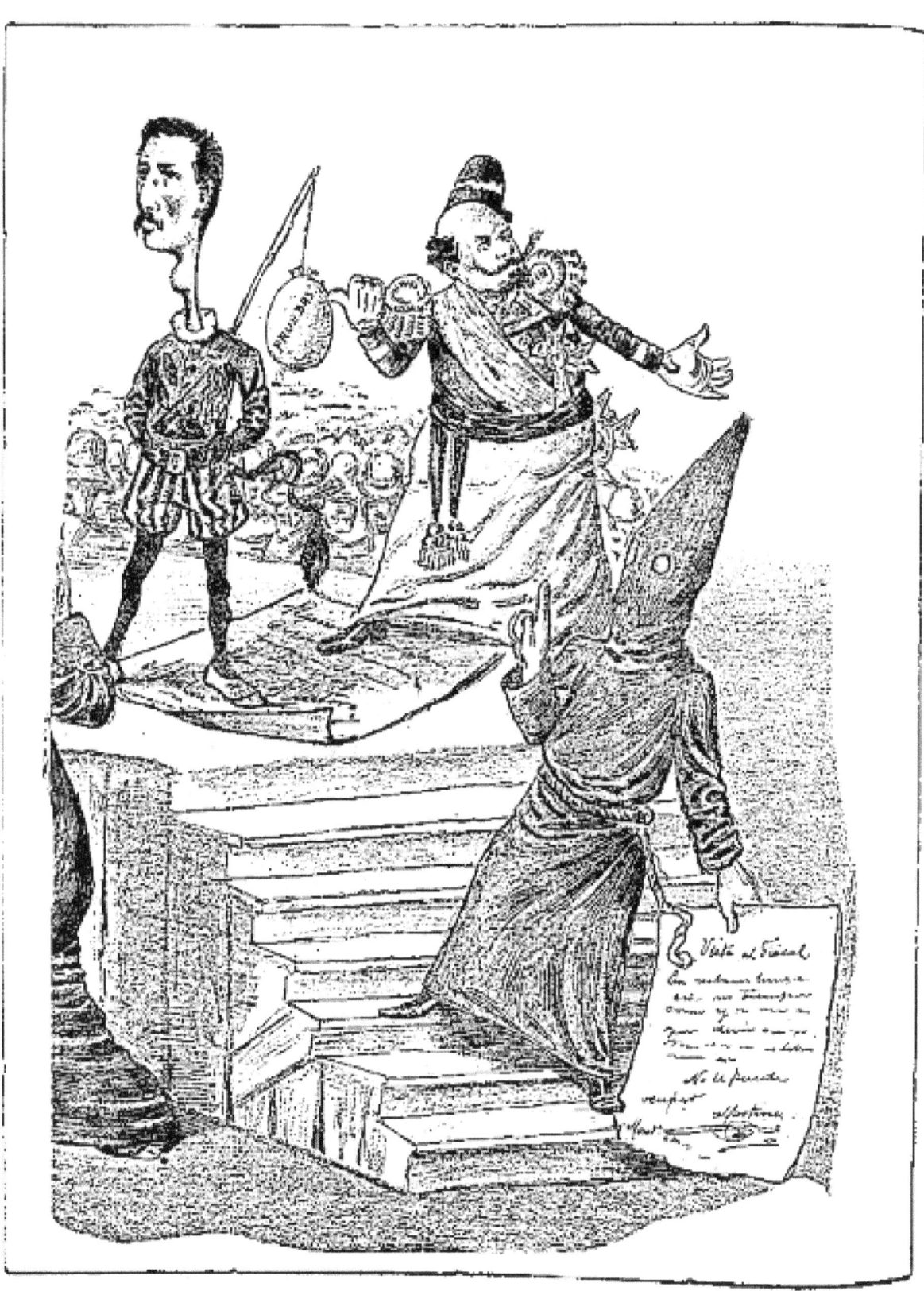

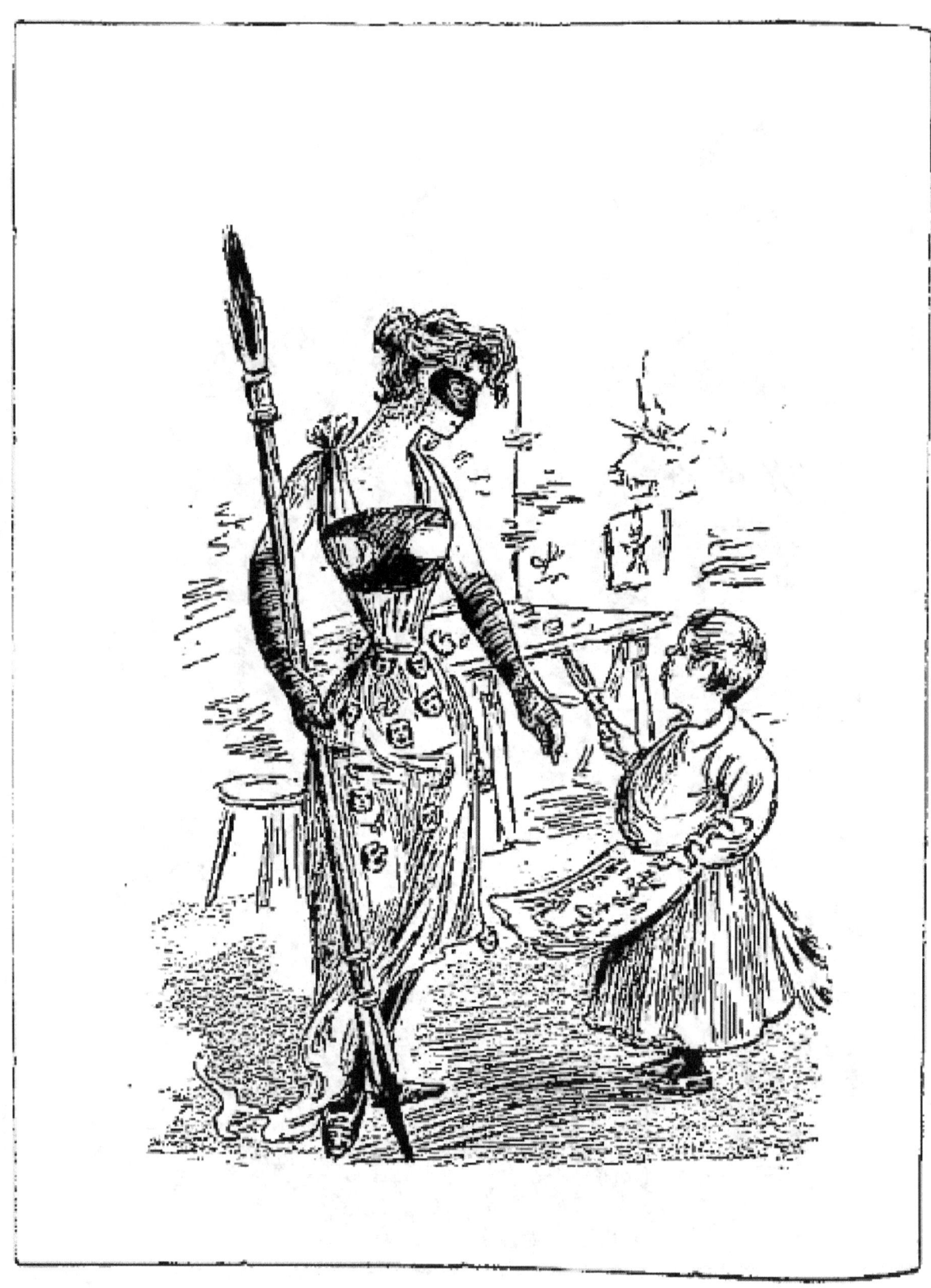

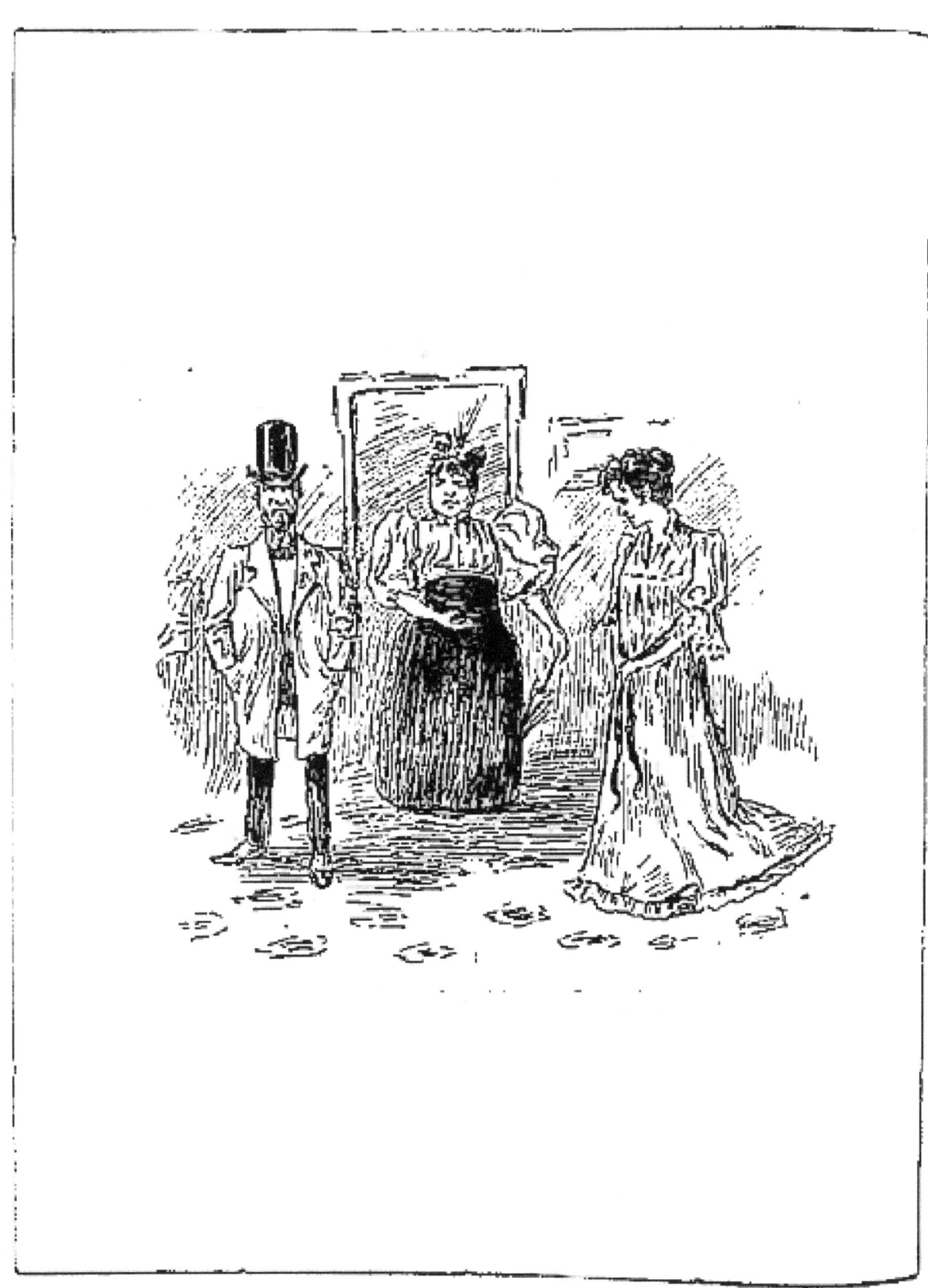

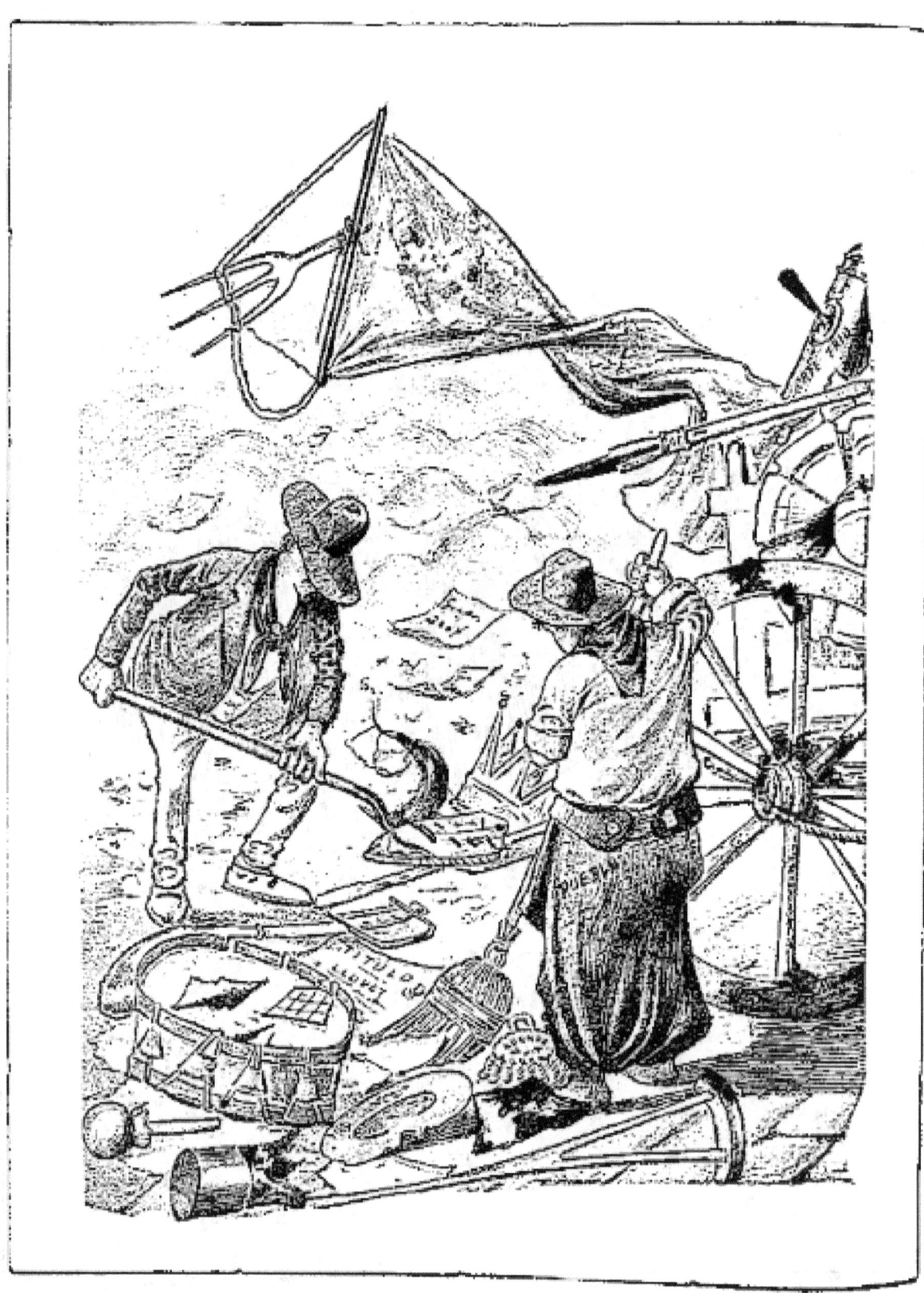

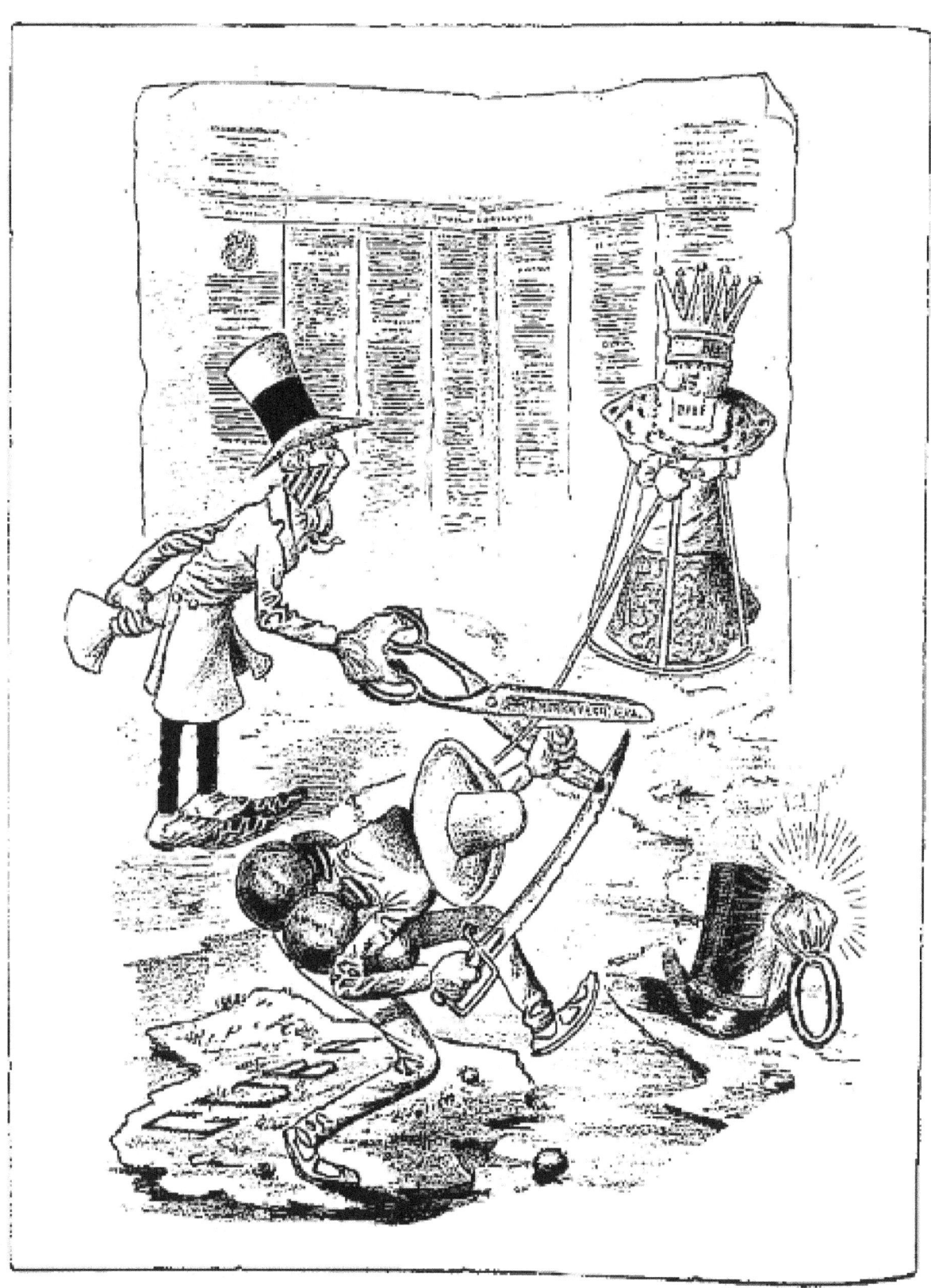

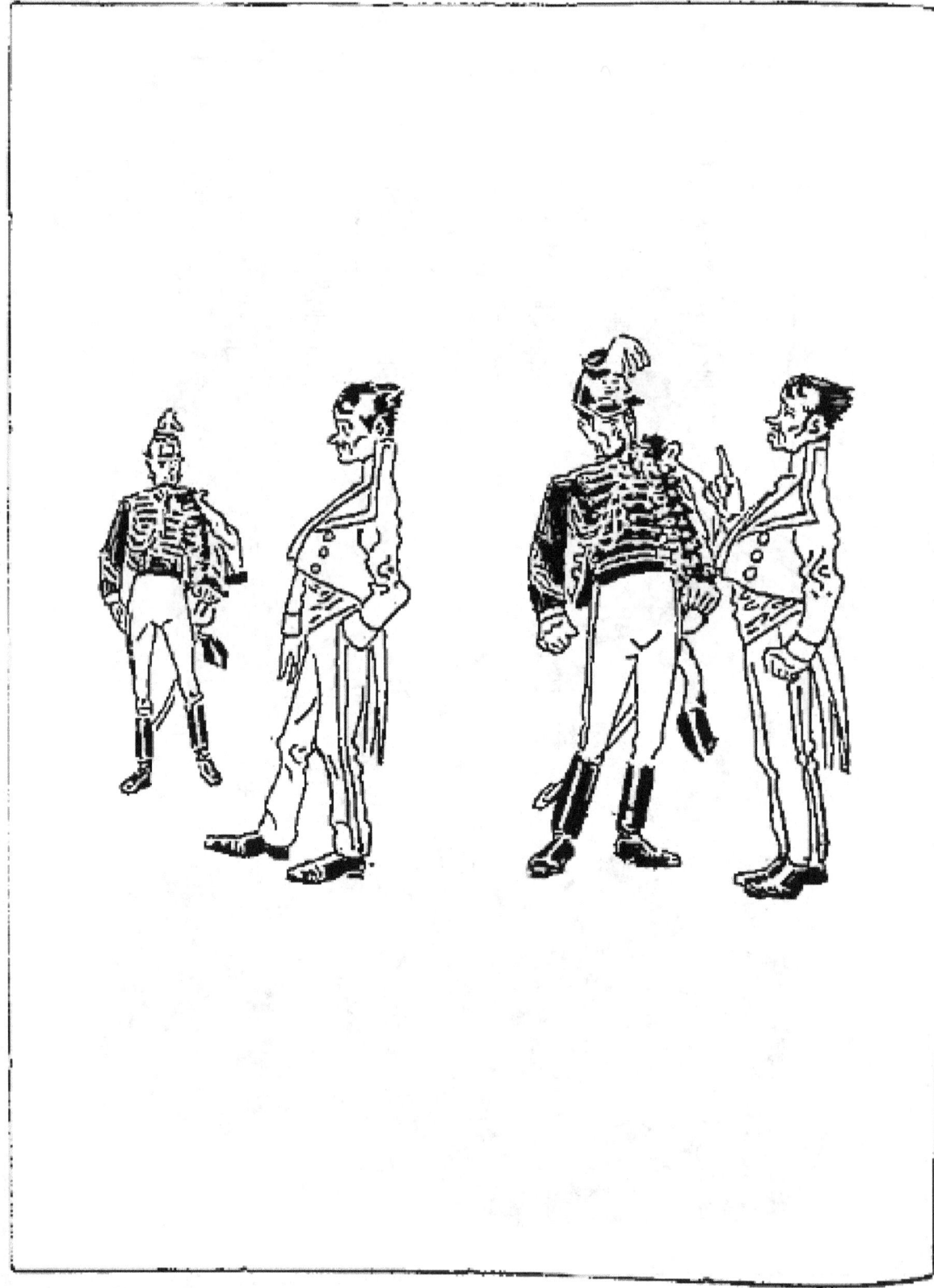

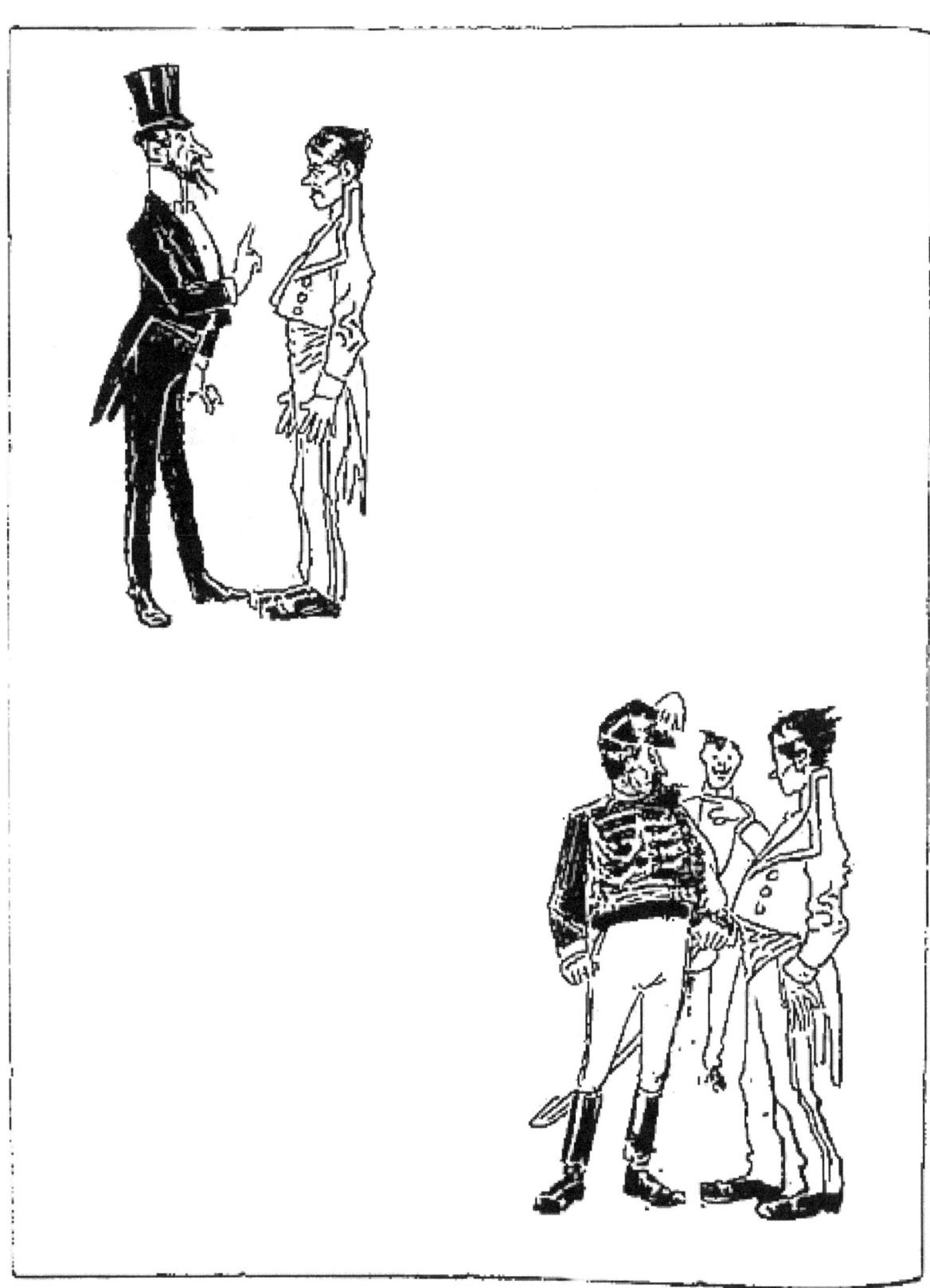

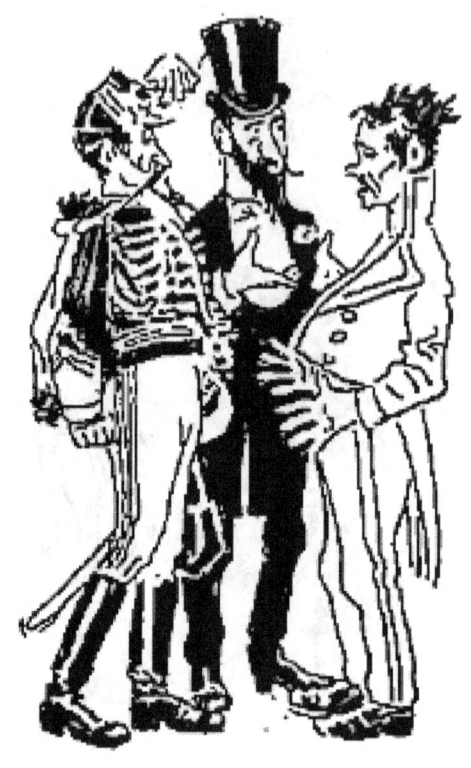
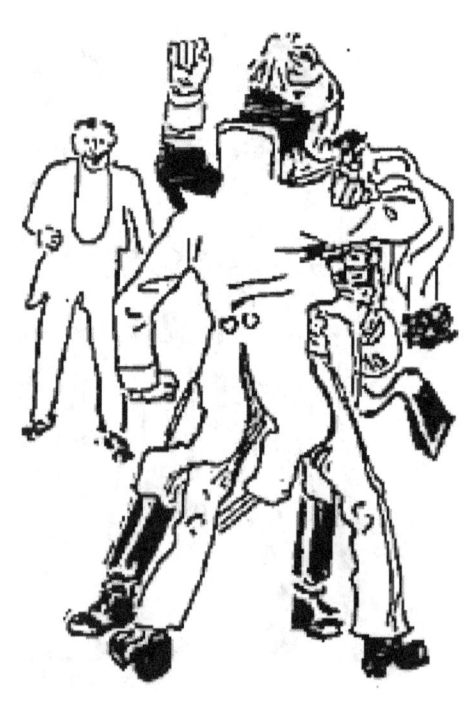

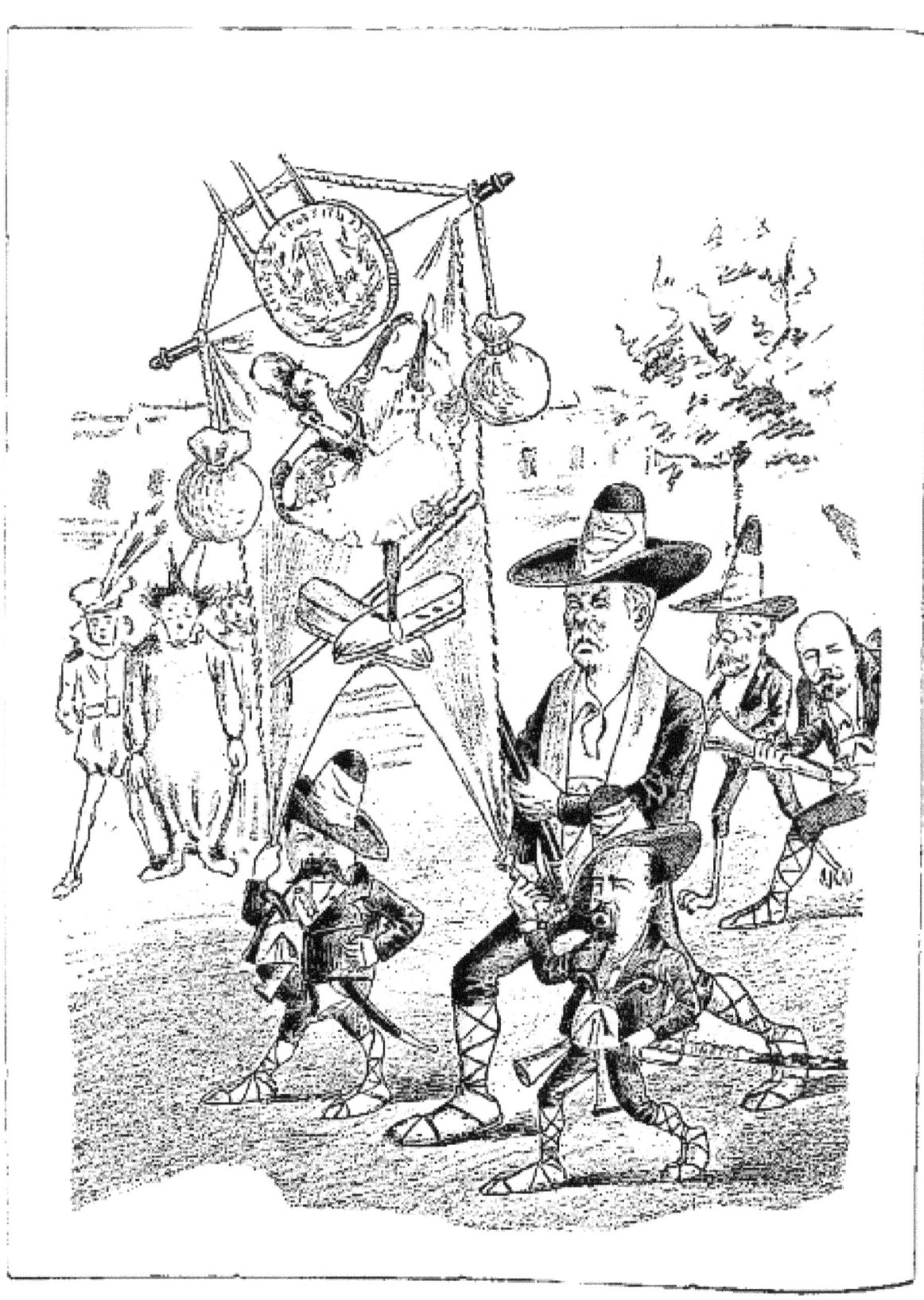

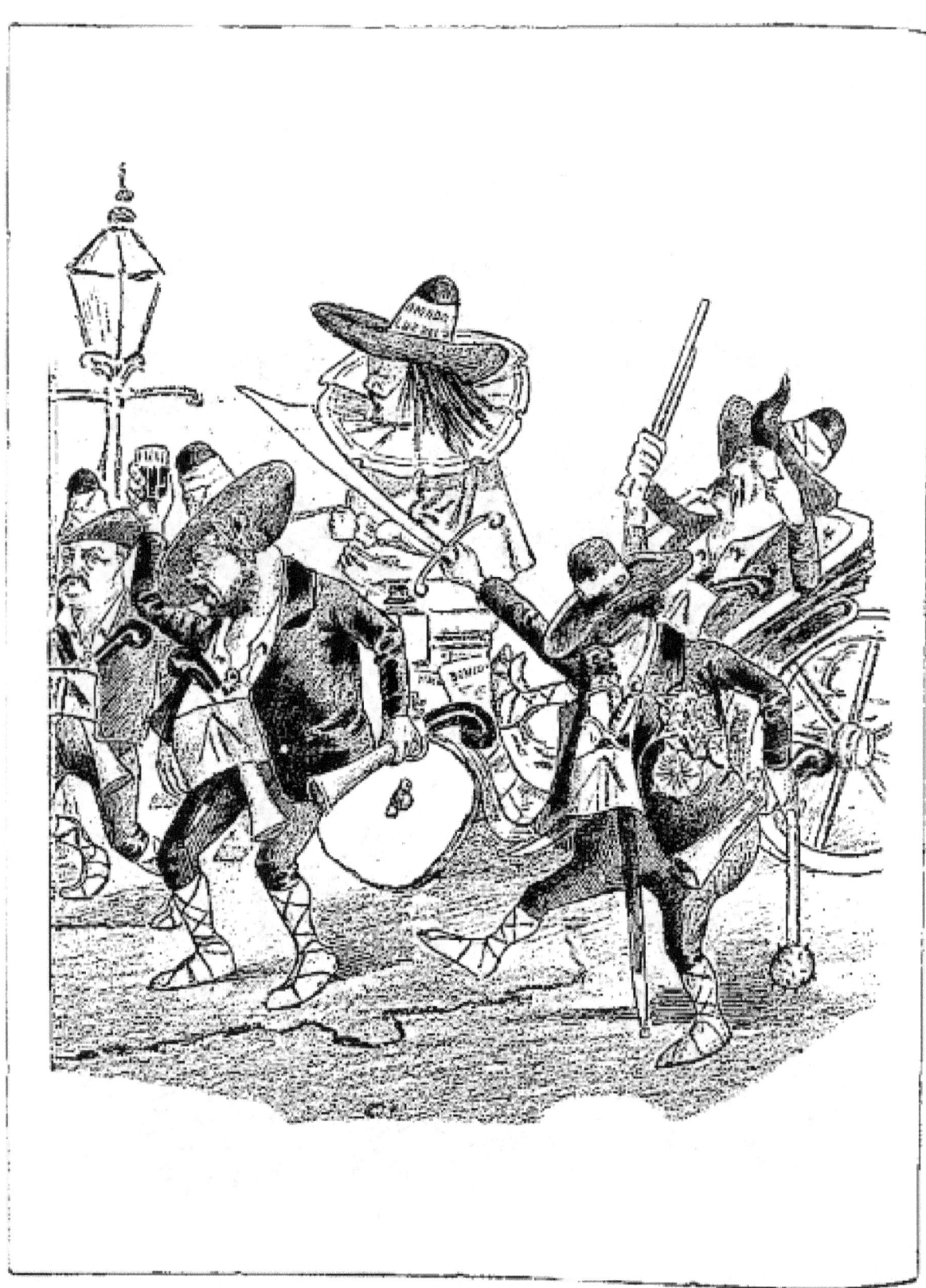

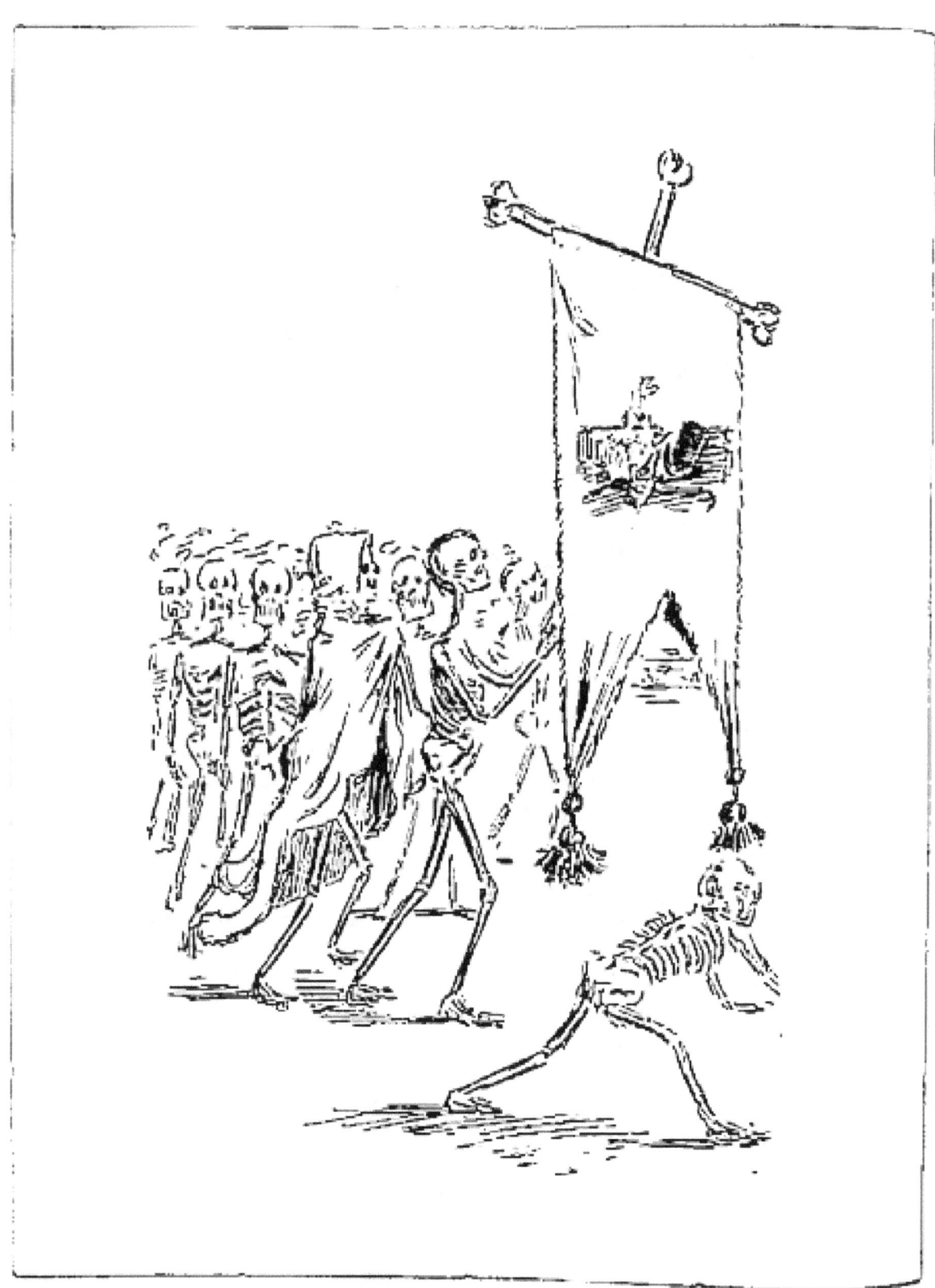

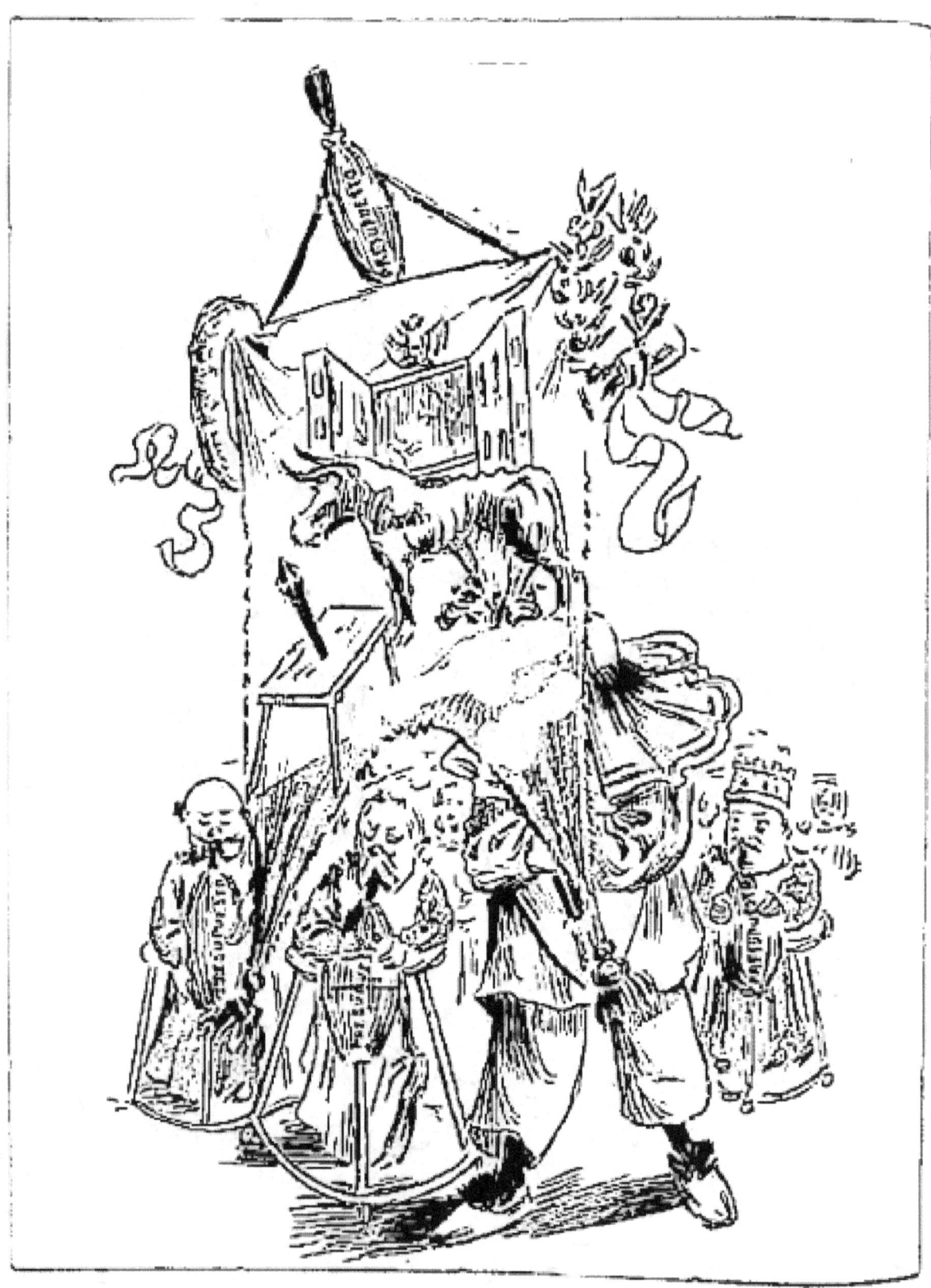

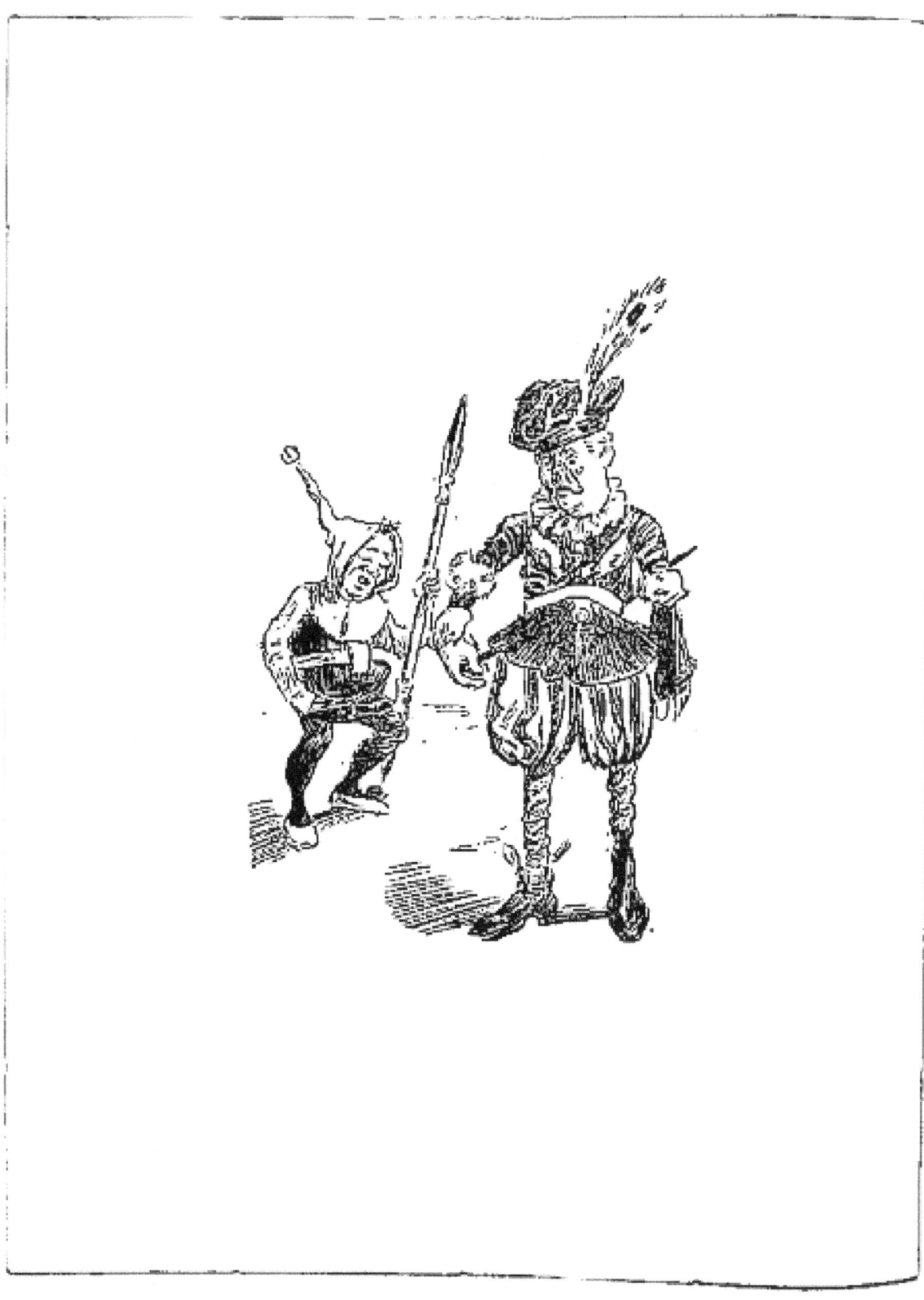

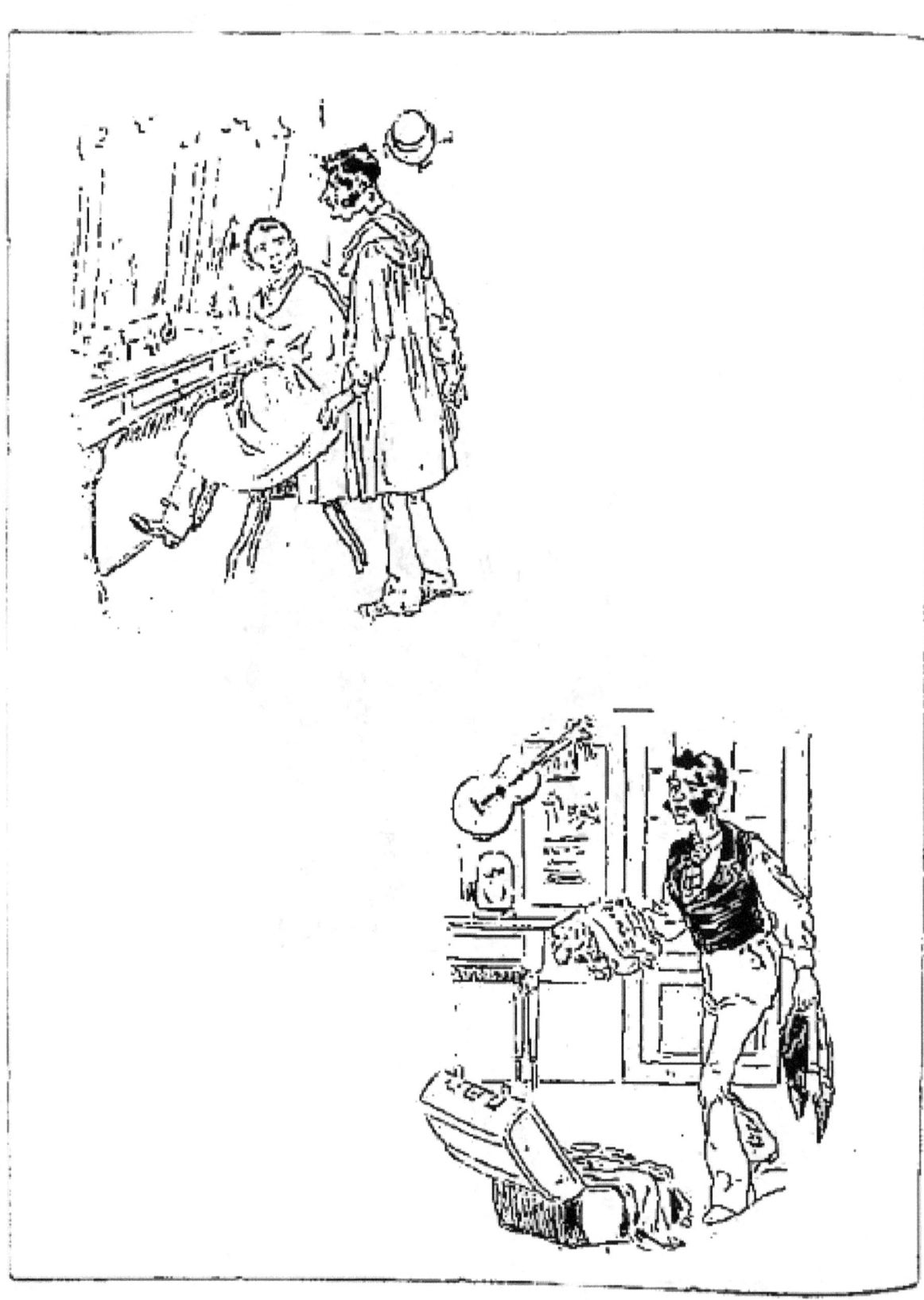

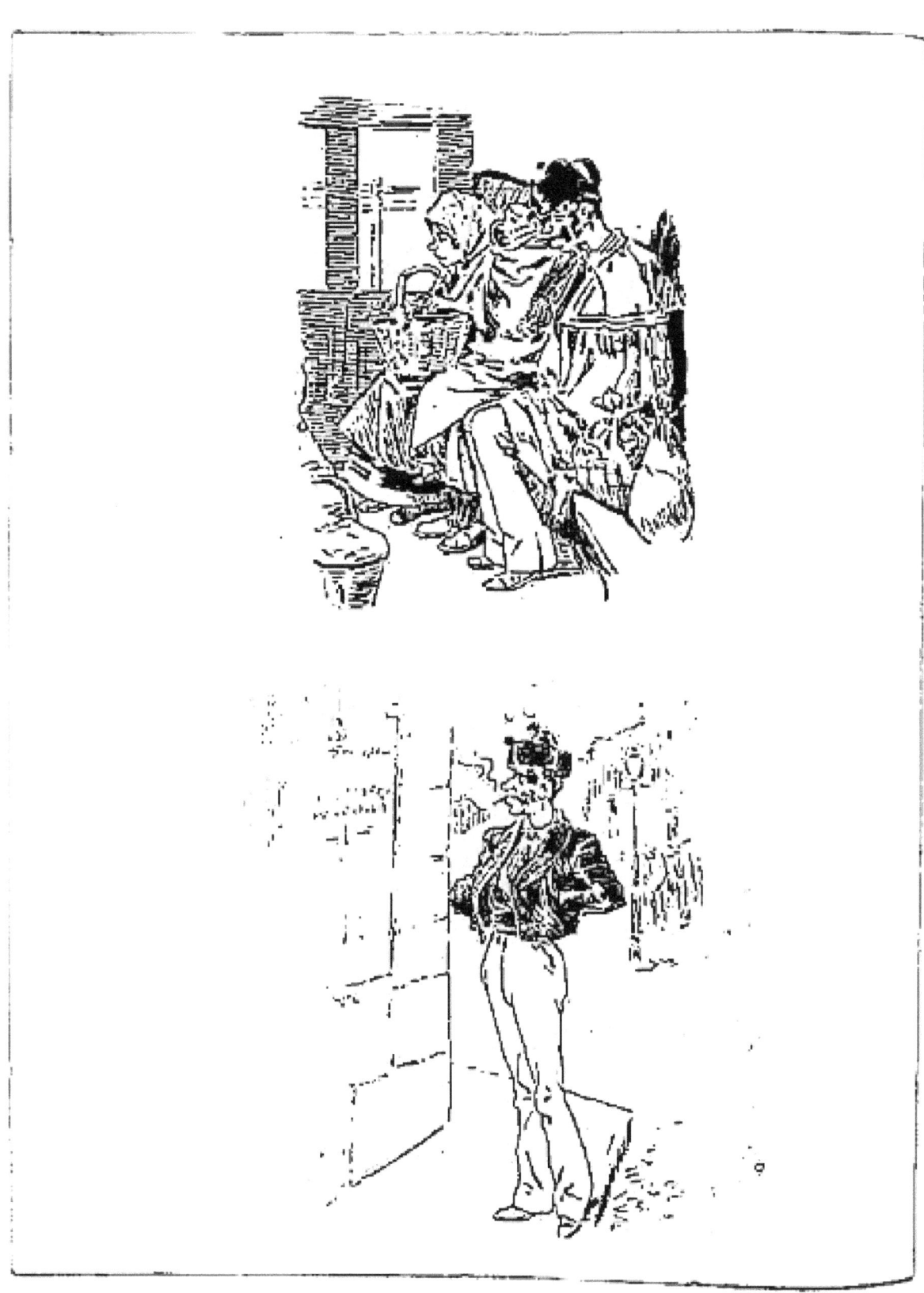

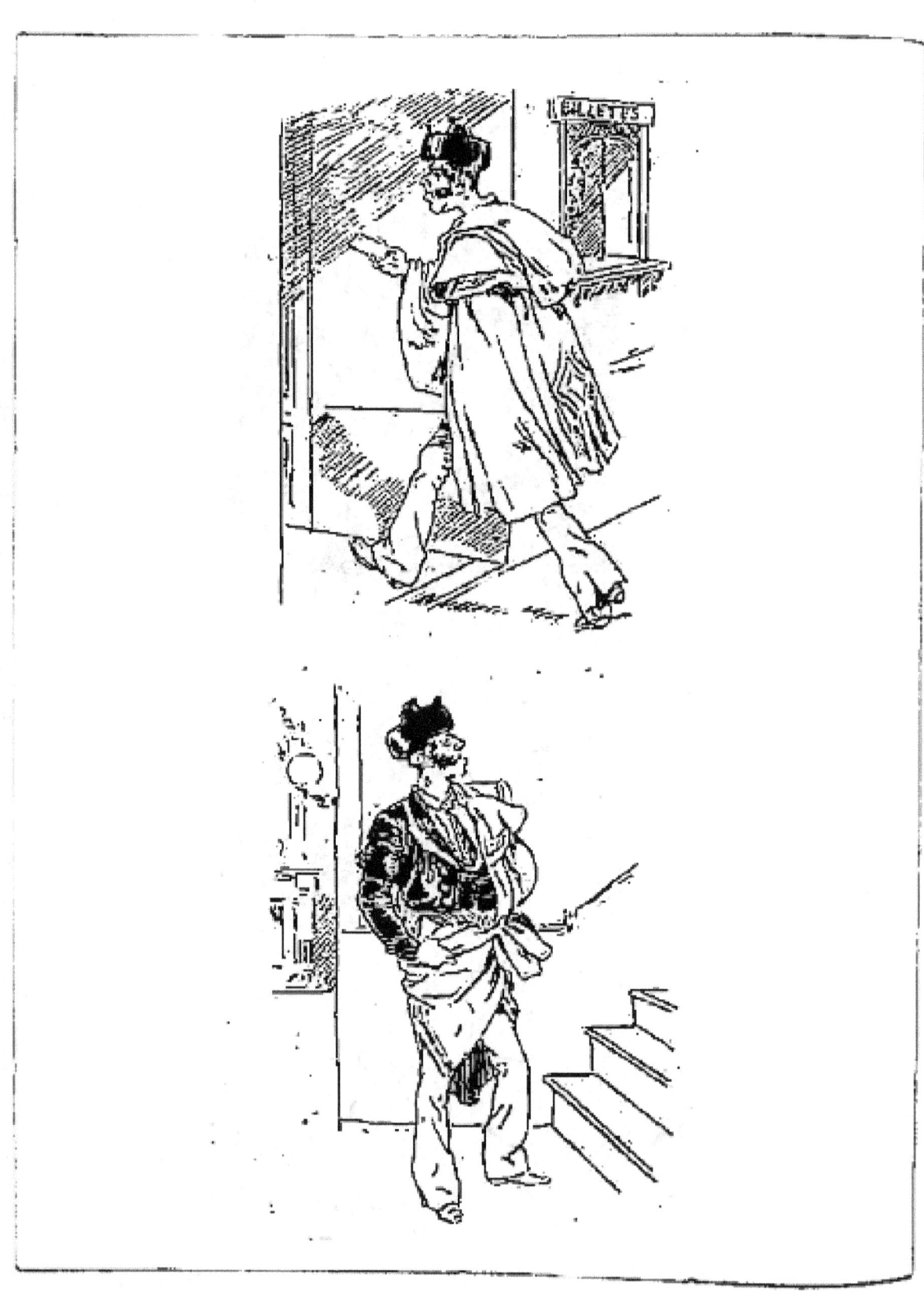

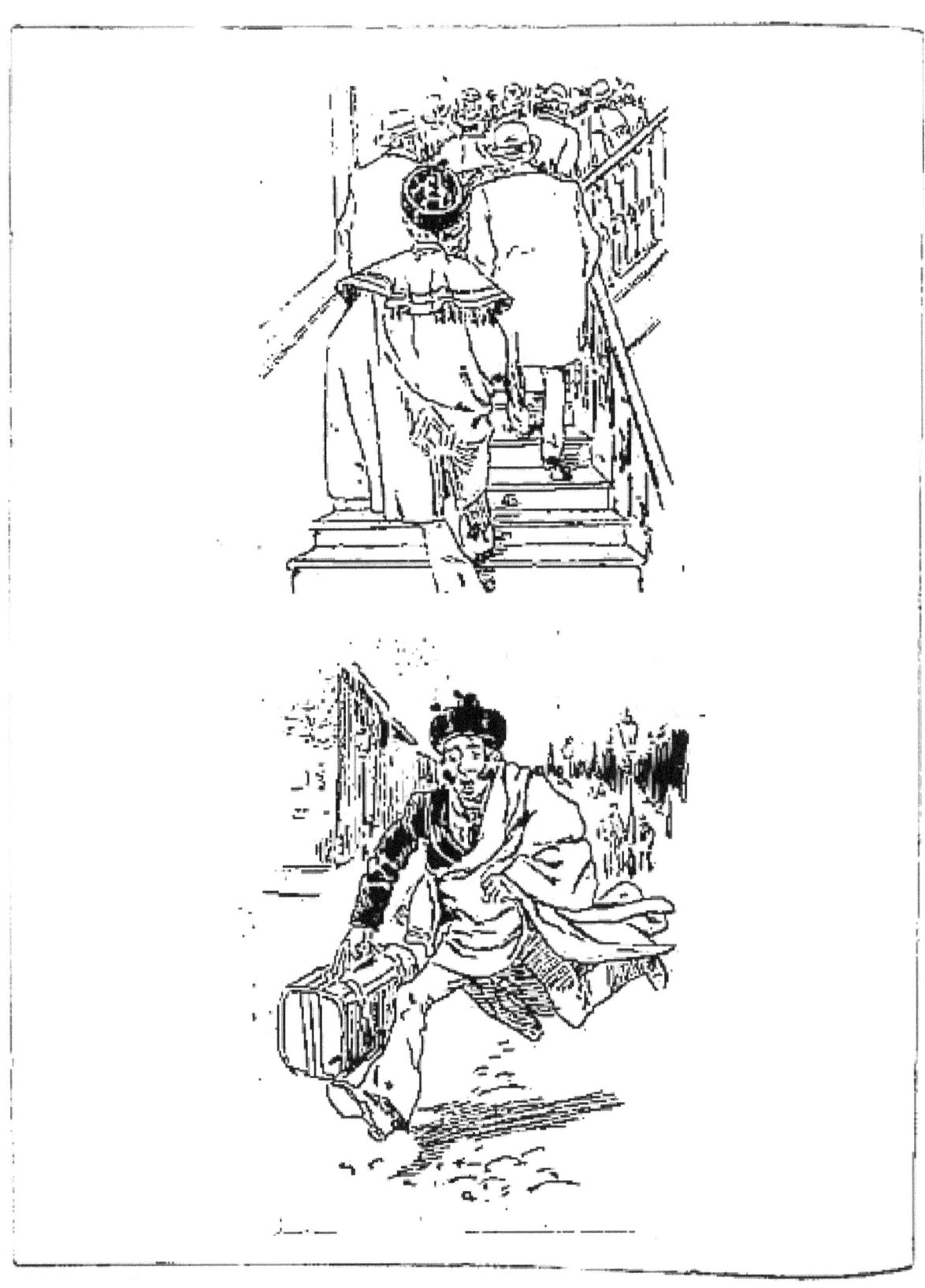

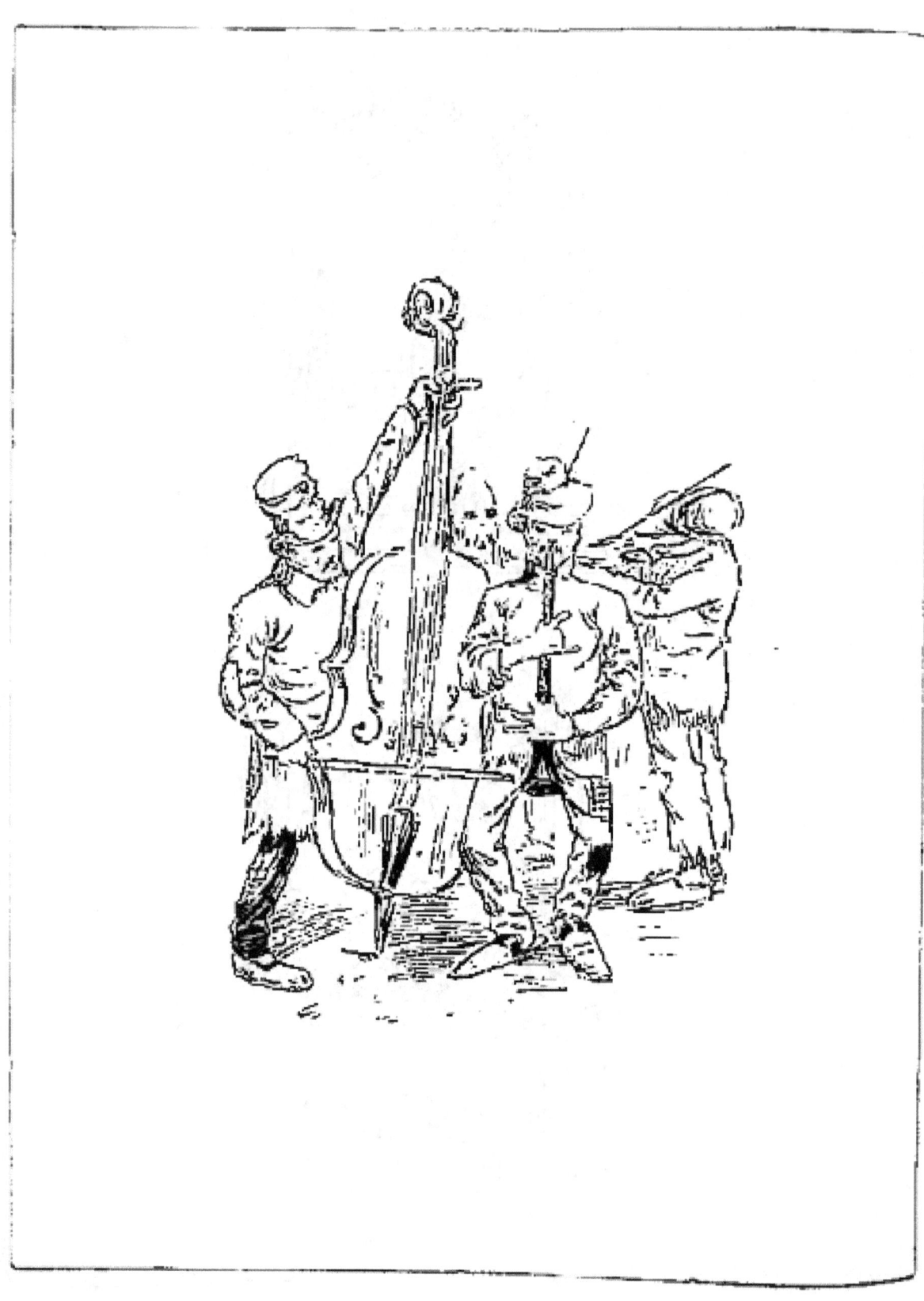

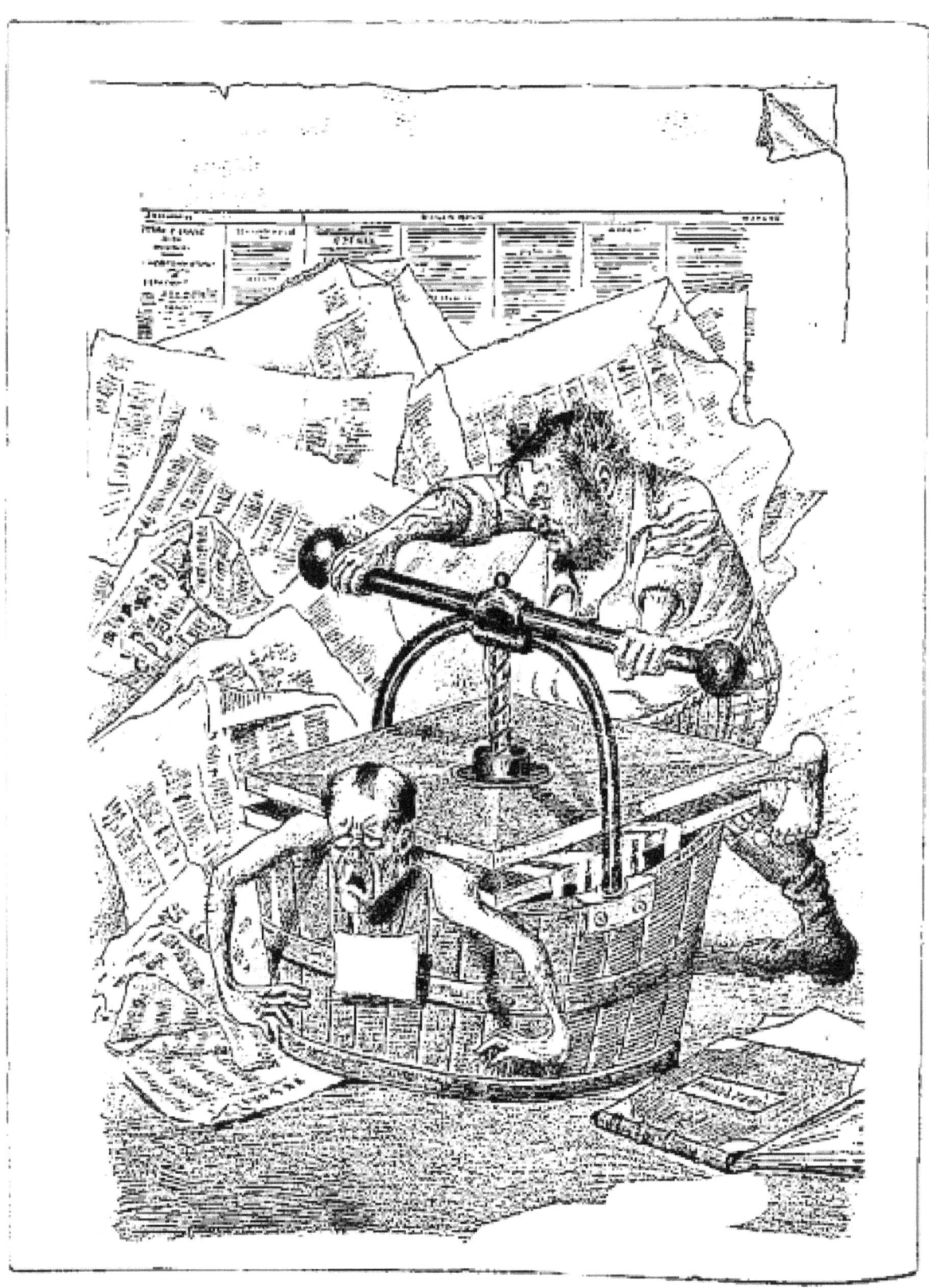

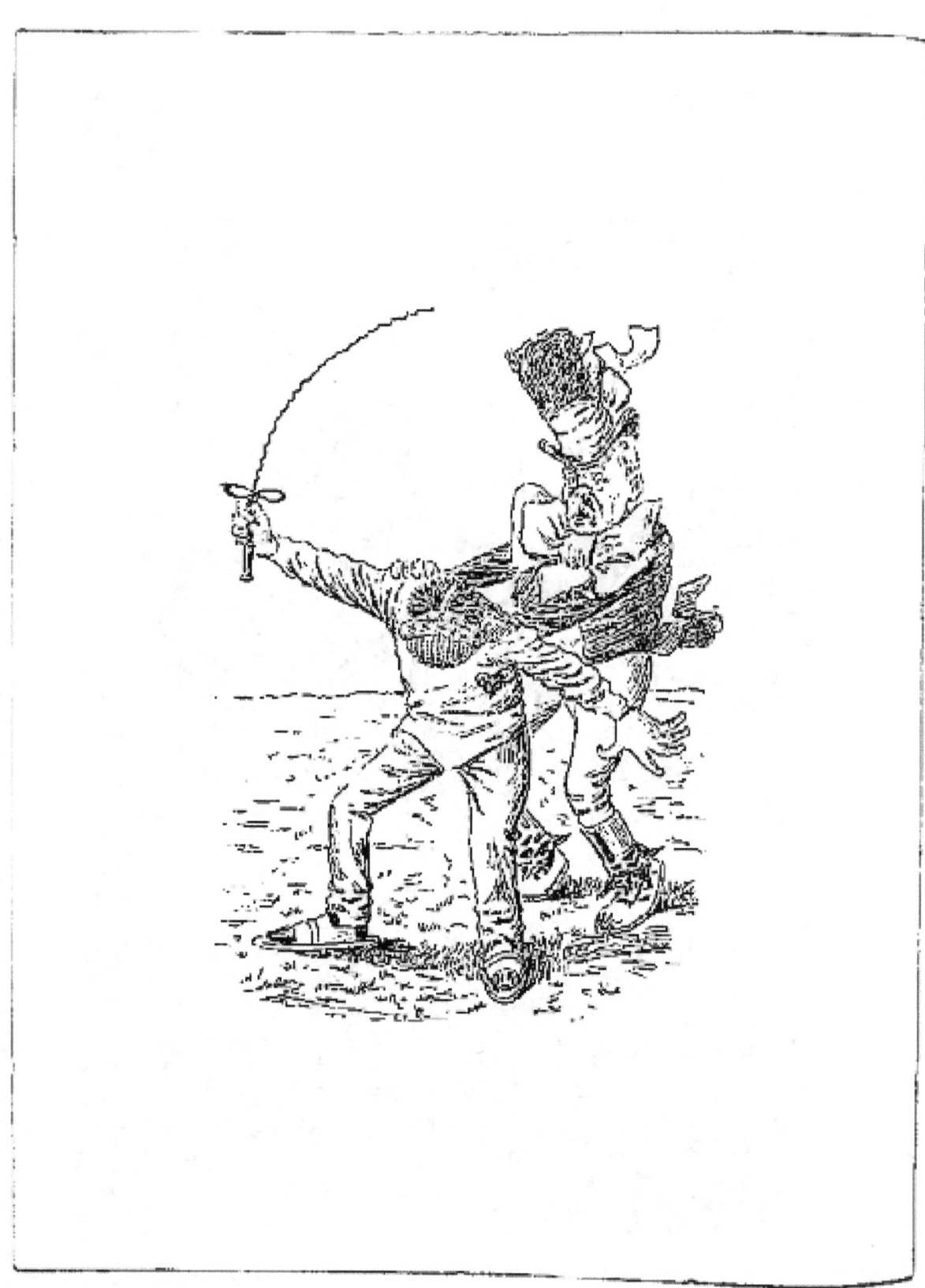

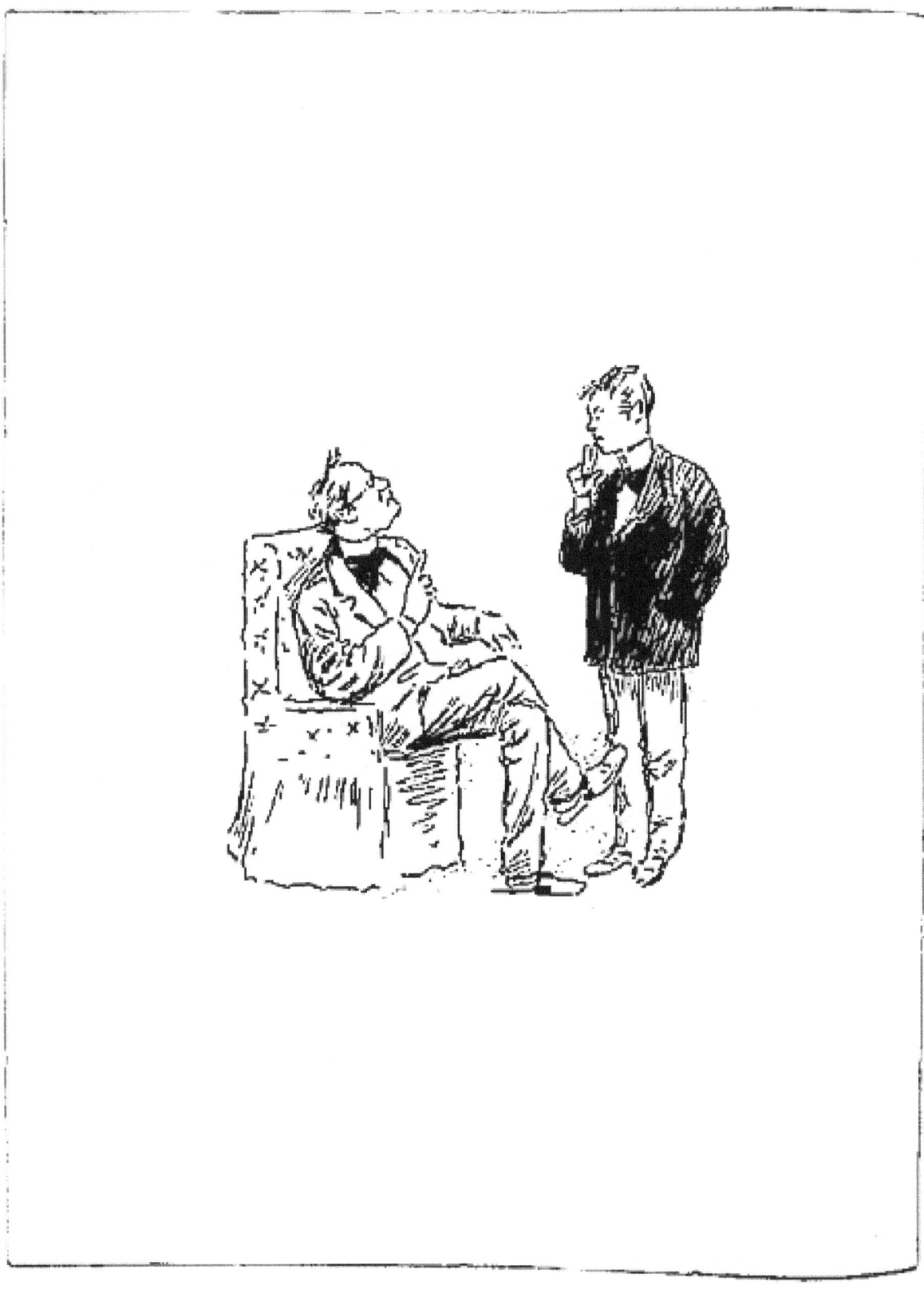

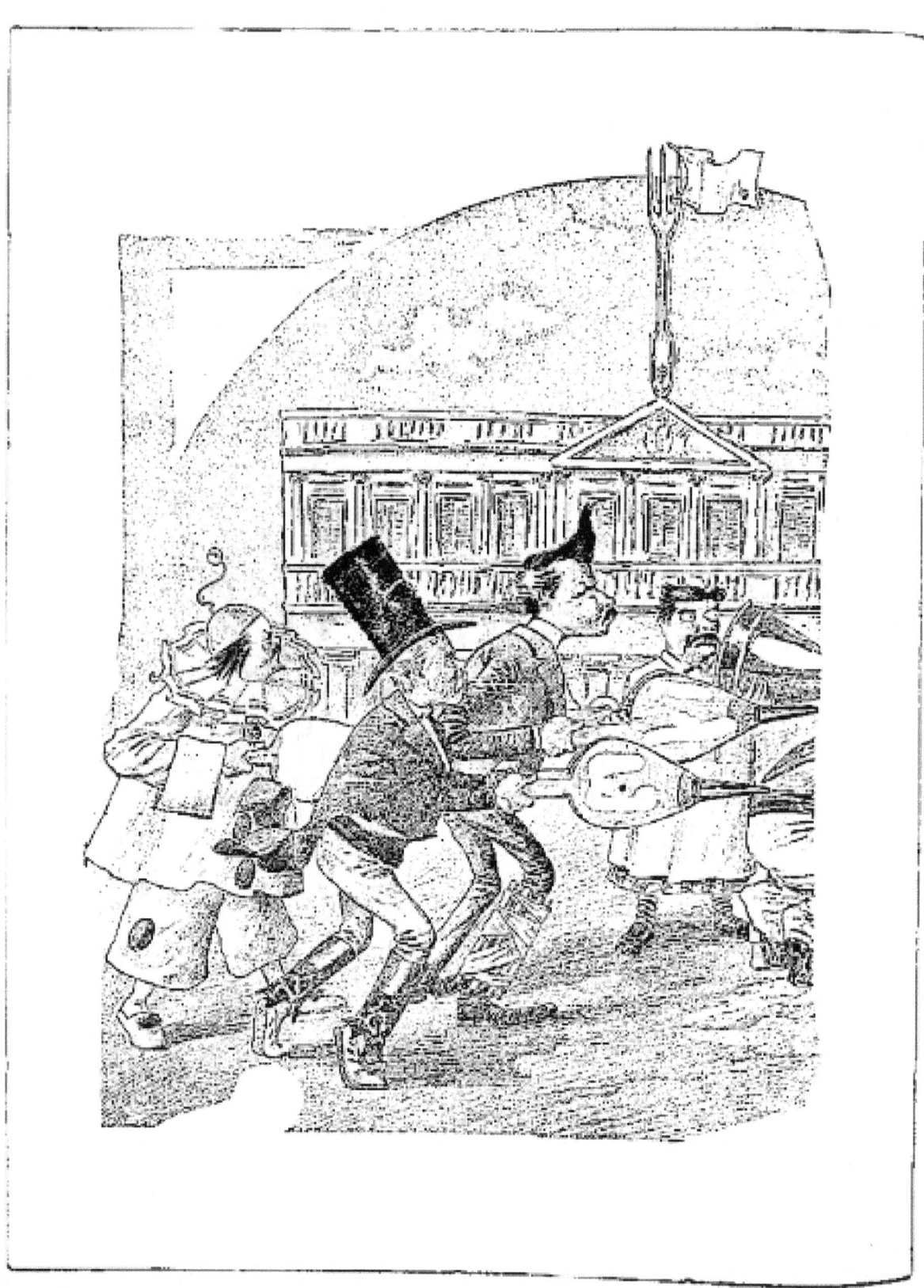

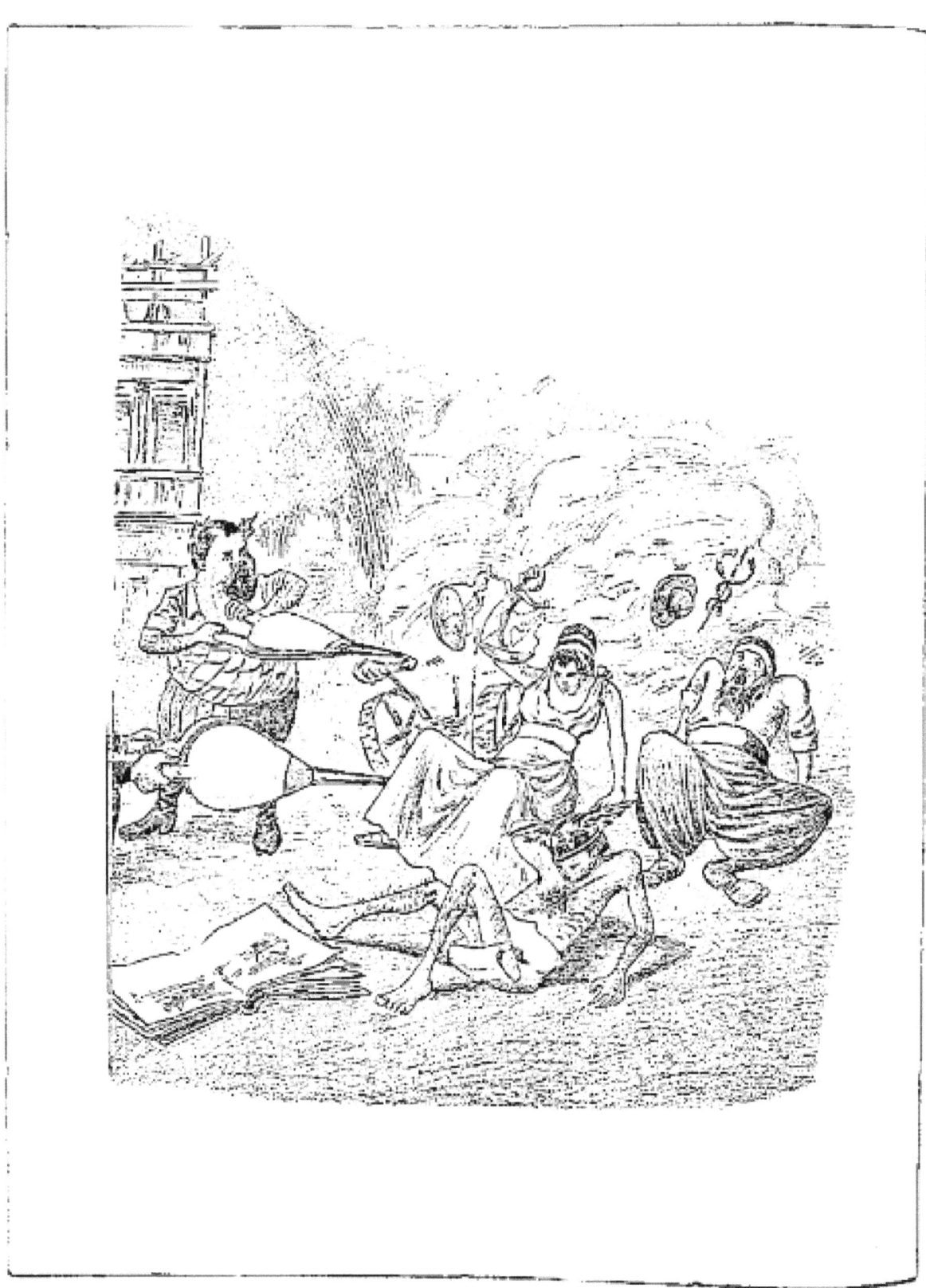

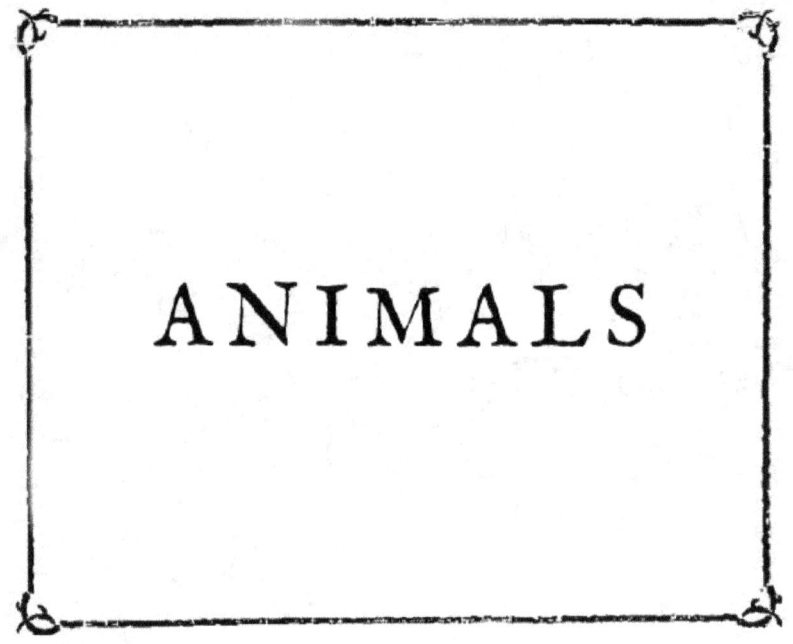

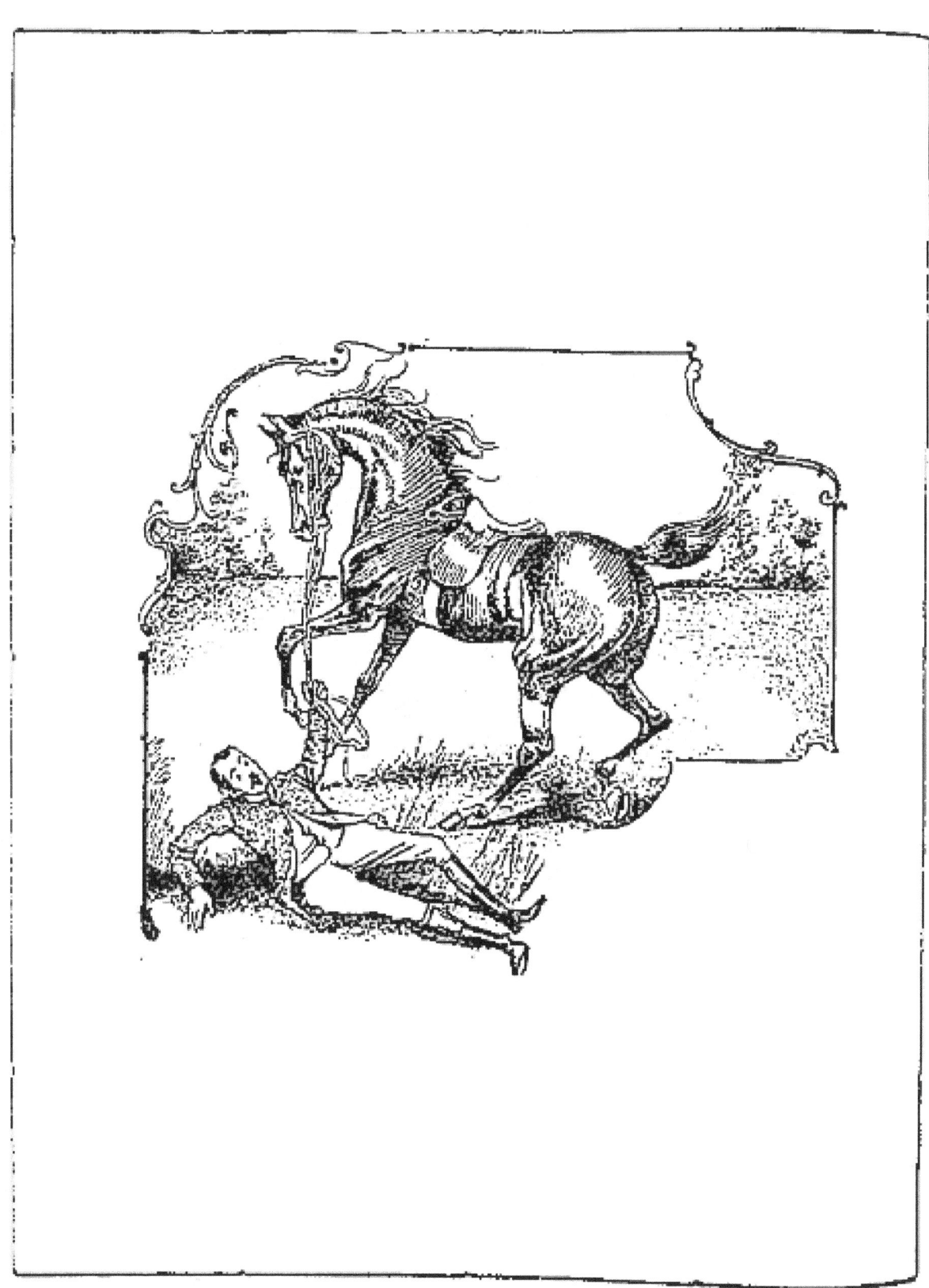

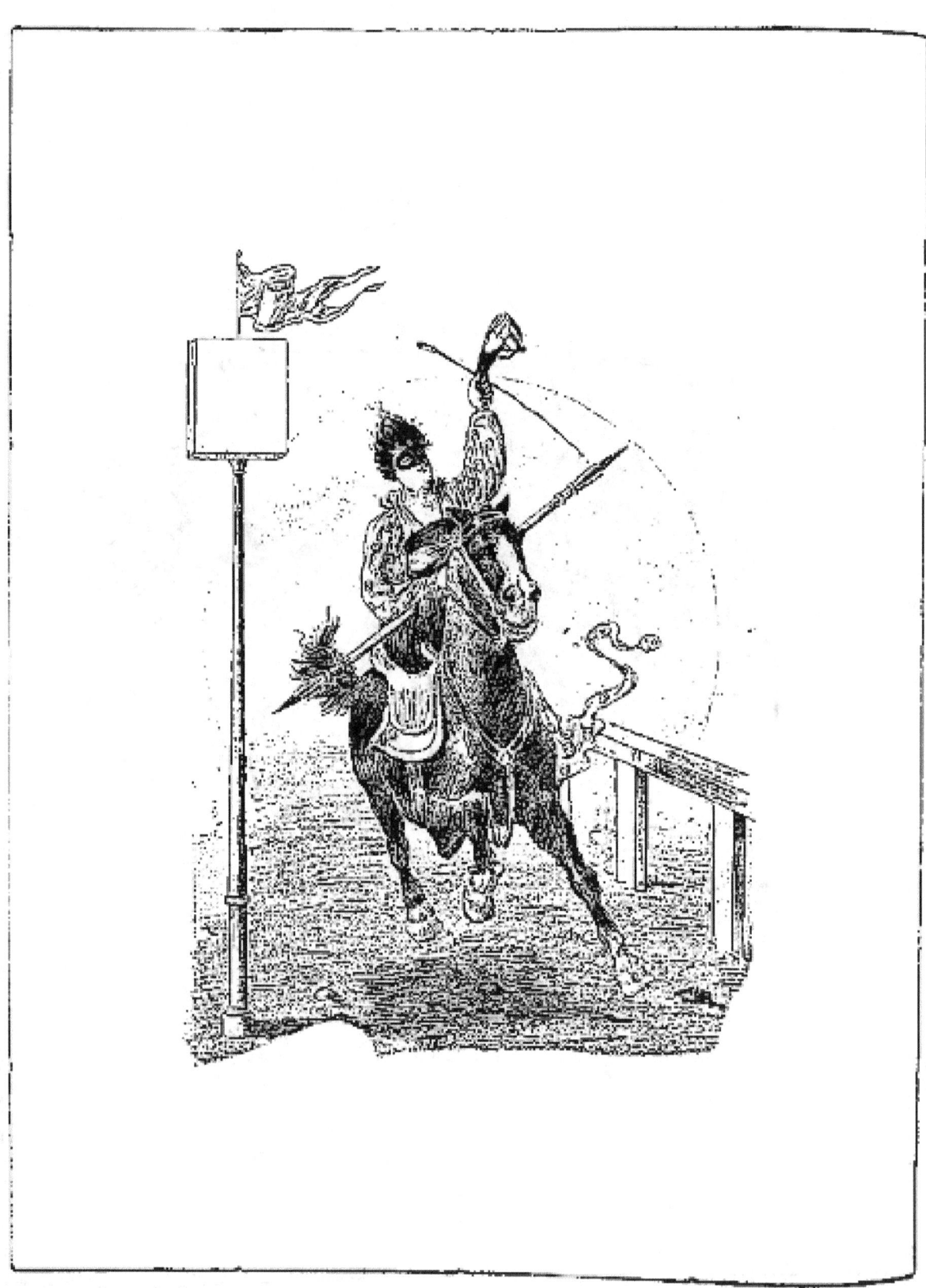

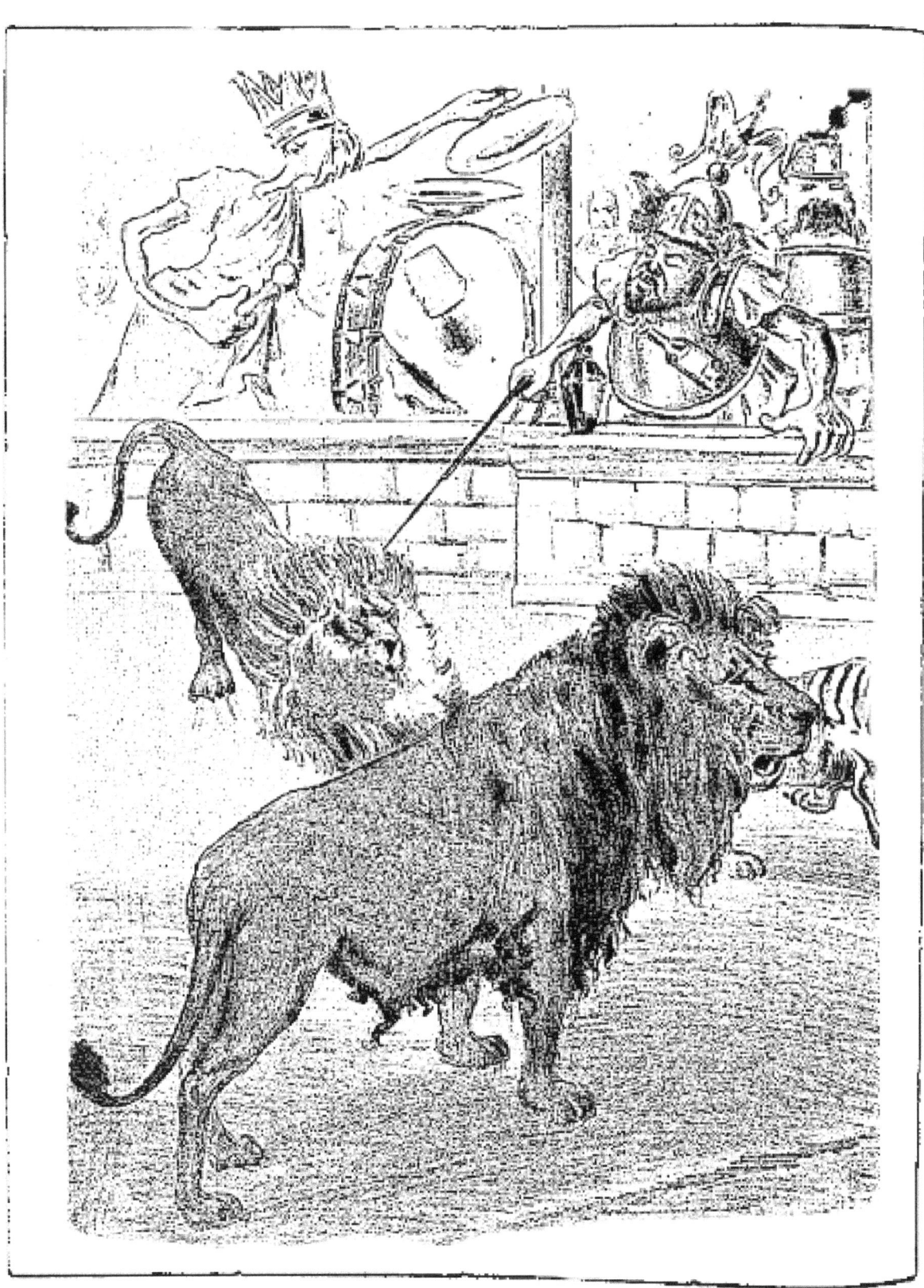

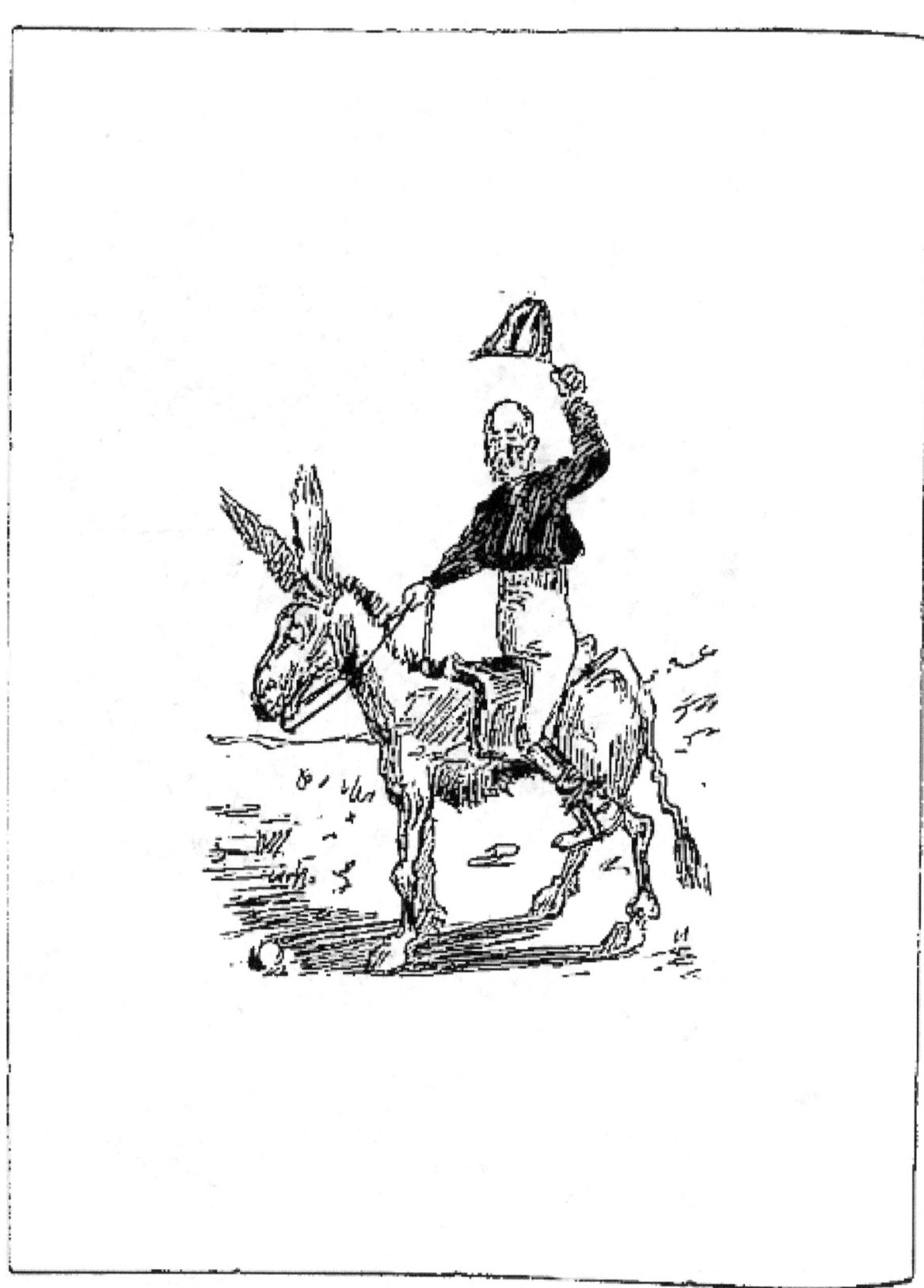

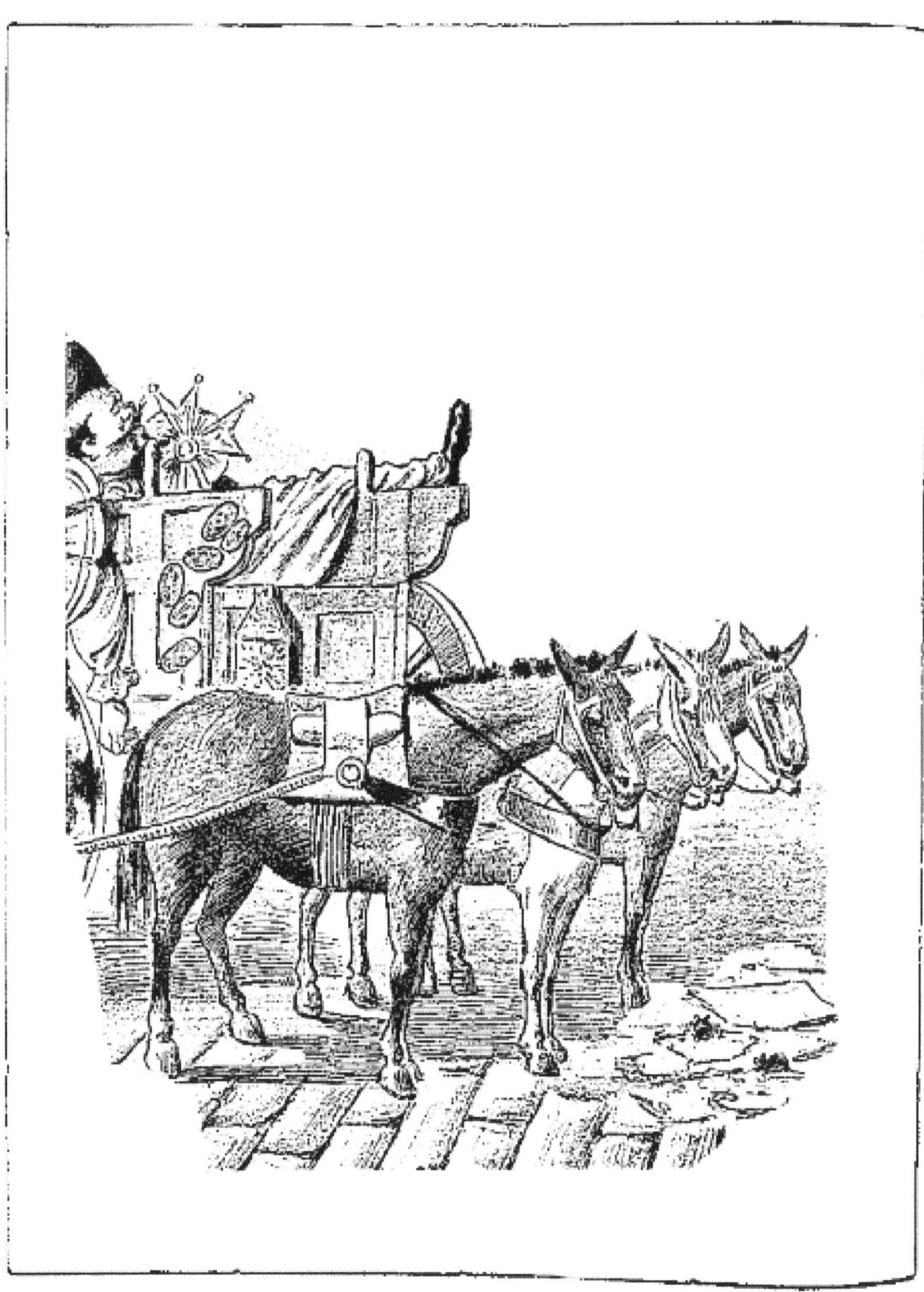

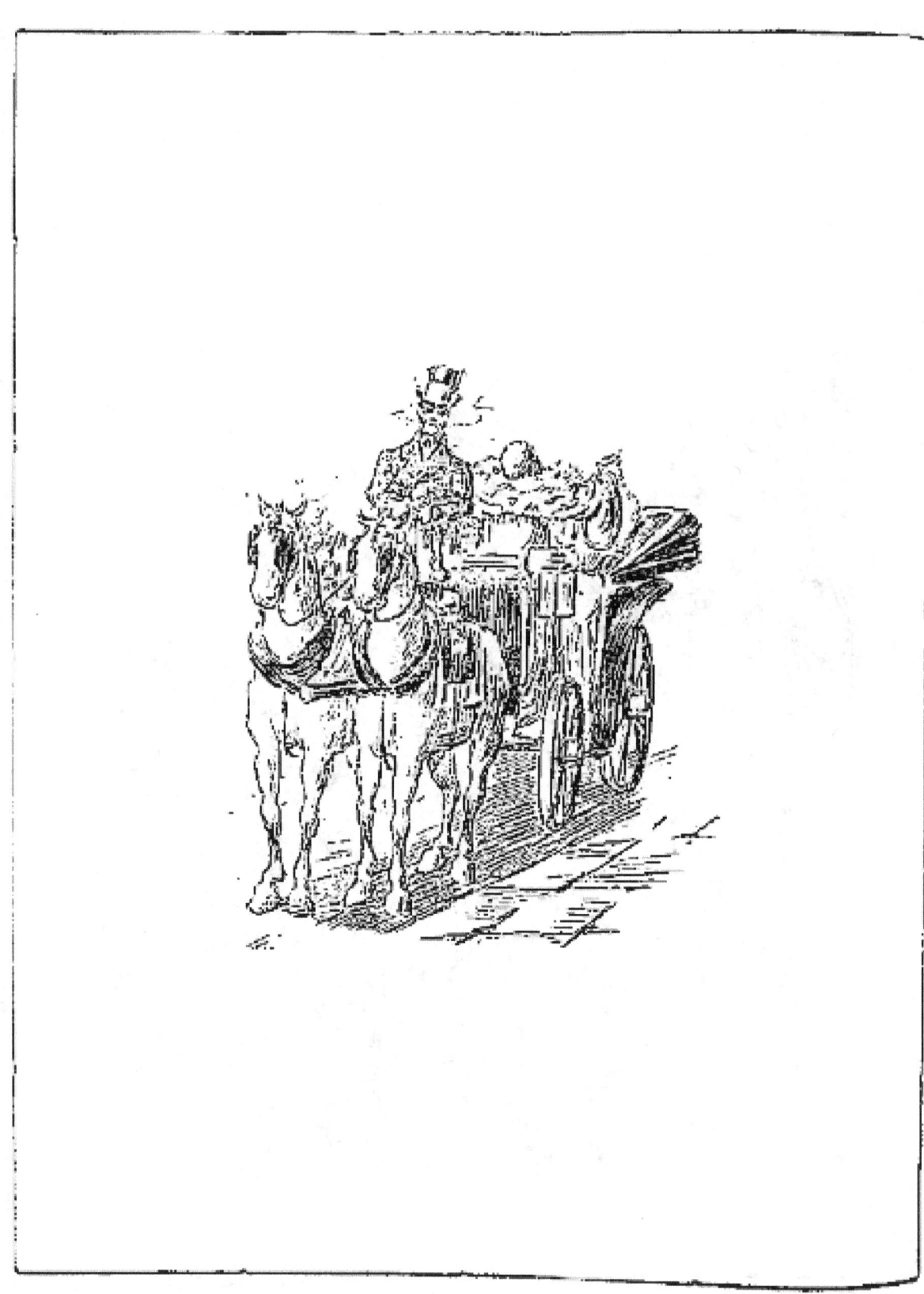

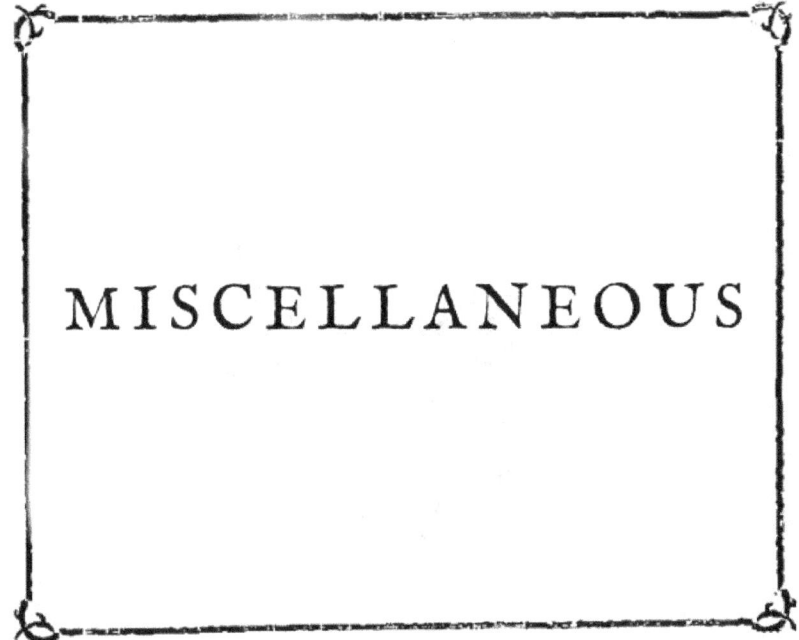

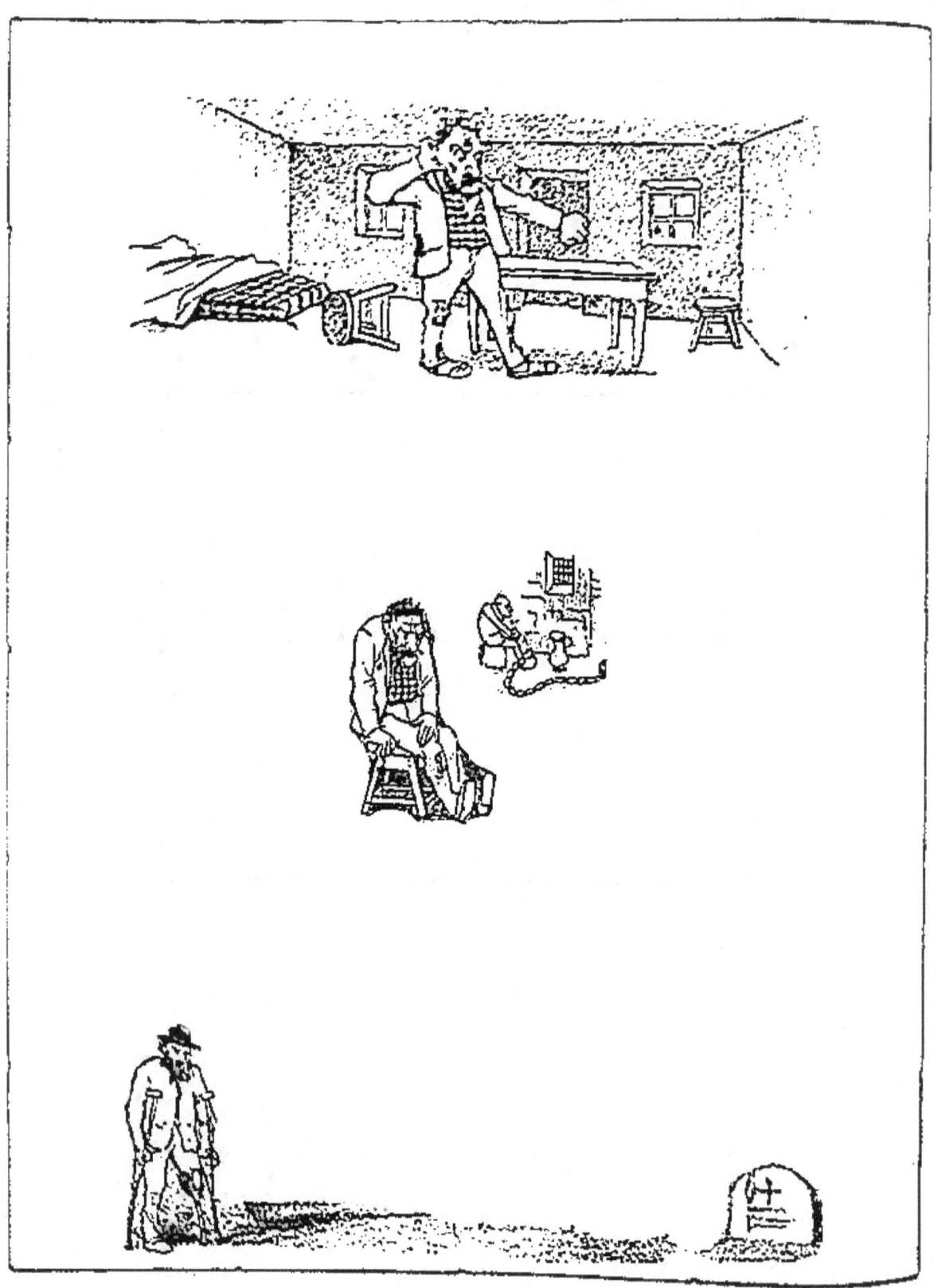

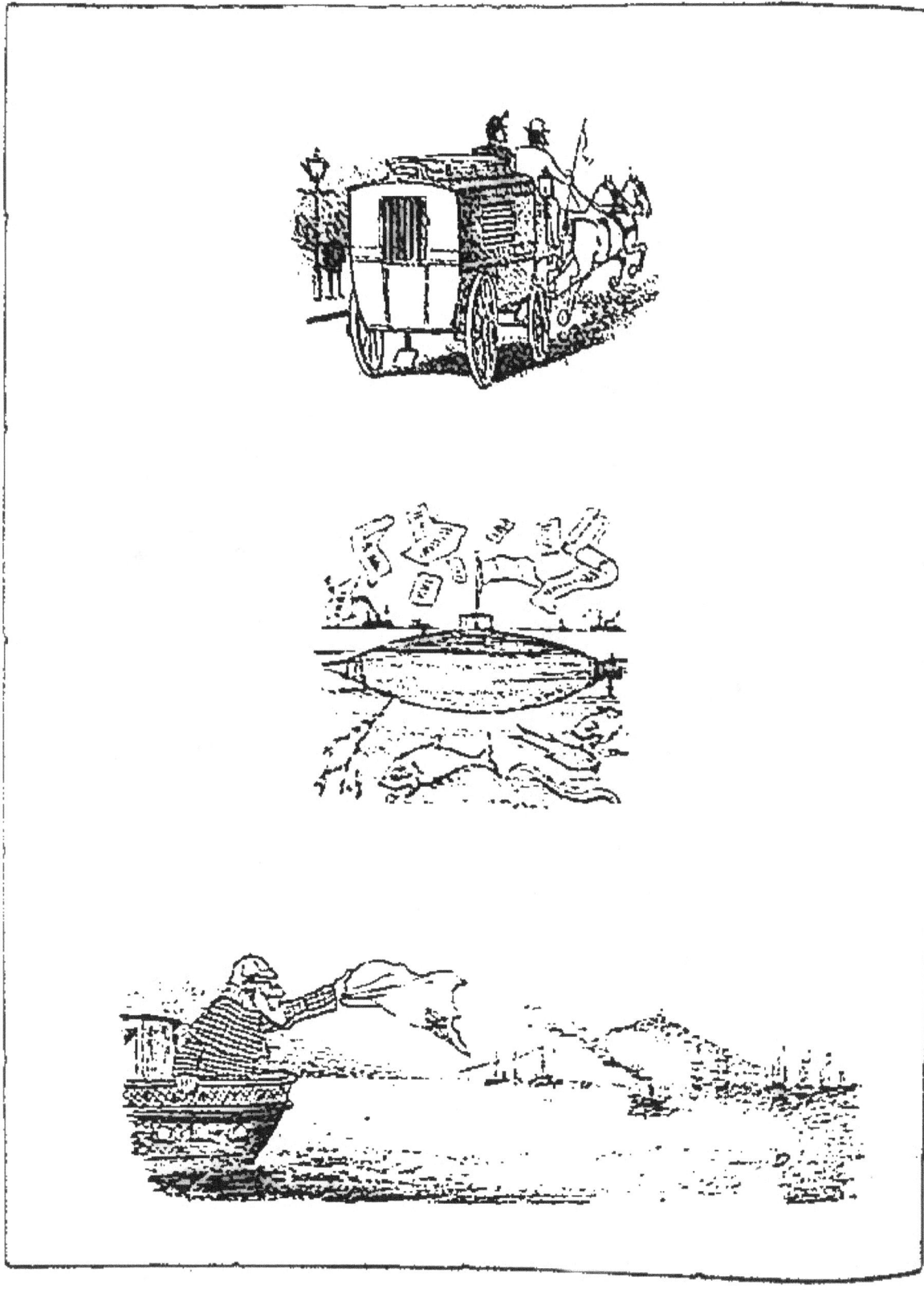

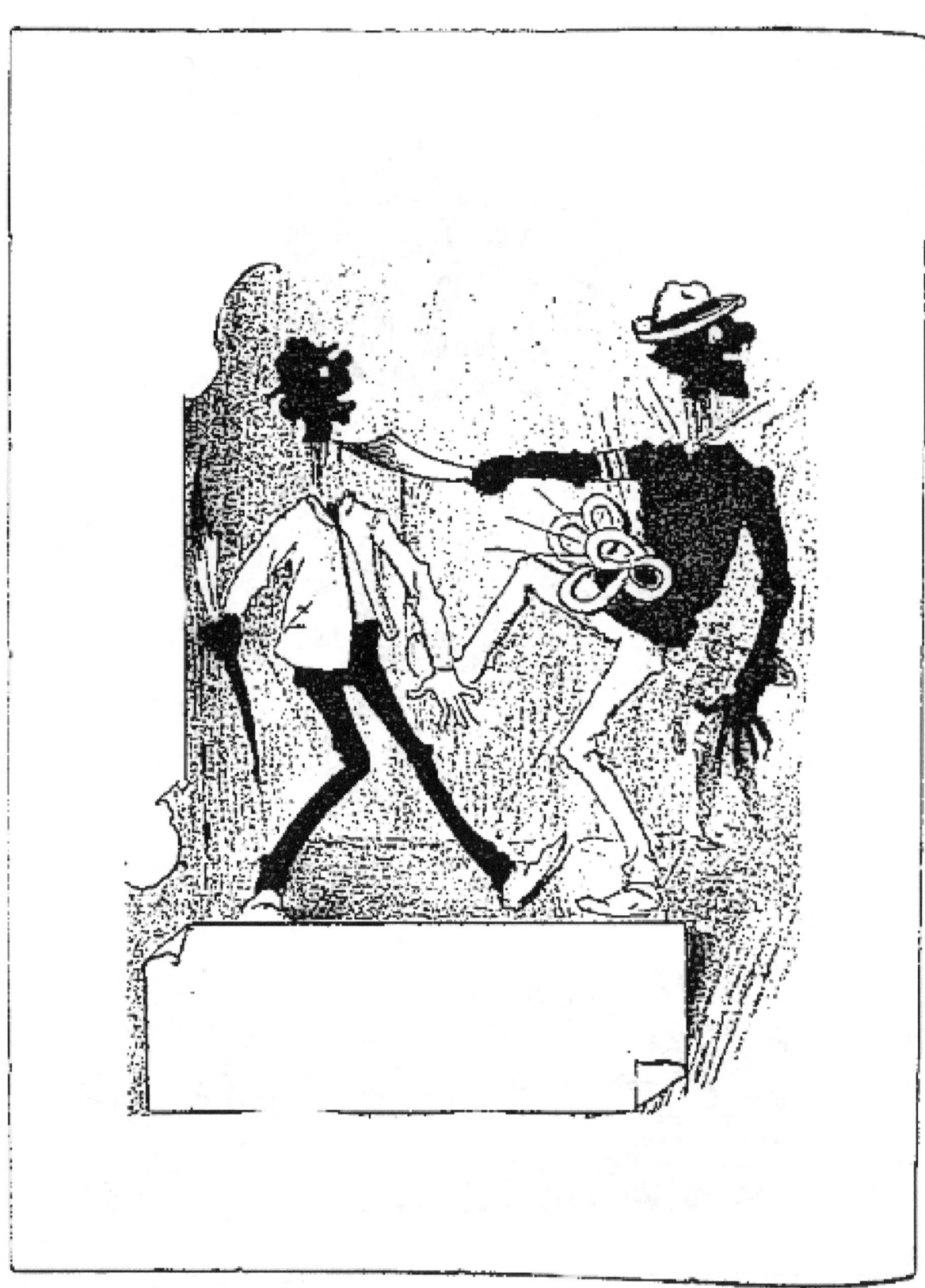

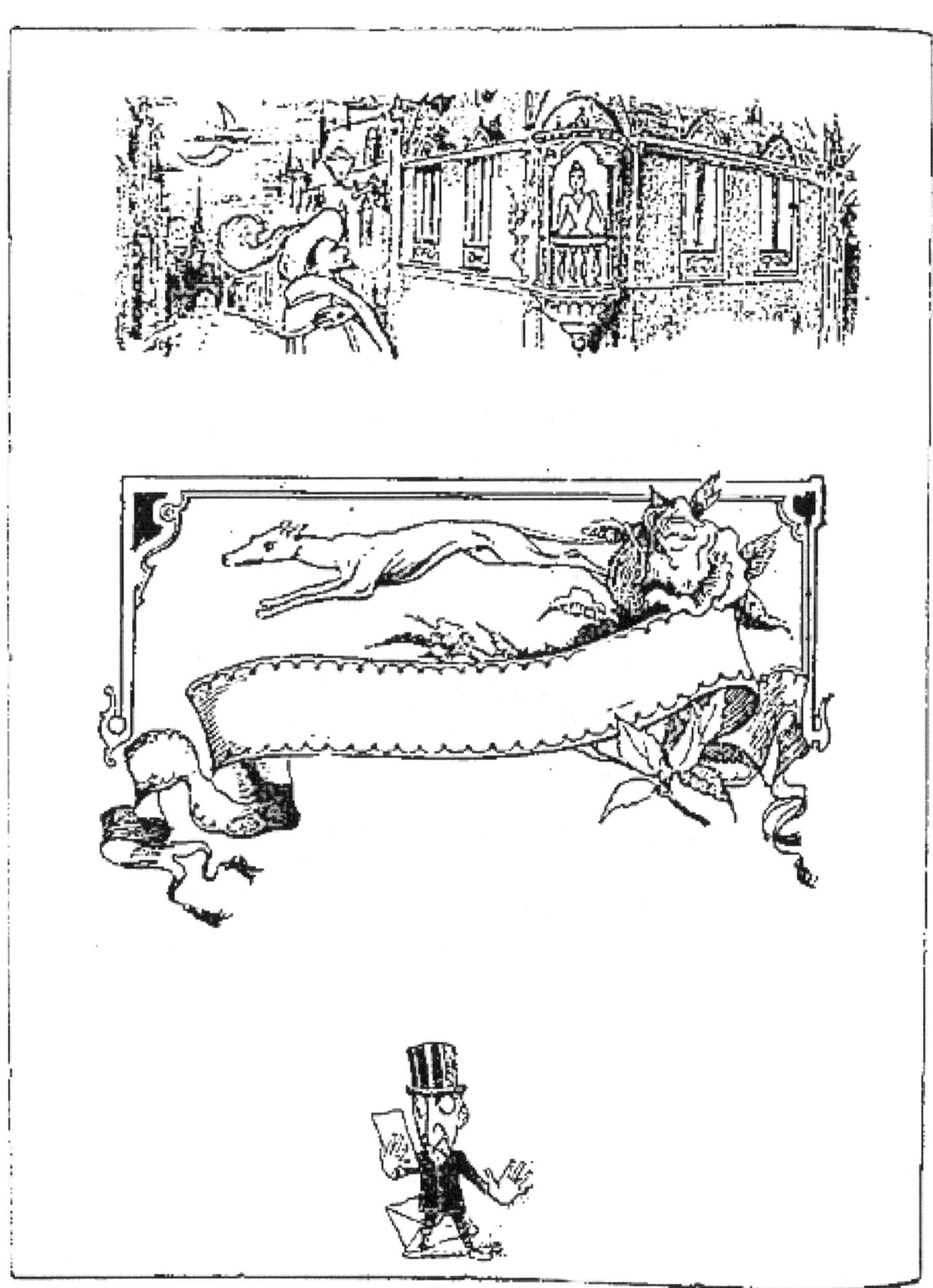

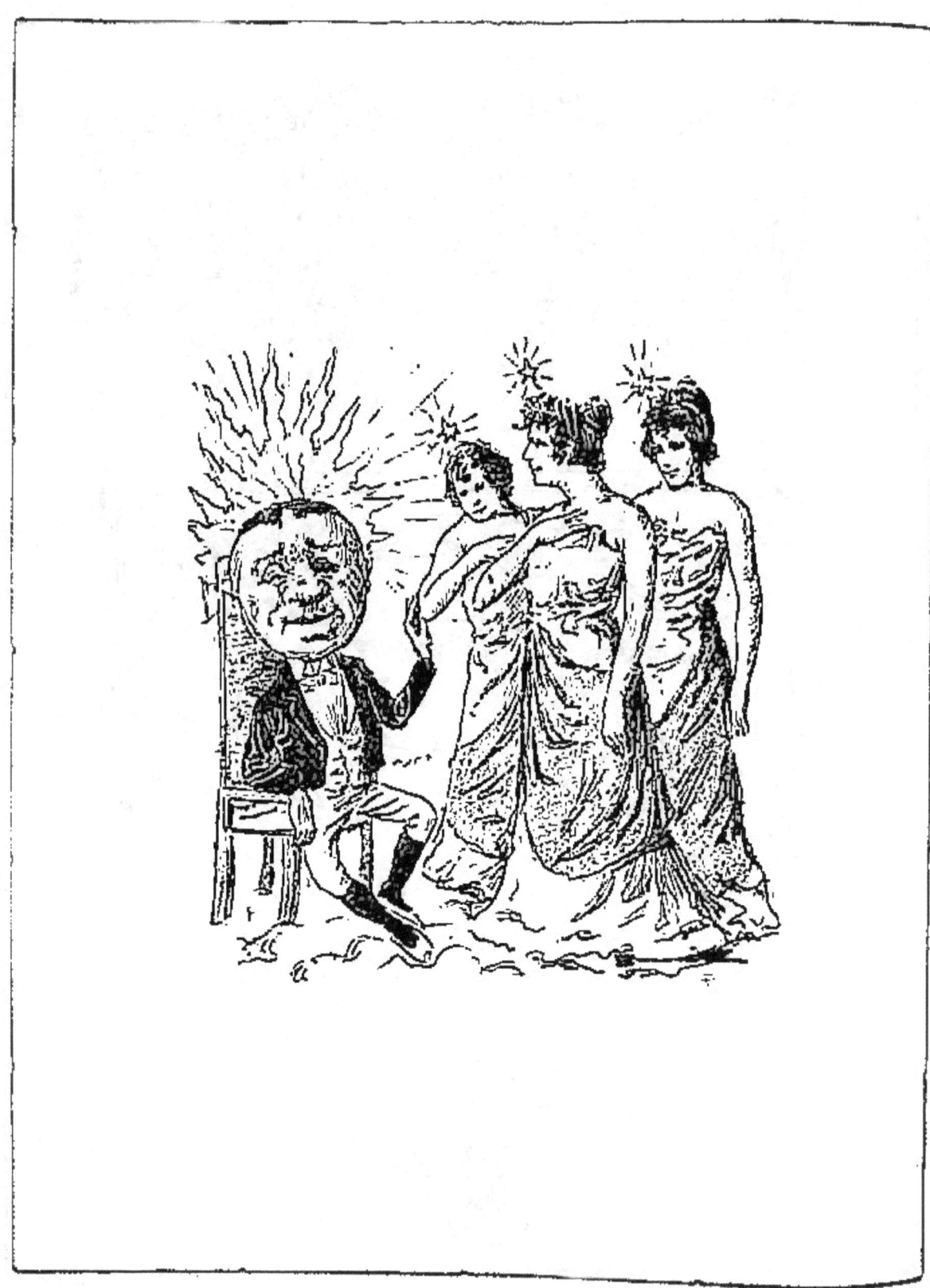

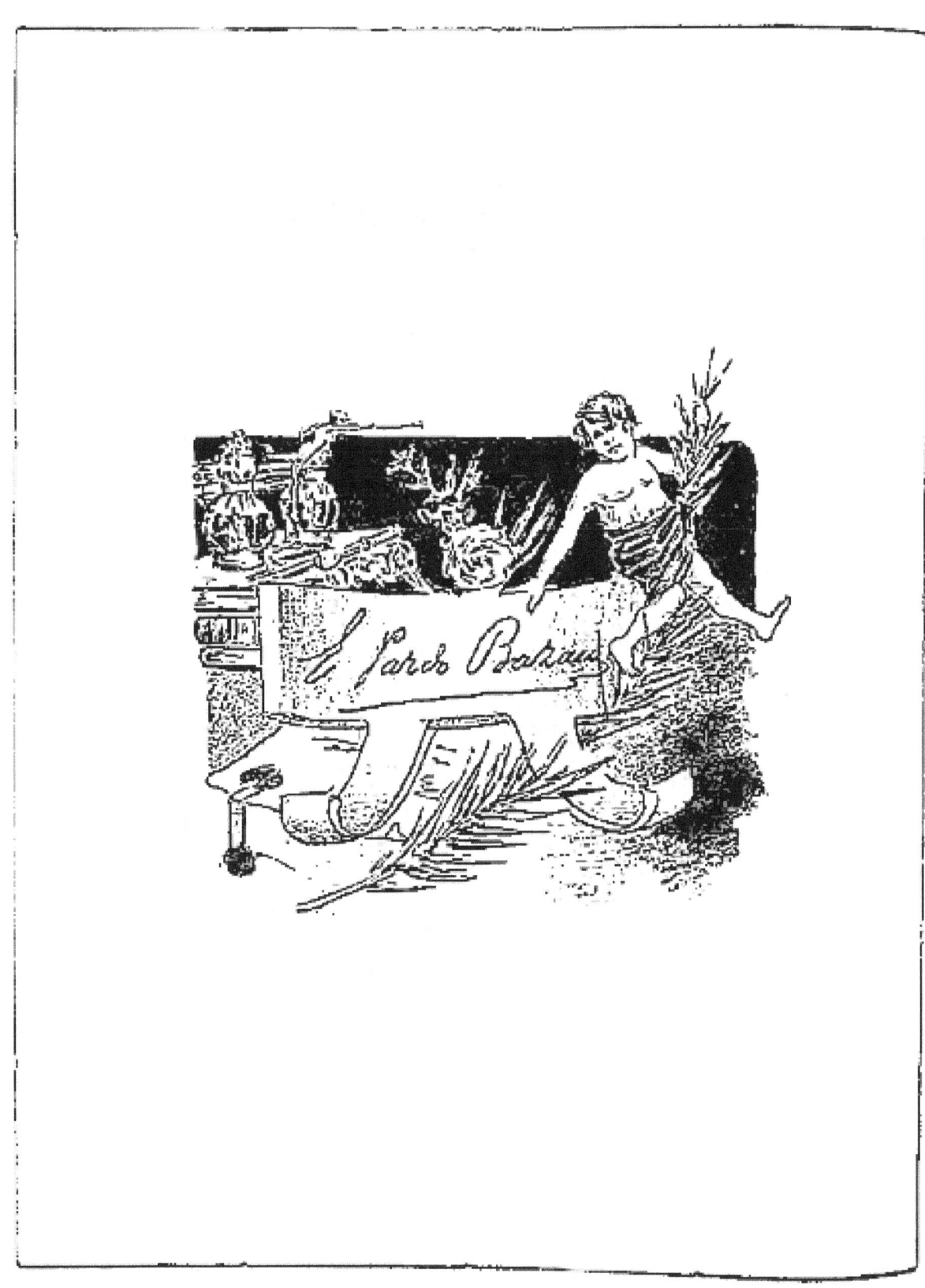

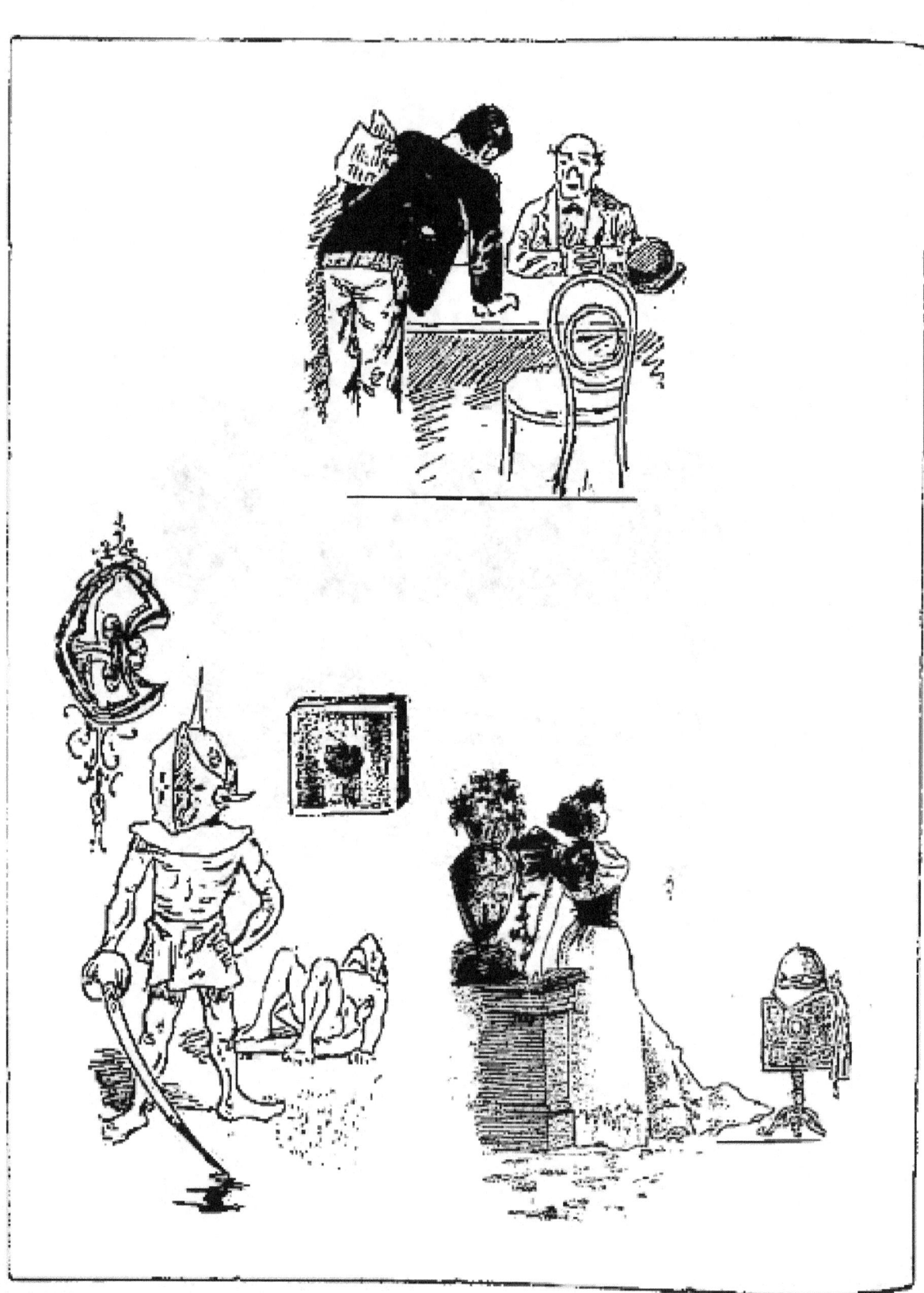

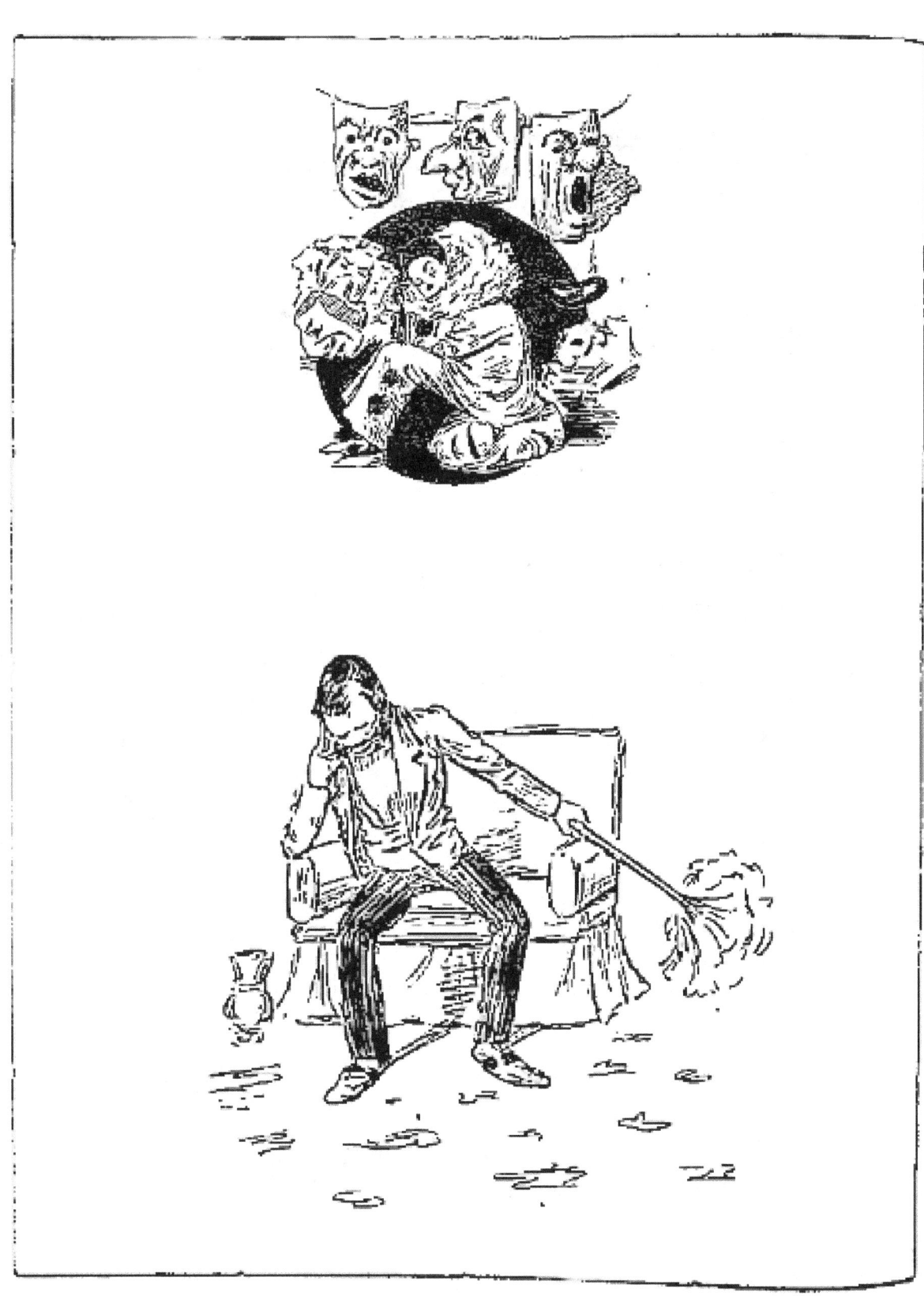

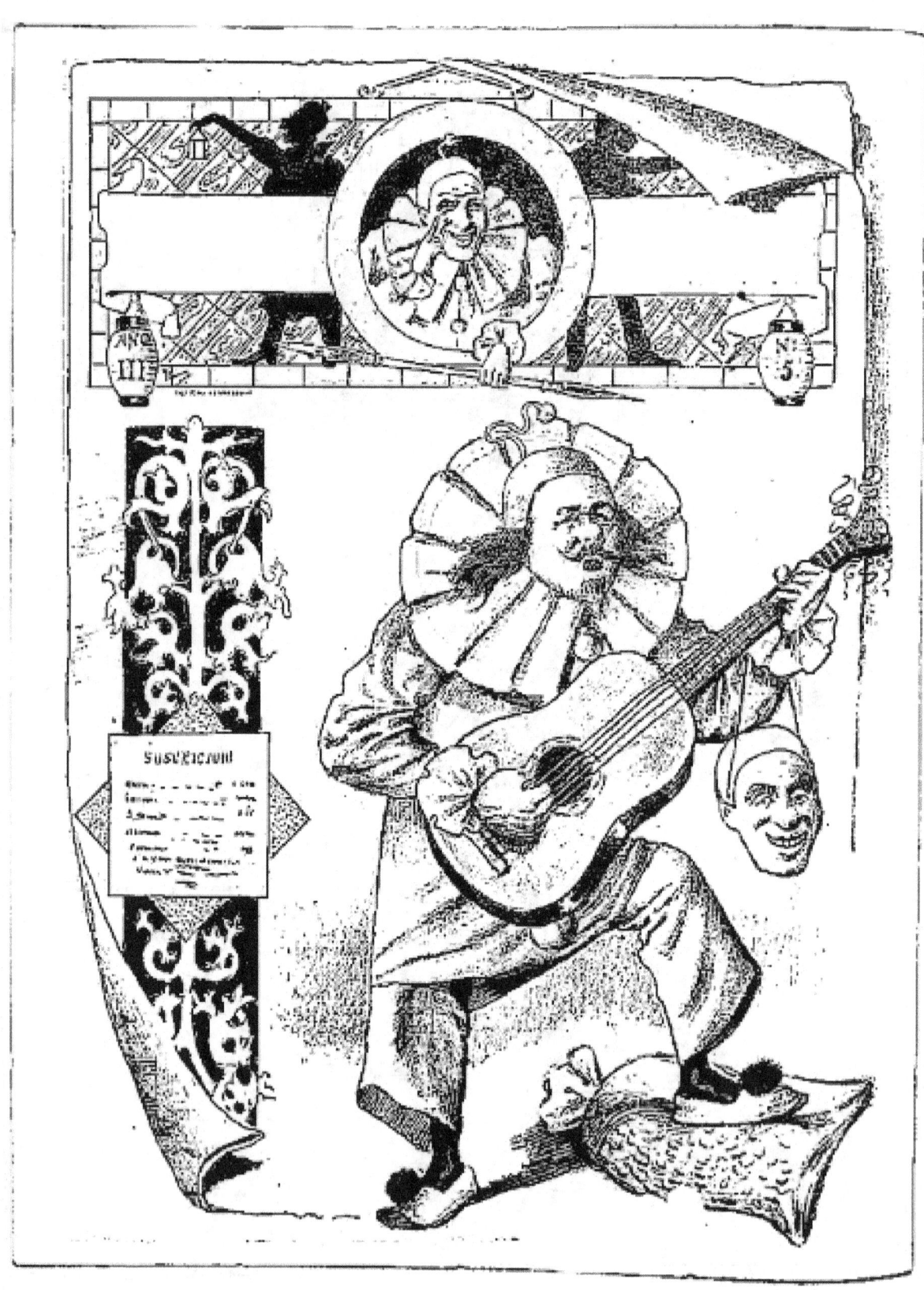

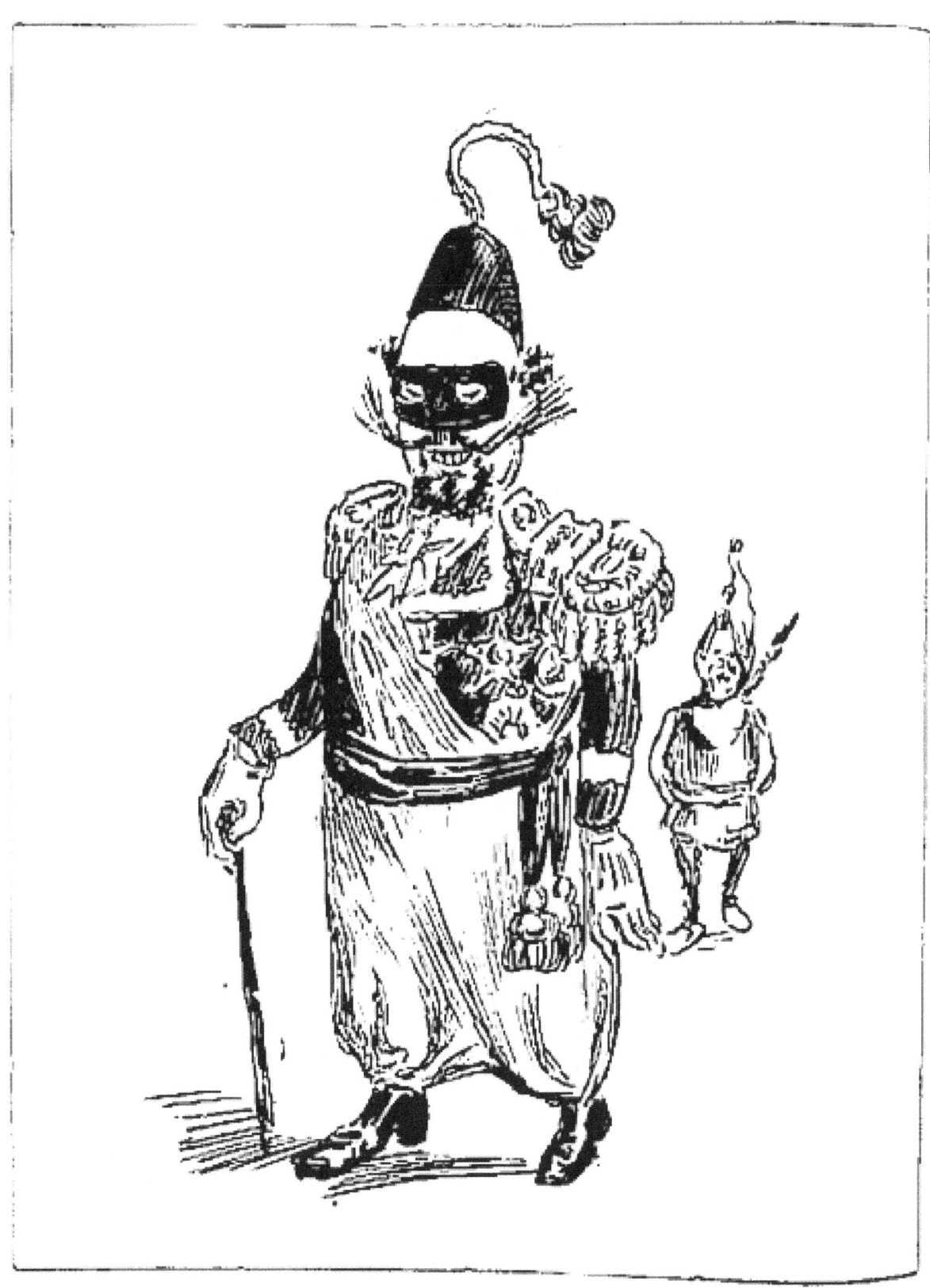

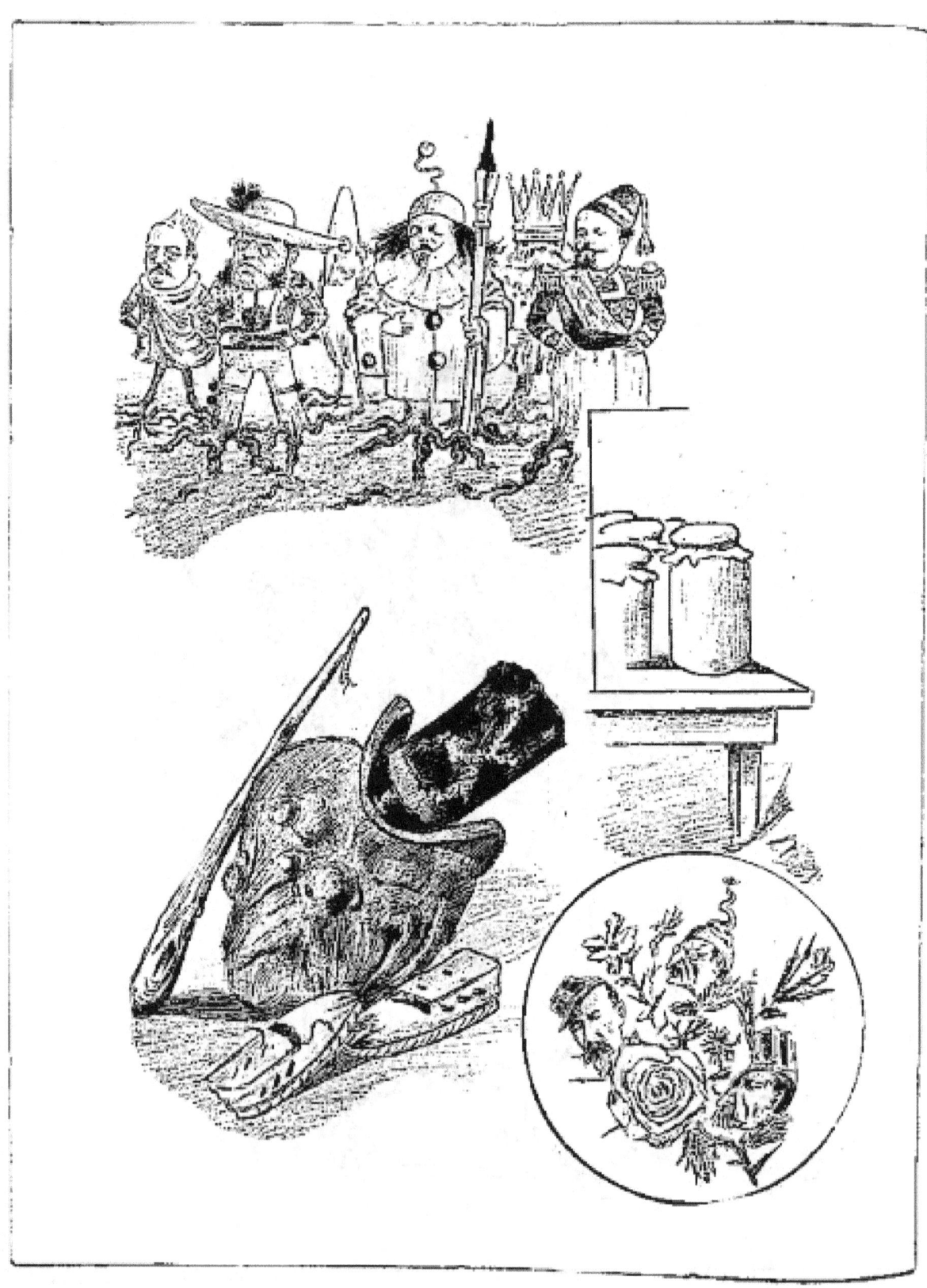

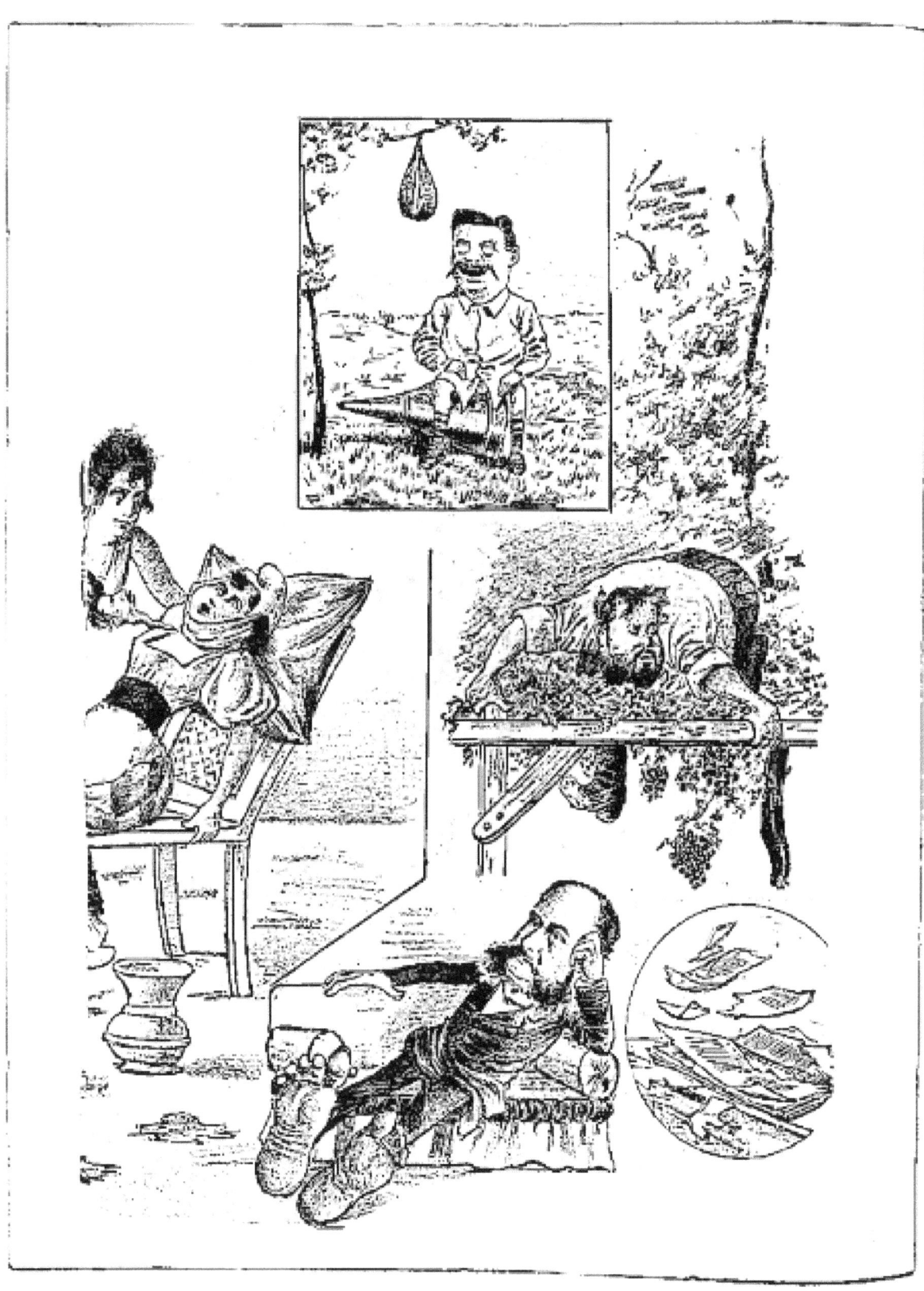

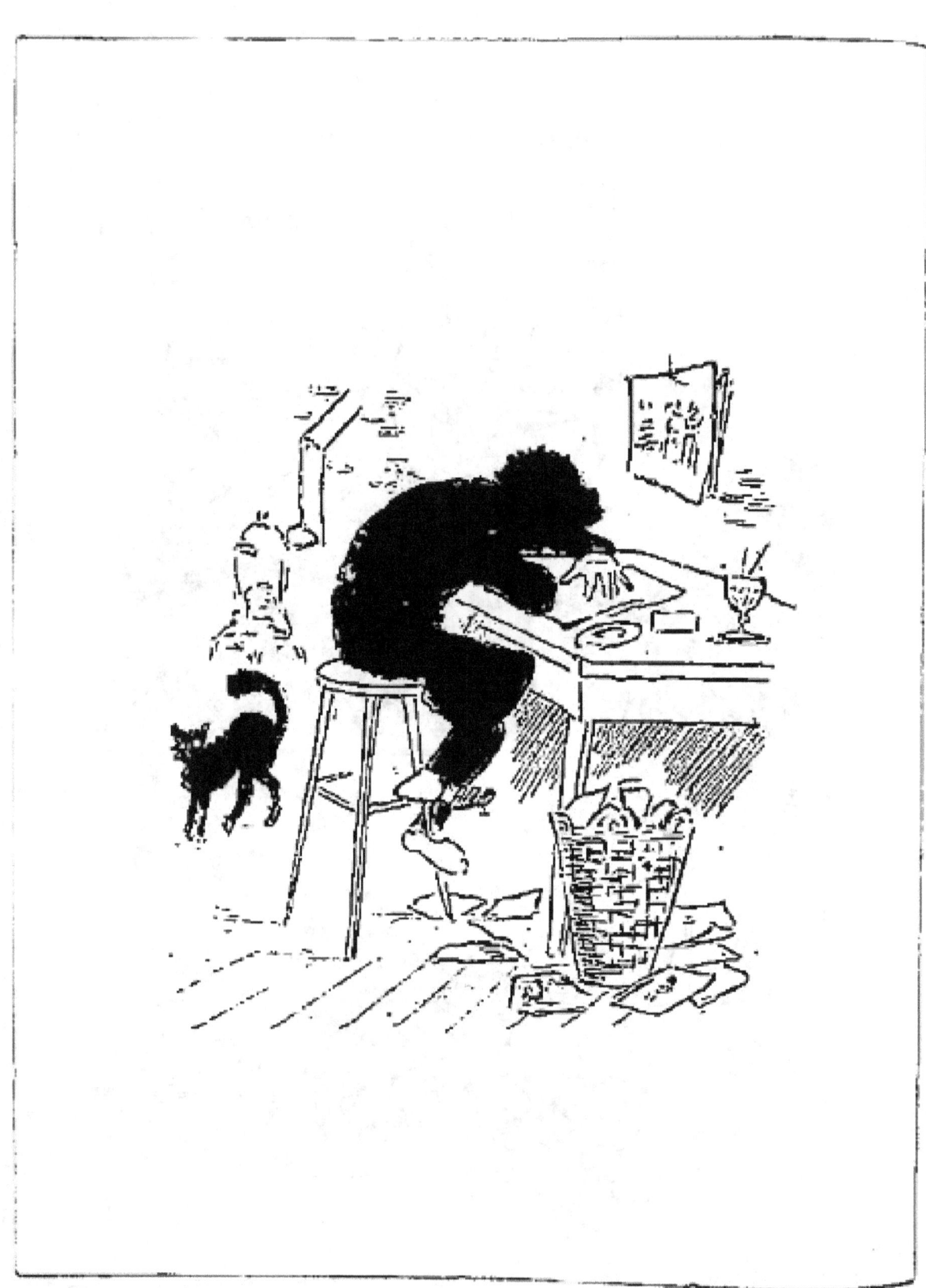

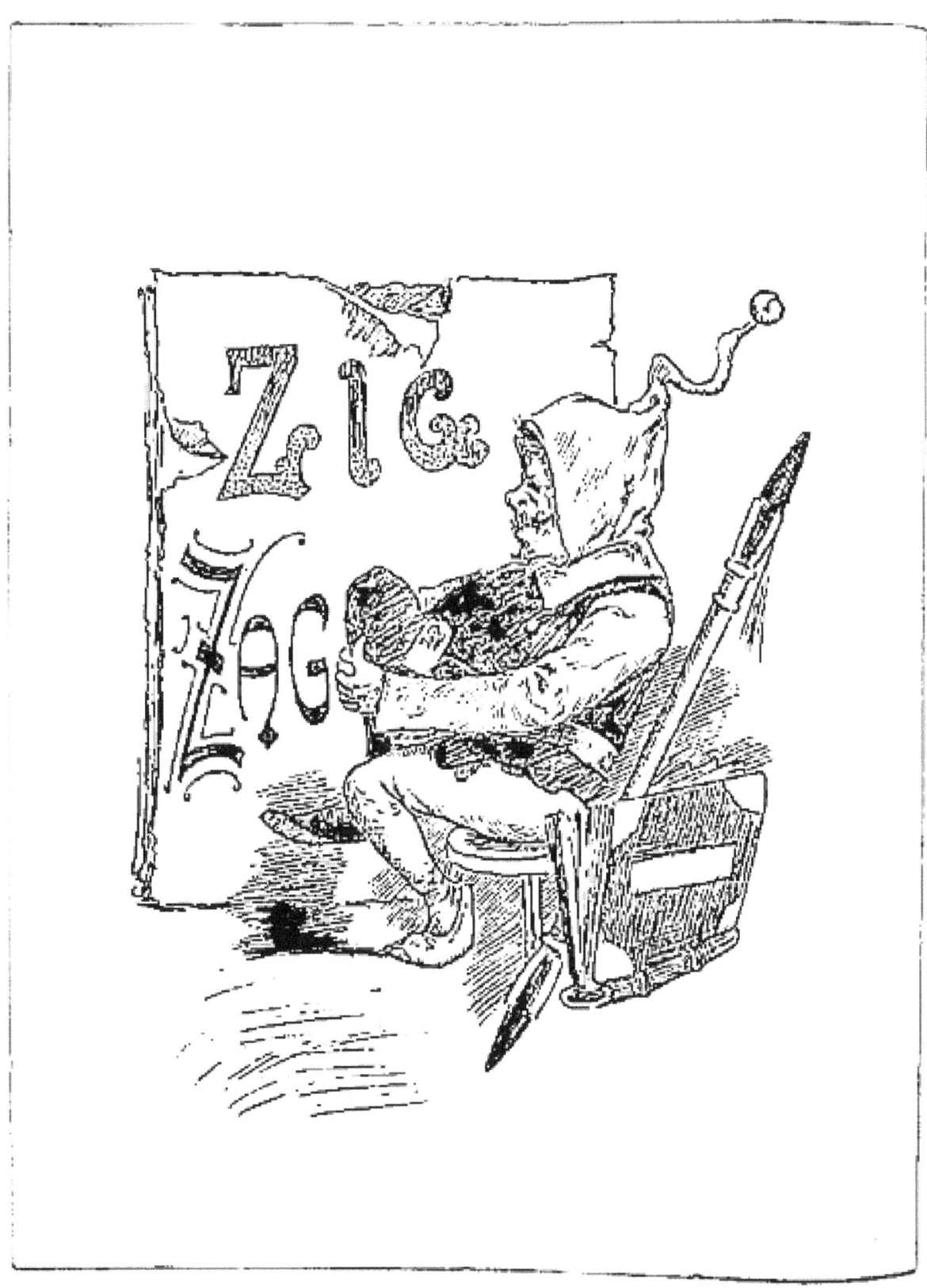

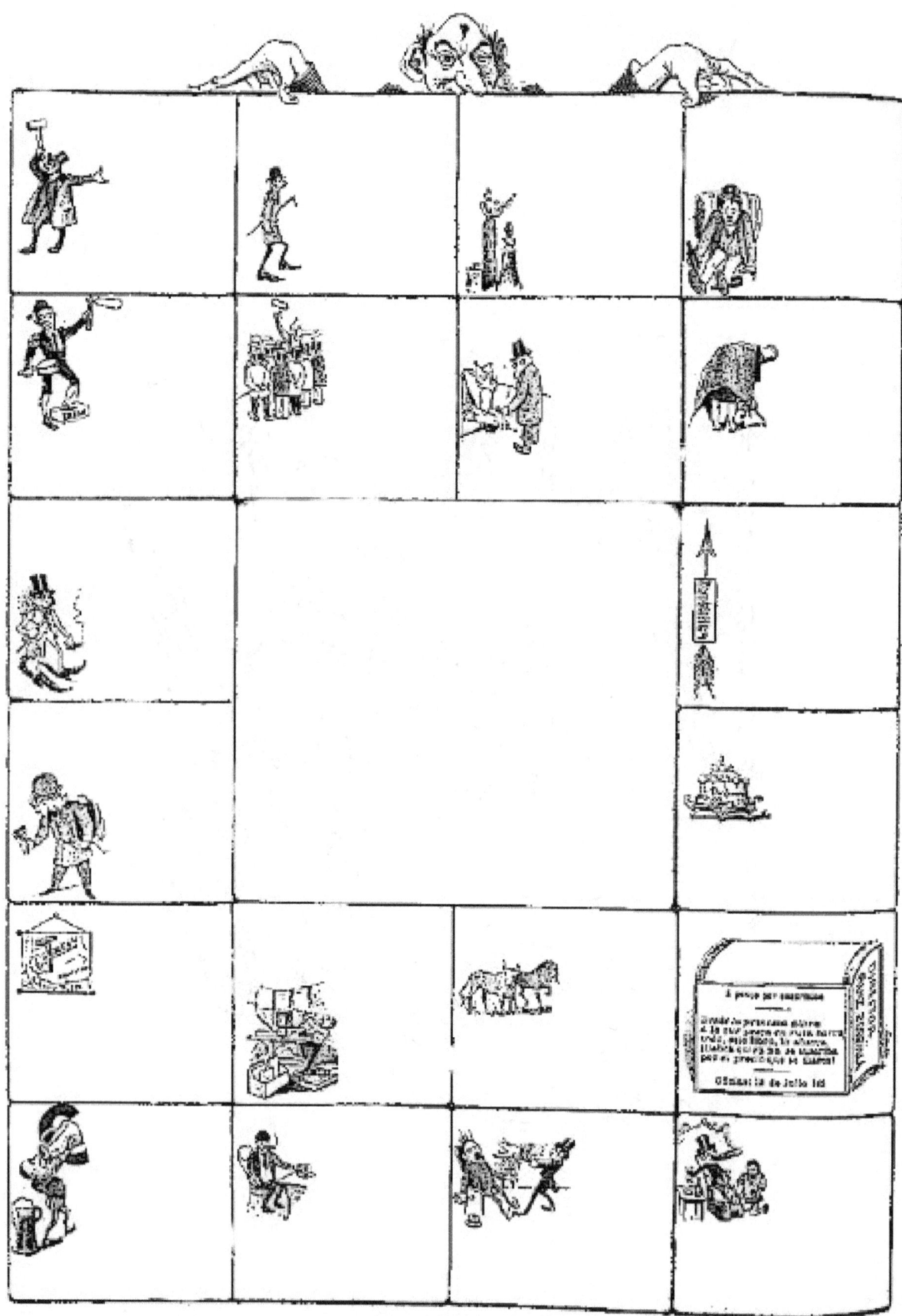

References

Download

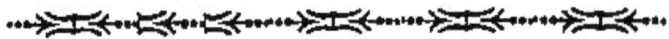

Download link that provides instant access to all images featured. It provides access to both the images and magazines from which the illustrations were obtained.

The short link

https://chl.li/amazingmagazineillustrationsI

The impossible link

https://drive.google.com/file/d/1TZbfKX7iHsfedtl83h3fA097aGag9Isz/view?usp=sharing

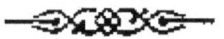

Password

Funes1894@Memorioso1960

Women

Page 8 - Illustrator: Charles Schütz. Caras y Caretas. Number 11. September 1890.

Page 9 - Illustrator: Charles Schütz. Caras y Caretas. Number 11. September 1890.

Page 10 - Illustrator: Aurelio Giménez Pastor. Caras y Caretas. Number 108. March 1896.

Page 11 - Illustrator: Aurelio Giménez Pastor. Caras y Caretas. Number 108. March 1896.

Page 12 - Caras y Caretas. Number 108. March 1896.

Page 13 - Caras y Caretas. Number 106. March 1896.

Page 14 - Illustrator: Aurelio Giménez Pastor. Caras y Caretas. Number 106. March 1896.

Page 15 - Illustrator: Aurelio Giménez Pastor. Caras y Caretas. Number 105. March 1896.

Page 16 - Caras y Caretas. Number 104. February 1896.

Page 17 - Caras y Caretas. Number 104. February 1896.

Page 18 - Illustrator: Aurelio Giménez Pastor. Caras y Caretas. Number 103. February 1896.

Page 19 - Illustrator: Aurelio Giménez Pastor. Caras y Caretas. Number 101. February 1896.

Page 20 - Illustrator: Charles Schütz. Caras y Caretas. Number 100. January 1896.

Page 21 - Illustrator: Charles Schütz. Caras y Caretas. Number 100. January 1896.

Page 22 - Illustrator: Wimplane II. Caras y Caretas. Number 99. January 1896.

MEN

Page 24 - Illustrator: Charles Schütz. Caras y Caretas. Number 11. September 1890.

Page 25 - Illustrator: Charles Schütz. Caras y Caretas. Number 11. September 1890.

Page 26 - Illustrator: Charles Schütz. Caras y Caretas. Number 11. September 1890.

Page 27 - Caras y Caretas. Number 108. March 1896.

Page 28 - Caras y Caretas. Number 106. March 1896.

Page 29 - Caras y Caretas. Number 105. March 1896.

Page 30 - Illustrator: Aurelio Giménez Pastor. Caras y Caretas. Number 104. February 1896.

Page 31 - Caras y Caretas. Number 103. February 1896.

Page 32 - Illustrator: Aurelio Giménez Pastor. Caras y Caretas. Number 103. February 1896.

Page 33 - Caras y Caretas. Number 103. February 1896.

Page 34 - Illustrator: Aurelio Giménez Pastor. Caras y Caretas. Number 101. February 1896.

Page 35 - Caras y Caretas. Number 101. February 1896.

Page 36 - Illustrator: Aurelio Giménez Pastor. Caras y Caretas. Number 100. January 1896.

Page 37 - Caras y Caretas. Number 100. January 1896.

Page 38 - Illustrator: Aurelio Giménez Pastor. Caras y Caretas. Number 100. January 1896.

Page 39 - Caras y Caretas. Number 100. January 1896.

Page 40 - Caras y Caretas. Number 100. January 1896.

Page 41 - Caras y Caretas. Number 100. January 1896.

Page 42 - Illustrator: Wimplane II. Caras y Caretas. Number 99. January 1896.

Groups & Scenes

Page 44 - Illustrator: Charles Schütz. Caras y Caretas. Number 11. September 1890.

Page 45 - Illustrator: Charles Schütz. Caras y Caretas. Number 11. September 1890.

Page 46 - Illustrator: Charles Schütz. Caras y Caretas. Number 11. September 1890.

Page 47 - Illustrator: Charles Schütz. Caras y Caretas. Number 11. September 1890.

Page 48 - Illustrator: Charles Schütz. Caras y Caretas. Number 11. September 1890.

Page 49 - Illustrator: Charles Schütz. Caras y Caretas. Number 11. September 1890.

Page 50 - Illustrator: Charles Schütz. Caras y Caretas. Number 11. September 1890.

Page 51 - Illustrator: Charles Schütz. Caras y Caretas. Number 11. September 1890.

Page 52 - Illustrator: Charles Schütz. Caras y Caretas. Number 11. September 1890.

Page 53 - Illustrator: Charles Schütz. Caras y Caretas. Number 11. September 1890.

Page 54 - Illustrator: Charles Schütz. Caras y Caretas. Number 11. September 1890.

Page 55 - Illustrator: Charles Schütz. Caras y Caretas. Number 11. September 1890.

Page 56 - Caras y Caretas. Number 108. March 1896.

Page 57 - Caras y Caretas. Number 108. March 1896.

Page 58 - Illustrator: Wimplane II. Caras y Caretas. Number 108. March 1896.

Page 59 - Illustrator: Wimplane II. Caras y Caretas. Number 108. March 1896.

Page 60 - Caras y Caretas. Number 108. March 1896.

Page 61 - Illustrator: Wimplane II. Caras y Caretas. Number 106. March 1896.

Page 62 - Caras y Caretas. Number 106. March 1896.

Page 63 - Caras y Caretas. Number 106. March 1896.

Page 64 - Caras y Caretas. Number 106. March 1896.

Page 65 - Caras y Caretas. Number 105. March 1896.

Page 66 - Illustrator: Wimplane II. Caras y Caretas. Number 105. March 1896.

Page 67 - Illustrator: Wimplane II. Caras y Caretas. Number 105. March 1896.

Page 68 - Caras y Caretas. Number 105. March 1896.

Page 69 - Caras y Caretas. Number 105. March 1896.

Page 70 - Illustrator: Wimplane II. Caras y Caretas. Number 104. February 1896.

Page 71 - Illustrator: Wimplane II. Caras y Caretas. Number 104. February 1896.

Page 72 - Caras y Caretas. Number 104. February 1896.

Page 73 - Caras y Caretas. Number 103. February 1896.

Page 74 - Caras y Caretas. Number 103. February 1896.

Page 75 - Illustrator: Wimplane II. Caras y Caretas. Number 103. February 1896.

Page 76 - Illustrator: Wimplane II. Caras y Caretas. Number 103. February 1896.

Page 77 - Caras y Caretas. Number 103. February 1896.

Page 78 - Caras y Caretas. Number 103. February 1896.

Page 79 - Caras y Caretas. Number 103. February 1896.

Page 80 - Caras y Caretas. Number 103. February 1896.

Page 81 - Caras y Caretas. Number 103. February 1896.

Page 82 - Caras y Caretas. Number 103. February 1896.

Page 83 - Caras y Caretas. Number 103. February 1896.

Page 84 - Caras y Caretas. Number 101. February 1896.

Page 85 - Illustrator: Wimplane II. Caras y Caretas. Number 101. February 1896.

Page 86 - Illustrator: Aurelio Giménez Pastor. Caras y Caretas. Number 101. February 1896.

Page 87 - Caras y Caretas. Number 100. January 1896.

Page 88 - Illustrator: Wimplane II. Caras y Caretas. Number 100. January 1896.

Page 89 - Illustrator: Wimplane II. Caras y Caretas. Number 100. January 1896.

Animals

Page 91 - Illustrator: Charles Schütz. Caras y Caretas. Number 11. September 1890.

Page 92 - Illustrator: Wimplane II. Caras y Caretas. Number 106. March 1896.

Page 93 - Illustrator: Wimplane II. Caras y Caretas. Number 106. March 1896.

Page 94 - Caras y Caretas. Number 106. March 1896.

Page 95 - Illustrator: Wimplane II. Caras y Caretas. Number 104. February 1896.

Page 96 - Caras y Caretas. Number 104. February 1896.

Miscellaneous

Page 98 - Illustrator: Charles Schütz. Caras y Caretas. Number 11. September 1890.

Page 99 - Illustrator: Charles Schütz. Caras y Caretas. Number 11. September 1890.

Page 100 - Illustrator: Charles Schütz. Caras y Caretas. Number 11. September 1890.

Page 101 - Illustrator: Charles Schütz. Caras y Caretas. Number 11. September 1890.

Page 102 - Caras y Caretas. Number 108. March 1896.

Page 103 - Caras y Caretas. Number 106. March 1896.

Page 104 - Caras y Caretas. Number 105. March 1896.

Page 105 - Caras y Caretas. Number 104. February 1896.

Page 106 - Illustrator: Wimplane II. Caras y Caretas. Number 103. February 1896.

Page 107 - Caras y Caretas. Number 103. February 1896.

Page 108 - Illustrator: Wimplane II. Caras y Caretas. Number 101. February 1896.

Page 109 - Illustrator: Wimplane II. Caras y Caretas. Number 101. February 1896.

Page 110 - Caras y Caretas. Number 100. January 1896.

Page 111 - Illustrator: Wimplane II. Caras y Caretas. Number 100. January 1896.

Page 112 - Illustrator: Wimplane II. Caras y Caretas. Number 99. January 1896.

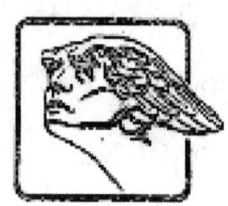

Old Century Books Publications

Montevideo, Uruguay

November 2020